# MIDRASH

## *Into the Kingdom*

*Contemporary Allegorical Midrash*

*Twenty-Five Modern Parables*

Bernd L Bergmann

ISBN: 979-8-218-81271-3

First Edition

Printed in the United States of America

*For Theresa*

*priest, editor, quilter, weaver, companion*
*who stitches light into everything she touches*
*and whose steady faith made this book possible.*

*You are the thread that holds the spiral together.*

# Preface

You are about to enter a book that does not behave the way most books behave.

It does not move in a straight line. It does not begin at the beginning and end at the end, at least not in the way those words are usually meant. It spirals. It circles inward, and as it circles, it descends, not into darkness exactly, but into depth, the way a well descends, the way a root descends, the way a prayer descends when it stops performing and starts meaning what it says.

This is a work of Contemporary Allegorical Midrash.

That phrase may be unfamiliar. Let me unpack it, not as a scholar, though scholarship informs what you will read, but as a writer who has spent years listening to ancient stories and asking them what they still have to say.

Midrash is an ancient Jewish interpretive tradition; a way of engaging sacred text that refuses to let the text sit still. The rabbis who practiced it believed that Scripture was not a closed book but a living conversation, that every verse, every word, every silence between words contained meanings that had not yet been discovered, that the act of interpretation was itself a form of devotion, a way of honoring the text by refusing to reduce it to a single reading.

There are two great streams of Midrash. Midrash Halakha concerns itself with law, with the practical question of how to live. Midrash Aggadah, the stream that feeds this book, concerns itself with story, with narrative, with the human hunger to understand not just what happened but what it means, not just what was said but what was left unsaid, not just what the text declares but what it whispers when you press your ear against it and listen with your whole attention.

The rabbis had a phrase for this. They said that Scripture has seventy faces. Turn it and turn it, for everything is in it. Seventy was not a literal number. It was a way of saying infinite, inexhaustible, alive. The text is never finished with you, and you are never finished with it. Every generation that encounters it discovers something the previous generation could not have seen, because every generation brings its own wounds, its own questions, its own particular darkness to the reading, and the text meets them there.

This book takes the parables of Jesus and does what the Midrashic tradition has always done. It turns them. It presses its ear against them. It asks what they sound like when they speak not in the idiom of first-century Palestine but in the language of contemporary American life, in the vocabulary of addiction and recovery, of healthcare denied and mercy extended, of veterans abandoned and strangers welcomed, of institutions that betray their purpose and individuals who fulfill theirs without knowing it.

The parables are not illustrations. They are not sermon fodder. They are not neat moral lessons with tidy applications. They are, as the scholar C. H. Dodd wrote in his book **The Parables of the Kingdom**, works that tease the mind into active thought. They are designed to unsettle, to provoke, to leave the hearer not with an answer but with a question that rearranges the furniture of the soul.

Jesus told these stories to people who were not looking for comfort. He told them to people who were looking for the Kingdom, which is to say, for a world rearranged according to mercy rather than power, according to grace rather than transaction, according to the last being first and the first being last and the door being open to everyone the respectable world had decided to exclude.

I have tried to honor that. I have tried to write stories that do not comfort prematurely, that do not resolve what the parables themselves leave unresolved, that sit with the discomfort and the mystery and the terrible beauty of a God who tells stories instead of issuing decrees.

The allegorical dimension means that these modern stories are not random. Each one is rooted in a specific parable, and the connections between the ancient story and the contemporary one are deliberate, structural, woven into the narrative at every level. But allegory here does not mean code. It does not mean that every character maps onto a biblical counterpart and the reader's job is to crack the cipher. It means that the parable's deep structure, its spiritual architecture, its way of seeing the world, has been transplanted into new soil. The roots are ancient. The branches are contemporary. The fruit belongs to both.

Some of these stories come from my own life. I am a recovering addict. I have worked as a welder, a broadcast television technical director, a school bus driver, a transport driver for Department of Corrections pre-release facilities, and most recently as a certified nursing assistant. I have sat with the dying. I have driven the forgotten. I have been the man in the parking lot at four in the morning wondering whether the engine would turn over and whether the day would hold. The material of these parables is not theoretical for me. It is the material of my actual days.

Other stories are imagined, or more precisely, they are listened into existence. I sat with each parable the way you sit with a person who is trying to tell you something important but has not yet found the words. I waited. I listened. I followed the parable's own logic into the contemporary world and wrote down what I found there. The characters are not me, but they are not not me either. They carry pieces of what I have seen, what I have survived, what I have been given by a grace I did not earn and do not fully understand.

The structure of this book is a spiral. It moves from the outer darkness inward toward the light, not in a straight line but in concentric circles, each one bringing you closer to the center, which is the Kingdom itself, which is the place where mercy and truth meet and the broken are made whole, not by being fixed but by being held.

Do not read this book quickly. Do not read it the way you read information. Read it the way you would walk through a cathedral you have never visited before, slowly, with your eyes open, letting the architecture do its work on you before you try to understand it. Let the stories accumulate. Let them talk to each other. Let the spiral carry you.

The Kingdom is not a destination. It is a way of seeing. And these twenty-five stories are twenty-five windows into that seeing, each one ground from a different angle, each one letting in a different quality of light, each one revealing a different face of the seventy faces that Scripture has always carried and will carry long after this book and its author have returned to dust.

Turn it and turn it.

Everything is in it.

# INTRODUCTION

## *Entering What Cannot Be Mapped*

You are standing at the entrance to something that cannot be mapped in advance.

This is not a tour. There is no itinerary. The places these stories will take you are not places that appear on any chart, because the Kingdom of Heaven, whatever else it is, is not a territory that submits to cartography. It submits only to entry. And entry, as every honest seeker knows, requires leaving behind the instruments that worked so well in the country you are leaving.

The parables of Jesus are the strangest stories ever told by the most influential teacher who ever lived. They are strange because they refuse to do what stories are supposed to do. They do not resolve cleanly. They do not reward the deserving and punish the undeserving. They do not confirm what the listener already believes. They detonate. They leave craters where certainties used to stand. They are, to paraphrase poet Scott Cairns, not so much windows as doors, and what lies on the other side of them is not a view but a world.

I have spent years walking through those doors. Not as a theologian. I have no seminary degree, no academic credentials in biblical studies, no letters after my name that would authorize me to speak about these things in the professional sense. I speak about them because they spoke to me first, in the particular language of a life that has included addiction and recovery, labor and loss, the company of the dying and the silence of the estranged, the four-in-the-morning darkness of a Montana winter and the first light that follows it when it comes.

These twenty-five stories are modern retellings of twenty-five of Jesus's parables. They are not translations. They are not paraphrases. They are not sermons disguised as fiction. They are acts of Midrash, which is the ancient Jewish practice of entering a sacred text so deeply that new stories grow from within it, the way new branches grow from old roots, the way light finds new surfaces when the sun moves to an angle no one anticipated.

Each chapter carries a parable inside it the way a seed carries a tree. The connection between the ancient story and the contemporary one is structural, woven into the narrative at every level, present in the architecture even when it is not announced in the text. Some readers will see the connections immediately. Others will discover them gradually, the way you discover the shape of a constellation, not all at once but star by star, until the pattern declares itself and you wonder how you ever looked at that stretch of sky without seeing it.

The chapters are arranged in a spiral. Not chronologically. Not by the order in which the parables appear in the Gospels. But in an order that moves from the outer darkness toward the interior light, from the margins toward the center, from the lost toward the found, from the scattered toward the gathered. The early chapters take place in the far country, in the places where people are most alone, most broken, most convinced that the distance between themselves and mercy is unbridgeable. The later chapters move inward, toward community, toward restoration, toward the feast that has been prepared and the table that has been set and the door that remains open even after midnight.

This is deliberate. It reflects the way the Kingdom actually works, which is not as a destination you arrive at but as a gravity you fall into, a pull you feel before you understand it, a homing instinct that operates below the level of conscious decision and draws you inward toward something you cannot name but recognize when you encounter it, the way you recognize a melody you have never heard before but somehow already know.

I should tell you what these stories are not.

They are not allegories in the mechanical sense, where every character maps onto a biblical counterpart and the reader's job is to decode the cipher. They are allegories in the older, deeper sense, where the ancient pattern lives inside the modern story the way a skeleton lives inside a body, providing structure without being visible on the surface, shaping everything without announcing itself.

They are not morality tales. The parables of Jesus are famously amoral in the conventional sense. The hero of the Dishonest Manager is a cheat. The father of the Prodigal Son rewards the wrong son. The Workers in the Vineyard are paid equally regardless of effort. These stories do not teach morality. They teach mercy, which is a different thing entirely, and mercy, as anyone who has received it knows, does not play by the rules.

They are not safe. I should warn you about this in advance because some of these stories go to places that will cost you something to visit. Addiction. Institutional abuse. The death of children. The failure of systems designed to heal. The particular cruelty of mercy withheld by people whose job it is to extend it. If you are looking for comfort, this is not the book that will provide it. If you are looking for the truth about what the Kingdom looks like when it breaks into the actual world, with all the blood and ash and awkward grace that implies, then come in. The door is open.

They are not finished. I mean this literally. Several of these stories end without resolution, without the neat closure that narrative convention demands, because the parables themselves end without resolution. Jesus was not interested in tying up loose ends. He was interested in leaving the listener inside the question, marinating in the discomfort, unable to escape into the false comfort of a conclusion. I have tried to honor that. Some of these endings will frustrate you. Good. Sit with the frustration. It is the parable doing its work.

What these stories are, I hope, is true. Not in the journalistic sense, though many of them draw from events I have witnessed or experienced. True in the sense that they accurately represent what it feels like to be human in a world that is simultaneously broken and

x

beloved, cruel and graced, falling apart and being held together by something that refuses to let go.

I wrote them for the people who stand at the edges of things. For the ones who have been told, by the world or by the church or by their own relentless inner voices, that they are too far gone, too broken, too stained by what they have done or what has been done to them to be included in whatever feast the Kingdom is preparing. I wrote them because I have stood at that edge myself, and what I found there was not the emptiness I expected but a door, and behind the door a table, and at the table a place set for me that I had not earned and did not deserve and could not refuse.

Enter.

The Kingdom does not require your credentials.

It requires only your willingness to be found.

CONTENTS

# CHAPTER 1
## TWENTY-FIVE FEET FROM THE EDGE OF FORGETTING

### The Dishonest Manager
*Luke 16:1–13*

There is a parable Jesus told that has troubled the careful minds of theologians for two thousand years, and I think I understand why.

A rich man discovers his manager has been squandering his possessions. He calls him in and says: give me an accounting of your management, because you can no longer be my manager. The window is closing. The authority is expiring. Whatever this man has left to do with what he has been given, he must do it now, in the narrowing interval between the verdict and its execution.

The manager does not collapse. He does not beg. He does not waste a single moment of what remains available to him in denial or self-pity or the manufacture of excuses. He thinks clearly, acts decisively, and uses every resource still in his hands to do something real and lasting before the door closes. He calls in the debtors. He reduces their burdens. He builds something that will outlast his authority, something that will remain after the accounting is complete and the position is gone.

And Jesus — to the perpetual confusion of everyone who has ever read this parable carefully — commends him. Not for what he did before he was caught. For what he did after. For seeing the moment clearly and spending himself completely in it. For understanding, with the fierce intelligence of a man who has nothing left to lose, that the only thing that matters now is what you do with what you still have before the window closes entirely.

I have thought about this parable for a long time without fully understanding it.

"

And then I took a gentle, pleasant man to his wife's funeral, and I understood.

I work in a place where time moves differently. Not the clean mathematics of clocks, but the strange geometry of ending. A care and rehabilitation facility, once a hospital where bodies were mended, now a home for people whose lives have narrowed into wings and hallways, into the small territories of the frail. I drive them where they need to go: dialysis three times a week, eye appointments to see a world growing dim, Walmart for necessities whose names they sometimes forget, family reunions where they are loved and partly recognized. Ordinary destinations for people whose days are anything but ordinary, whose hours are measured not in minutes but in the slow counts of breath, of pills, of visits that come or do not come.

One wing holds those whose memories have thinned to threads. Dementia. Alzheimer's. The slow unspooling of a life once fully known, once tightly wound. In that wing, the past is not past but constantly present and constantly vanishing, a shoreline being eaten by an implacable tide. I have learned to move carefully in that wing. Not because the residents are fragile in body, though some are, but because the world they inhabit is different from the world I drive through on my way to work. It is a world where a man can look at his own hands and not be certain whose hands they are. Where the face of a daughter becomes the face of a stranger. Where sixty years of a life, the texture and weight and specific gravity of everything experienced, loved, and lost, can recede in a morning like water draining from a basin, leaving only the smooth bare floor of the present moment, clean and empty and without history.

The manager of that parable understood something about time that most of us refuse to understand until we have no choice. That the authority to act does not last forever. That the window is always, always closing. That the accounting will be called in, and when it is, the only question that will matter is what you did in the interval.

I did not know this yet on the morning I pulled the van around to the memory care wing and helped a gentle, pleasant man into the passenger seat. I knew his name. I knew his destination. I did not yet know what the day was going to teach me about what it means to be given time and what it means to spend it.

He had been preparing, in whatever way the mind allows when preparation itself keeps sliding away, to leave the facility and return home to her. Instead, he was returning home from her. From the warm fact of her presence to the cold fact of her absence. There is a quiet tragedy in that reversal that no manual teaches you how to hold, no training prepares you to carry. He sat in the passenger seat with his hands folded in his lap and looked out at the streets of the town he had lived in for most of his life, and he looked at them the way you look at a painting you almost recognize, almost certain you have stood before it before, almost certain it means something, unable to say what.

I stayed in the van during the graveside service. Twenty-five feet away. Close enough to see faces tighten and soften with grief. Far enough to remain invisible, a witness behind glass.

It was not a burial in the earth. No casket lowering into darkness. Just an urn small enough to hold in two hands, a small circle of mourners, and a sun that broke through the January clouds as if it had been waiting backstage for its cue, as if even the weather knew its duty to the occasion. A baker's dozen of people, perhaps fewer. Children whose faces carried her features. Grandchildren who had her eyes. Siblings grown old together. Friends whose own days were likewise numbered. A family knit tightly by loss, huddled against the January cold like survivors of some ancient shipwreck, doing what grief has taught the human animal to do since the first burial: hold each other, whisper the promises that the dead cannot hear, steady themselves against the cold that comes from without and within.

Then I saw him. Her son, I guessed from the shape of his sorrow. He stepped away from the group with the particular gait of someone trying to hold himself together, trying not to break before he reached privacy.

He walked to his pickup truck, bent over the bed of it, and sobbed into the metal. His face flushed red, his shoulders shaking with a violence that seemed to come from somewhere deeper than lungs. In that moment, grief had no ceremony, no script, no dignity. It was simply a human being breaking open in the only place he could, his forehead against cold steel, his body wracked by the knowledge that she who had given him life was gone, and all the words spoken at graveside could not call her back.

Watching him from my twenty-five feet, watching this stranger's private devastation made public only by my accidental witness, I felt something shift inside me. Not pity, which stands above suffering and looks down at it. Something more like recognition. This was the raw face of humanity in its most unguarded hour. Not performed for any audience. Not arranged for any camera. Just unbearably, irreducibly real. This was what we look like when the masks fall, when there is no strength left for courage, when love has nowhere to go but into the side of a truck.

And yet, for all that sorrow, for all the authenticity of that man's breaking, the gathering was small. Too small. Thirteen people, perhaps, to mark the passage of a woman who had lived seventy, eighty years — I did not know her age, but I knew the mathematics did not balance. It made me wonder, with the cruelty of an outsider's arithmetic, why so few had come to stand at the edge of her life and bear witness to its ending. Had distance swallowed the others? Had time done its slow erosion of the connections that once bound a wider circle to this woman's life? Or was this simply what a life looks like now, in our scattered age, when funerals compete with obligation and the ordinary drift of years?

The window closes, Jesus said. The accounting is called in. And what we find in the ledger is what we actually did with what we had, not what we intended, not what we meant to do, not the visits we planned but never made, not the calls we started to dial and then set down. What we actually did.

4

Later, back at the facility, I asked the CNA — a woman who tends to the forgotten ones with a patience that seems almost saintly, who moves through those hallways with the particular grace of someone who has made peace with the fact that her work will never be finished and does it anyway — I asked her if the man I had driven ever received visitors.

She looked at me with eyes that had seen too much and yet remained kind. "No," she said. "Not once."

Two words. Not once. Not in however many months or years he had been there, in whatever seasons had passed outside his window while he sat in his chair and looked at his hands. Not once had someone driven down these roads, walked these hallways, sat in that room where he waited without knowing he was waiting. The grandchildren who had stood at the graveside and told him they loved him, that they would visit soon — their words had floated in the cold January air, warm and hopeful and already beginning their long arc toward the ledger where such things are recorded.

He would not remember their promises. That is the mercy and the terror of it simultaneously. The forgetting that protects him from the daily wound of their absence also releases them from the accountability of their presence. You cannot be held to a promise by someone who cannot remember you made it. The window closes and the one who might have called you to account has already lost the thread.

But the manager in the parable was not commended because his master forgot to hold him accountable. He was commended because he acted before the window closed. Not after. Before. While the authority remained. While the resources were still in his hands. While there was still something he could do with what he had been given.

This is the question I carried home from that cemetery, that has lived in me in the weeks since, that I turn over in the dark the way you turn over a stone to see what lives beneath it.

What do we do with the time before the forgetting?

Not the forgetting of the one in the memory care wing, though that forgetting is real and its mercy is real and its terror is equally real. The forgetting of all of us. The slow erosion of connection that happens not because of disease but because of distance and obligation and the ordinary momentum of days that fill themselves with everything except the things that matter most. The forgetting that happens not in a wing of a care facility but in the daily choices of ordinary lives, in the calls not made, the visits not taken, the words not said while the window was still open and the person who needed to hear them was still there to receive them.

The manager used what he had, while he had it, in the service of the people the moment required. He did not wait for a better set of tools. He did not wait for a more convenient season. He acted in the interval, with whatever remained available, before the door closed.

That is the parable. That is what Jesus was commending. Not the dishonesty of the before. The urgency of the after.

Before we left the cemetery, before I drove him back to the place he could not remember was now his home, I heard the teenage grandchildren tell him they loved him. That they would visit soon. Their words floated in the cold air — warm, hopeful, and carrying in them the particular hollowness of promises made in the presence of death. That ancient human impulse to offer something, anything, against the dark. Maybe I am being judgmental, sitting in my van with my driver's distance and my professional remove. Maybe they meant every syllable with the full force of their young hearts. But something in their tone carried the feeling of ritual rather than intention, of words said because words must be said, because silence at a grave is unbearable.

And then the strange mercy arrived, the mercy that is also a kind of curse.

He would not remember their promises.

He would not remember their faces, already fading like photographs left in the sun.

He would not remember the funeral, the urn, the snow, the man sobbing into his truck.

He would not remember that she was gone.

He would not remember the woman he had loved, perhaps for fifty years, perhaps since they were young and the world was wide before them.

As we drove back through town — the CNA in front, speaking to him gently, me behind the wheel navigating streets I was still learning — he looked out at the buildings, the church where he may have been married, the park where he may have played as a boy, the houses he had passed ten thousand times, and asked with the innocent curiosity of a child whether he had ever been there before. The CNA told me later, her voice carrying the particular sadness of those who work among the forgetting, that every street we passed had once been part of his story. This corner store. That school. Those houses. All of it had been the geography of his life, the map of his existence, the ledger of his days.

Memory had taken the map from him. Left only a faint sense of familiarity, like a dream almost recalled but not quite grasped, like a song whose melody had gone but whose feeling remained — haunting and unplaceable.

The manager in the parable understood that the map does not last forever. That the authority to act expires. That the moment between the verdict and the execution is not a waiting room. It is the whole point. It is the only opportunity that remains.

Now, in the hours since, sitting in the silence of evening, reflecting on the day and all it contained, I feel a sadness I cannot quite name. Not grief, which requires relationship, but something more existential, more terrible in its implications. The graveside service felt thin. Threadbare. Almost unfinished. No celebration of life with its stories and laughter through tears. No remembrances shared. No one stood to say what she had meant, what she had been, what the world had lost with her passing. Just a duty performed in the snow, a ritual completed because rituals must be completed, but without the fullness, the richness, the human texture that makes ritual more than empty form.

And I keep asking myself, knowing there are no clean answers, knowing that some questions exist only to be held:

Did I simply carry an empty vessel that day — a body without memory, surrounded by strangers he no longer recognized, a participant in a ceremony that had meaning for everyone except the one person it was ostensibly for?

Was this truly for him, this gathering, these words, this cold standing in snow? Or was it for the family who needed to be seen — by themselves and perhaps by each other — doing the right thing, discharging their duty to the dead?

What does it say about us, about humanity in this late hour, when the one person most connected to the loss, most devastated by it, cannot remember five minutes of it, cannot hold the loss long enough to grieve?

And what weight do we give to promises made to those who cannot hold us accountable? Whose forgetting releases us before we have even failed?

The Dishonest Manager did not wait to be released. He acted before the release came, in the full knowledge that the window was closing, with the complete commitment of a man who understood that what you do in the interval is the only thing that was ever truly yours to give.

Maybe the funeral was for the living, as all funerals are. The dead, after all, are past our ceremonies, past our need to mark and mourn.

Maybe it was for the son who sobbed into his truck, for the grandchildren learning what loss looks like up close, for the siblings who had lost not just a sister but a piece of their own history. Maybe the gathering, however small, was exactly what it needed to be for the people who needed it.

And maybe forgetting is the only mercy given to the one who had lost the most — released from the daily knowledge of absence, from the fresh wound that would not heal, from the reaching for someone who will not be there.

But the parable does not end with mercy. It ends with a question directed at the living. At us. At the ones who still have the map. At the ones whose memories have not yet thinned to threads, whose windows have not yet closed, whose authority to act has not yet expired.

What are you doing with what you have, while you still have it?

Twenty-five feet. That was the distance. Close enough to witness. Far enough to remain outside the circle.

Perhaps that is where we all stand, in the end. At the edge of each other's forgetting. Holding what we can of what is slipping away. Making our small promises against the dark.

But the manager did not stand twenty-five feet away and watch the window close. He moved. He acted. He used what remained in the interval between the verdict and the silence. Not because he was righteous. Not because the timing was convenient. Because the moment required it and the moment was all he had.

The kingdom does not wait for us to find a better time.

The kingdom is the time we have.

Use it.

Now.

While the map is still in your hands.

While the faces are still familiar.

While the window is still open and the one who needs you is still there to receive what you have to give.

Go. Not tomorrow. Not when things settle. Not when life makes room.

Now.

Before the accounting is called in.

Before the tide takes the shoreline.

Before the window closes on everything you meant to say and never said, everything you meant to do and never did, everything you meant to be to the person twenty-five feet away who is waiting, without knowing they are waiting, for you to close the distance.

That is the kingdom.

That has always been the kingdom.

Not the place where the righteous dwell in their rightness.

The place where the manager acts in the interval.

The place where the distance gets closed.

The place where someone drives through the streets of a town they are still learning and understands, somewhere between the church and the school and the corner store, that the map is a gift.

And gifts, by their nature, do not last forever.

Use them while you can.

Into the Kingdom of Forgetting.

Into the Kingdom.

## CHAPTER 2
### THE FIELD OF UNKNOWING

*The Wheat and the Weeds*
*Matthew 13:24–30, 36–43*

The intake room at Covenant House smelled of industrial cleaner and something older, something layered beneath the pine-scented surface that no amount of mopping could fully reach. It was the smell of a hundred bodies cycling through in various states of chemical dependency, a thousand confessions made under fluorescent lights to counselors who had heard it all before, a building that had absorbed so much human wreckage that the walls themselves seemed to carry a residual grief, a molecular memory of every man and woman who had sat in these plastic chairs and tried to explain, to a stranger with a clipboard, how they had arrived at the place where arriving here was the best option left.

Elijah Watts sat in one of those chairs, his hands clasped between his knees, his right leg bouncing with the involuntary percussion of a body that had not been fully sober in nine years. He was thirty-four. He looked forty-seven. The arithmetic of addiction does not follow the standard tables. It multiplies certain things and divides others, compressing decades of physical deterioration into a few violent years while simultaneously stretching each hour into something that feels eternal, an endless present tense of need and procurement and the brief chemical reprieve that makes the need temporarily survivable.

He had been a welder. Before the pills. Before the pills became the powder. Before the powder became the needle. Before the needle became the only truth his body recognized, the only language it still spoke fluently. He had been good at welding. He had liked the precision of it, the way the arc bridged two pieces of metal and fused them into something that was neither one nor the other but a third thing entirely, stronger at the joint than at any other point. He had liked the metaphor of it too, though he would never have used that word. Two broken things made whole by fire. That meant something to him, even then, even before he understood what it meant.

The counselor who processed his intake was a woman named Grace, which Elijah would later consider the most improbable and on-the-nose piece of evidence for a universe with a sense of humor that he had ever encountered. She was fifty-three, had been sober for twenty-one years, and had the particular quality of attention that belongs to people who have been where you are and have no interest in pretending otherwise. She did not soften. She did not sugarcoat. She looked at him across the desk with the level gaze of someone who had seen a thousand Elijahs and knew that what he needed was not sympathy but accuracy.

"What are you using?" she asked.

He told her. She wrote it down without reaction, the way a mechanic writes down the symptoms of an engine problem, clinically, without moral judgment, interested only in the data that would determine the course of repair.

"How long?"

"Nine years."

"What happened nine years ago?"

He looked at the floor. The linoleum was cracked in a pattern that resembled a river delta. "My daughter died."

Grace set down her pen. Not dramatically. Just a small, deliberate lowering of the instrument, a gesture that said I am no longer recording. I am listening.

"How old was she?"

"Three."

"What was her name?"

"Lily."

Grace was quiet for a moment. Then she picked up the pen again. "Okay, Elijah. Here's what's going to happen. You're going to detox, which will be the worst three days of your life, and I'm not going to lie to you about that because you deserve the truth. After detox, you enter the residential program. Twenty-eight days minimum. The program includes individual counseling, group therapy, medical monitoring, and a work component. You will be expected to participate in all of it. You will be expected to show up. You will be expected to tell the truth, even when the truth is the last thing you want to tell. Especially then."

"And if I can't?"

"Then you leave. And you go back to what you were doing before you walked through that door. And that's your right. Nobody's going to chain you to a bed. But I'll tell you this: the door you walked through today is not always open. It's open now. It won't always be."

He looked at her. "You been through this?"

"I've been exactly where you're sitting. Different substance. Same chair."

"And you made it."

"I'm here," she said. "That's not the same thing as making it. Making it implies you arrive somewhere. I haven't arrived anywhere. I just keep showing up."

The detox was everything Grace had promised. Three days of a body in revolt, a mutiny of every system, every nerve ending, every cell that had been reconfigured over nine years to require what he was now denying it. He sweated through sheets. He vomited until there was nothing left and then vomited the nothing. His muscles cramped in configurations he didn't know muscles could achieve. His mind produced hallucinations that were not the colorful, whimsical kind depicted in movies but the gray, grinding, terrifying kind, visions of Lily standing in the corner of his room at 3 AM asking why he hadn't been there, why he had left, why he had chosen the needle over her memory, questions he could not answer because the answers were the thing he was detoxing from.

On the third night, a man appeared in the doorway of his room. Not a hallucination. A person. Older, maybe sixty, with a face like a topographic map of hard living, every ridge and valley earned through decades of the kind of experience that leaves permanent marks. He wore the faded scrubs of a night-shift aide, and he carried a cup of water with the careful deliberateness of someone who understood that at this particular moment, a cup of water was the most important object in the world.

"Drink," the man said.

Elijah took the cup. His hands shook so badly the water sloshed over the rim.

"I know," the man said. He pulled a chair close to the bed and sat down with the unhurried patience of a person who had nowhere else to be. "I know what this is. I've been here. Not metaphorically. Literally. In this room. Bed by the window. Seventeen years ago."

Elijah looked at him.

"My name's Vernon," the man said. "And I'm going to sit here with you tonight. Not because it's my job, though it is. Because nobody sat with me, and I've spent seventeen years wishing someone had."

Vernon stayed until dawn. He did not offer wisdom. He did not share his story in the way of people who are eager to establish credentials of suffering. He simply sat, a quiet, solid presence in the room, occasionally refilling the cup of water, occasionally placing a cool cloth on Elijah's forehead, occasionally saying the only thing that needed to be said, which was I know, I know.

When the sun came up, Vernon stood. He placed his hand on Elijah's shoulder. The weight of it was startling, not its physical weight, which was ordinary, but its intentional weight, the way it communicated through flesh and bone a message that words could not adequately carry: you are here. You are alive. You have made it through the night.

"You're through the worst of it," Vernon said. "The rest is just the rest of your life."

The residential program unfolded in the particular rhythm of institutional recovery: structured, repetitive, designed to replace the chaos of addiction with a predictable sequence of expectations that served as scaffolding for a self that had collapsed. Morning meeting at seven. Breakfast at seven-thirty. Group therapy at nine. Individual counseling at eleven. Lunch. Work detail. Afternoon session. Dinner. Evening meeting. Lights out at ten.

Elijah moved through it with the mechanical compliance of a man who had not yet decided whether he wanted to be here but had nowhere else to go. He showed up. He sat in the groups and listened to other people's stories and occasionally told pieces of his own, the safe pieces, the surface pieces, the parts that could be shared without going too deep, without touching the thing at the bottom that he was not yet ready to touch.

But there was a man in the group named Curtis who had no interest in surface pieces.

Curtis was fifty-one and had been in the program for four months, which made him an elder by the standards of a place where most people's tenure was measured in weeks. He was a Vietnam veteran with a voice like gravel being poured into a metal bucket and an approach to group therapy that dispensed entirely with the gentle, affirming protocols the counselors had been trained to follow. Curtis did not affirm. Curtis did not validate. Curtis listened with the focused intensity of a sniper and then said, with no particular concern for your feelings, what he thought was actually going on.

"You're holding out on us," Curtis said to Elijah during his second week. The group was seated in the circle, nine men in various stages of recovery, the counselor, a young man named James who was good at his job but still learning the difference between what the textbooks said and what the room required.

Elijah looked at him. "I'm sharing."

"You're performing sharing," Curtis said. "There's a difference. You're giving us the version that sounds right. The version that gets a nod from James and makes the guys feel like we're all progressing. But you're not giving us the thing."

"What thing?"

"The thing you're still using over. The thing that's sitting in your chest like a hot coal that you've learned to live with because the alternative is picking it up and looking at it, and looking at it would mean feeling it, and feeling it is the one thing you've spent nine years arranging your entire life around not doing."

The room was quiet. James shifted in his chair.

"You don't know what you're talking about," Elijah said.

"Maybe not," Curtis said. "But I know what holding out looks like. I did it for three months. And you know what happened? Nothing. I didn't get better and I didn't get worse. I just stayed the same, and staying the same in here is the same as dying out there, it's just slower and the food is better."

Elijah didn't speak for the rest of the session. He went to his room. He sat on the bed, looked at the wall, and felt the hot coal in his chest doing exactly what Curtis had described, sitting there, radiating heat, a permanent source of pain that he had learned to organize his entire existence around because the alternative, the picking up and the looking and the feeling, was the one thing he could not do.

Except the wall was not interesting enough to look at for very long. And the silence was not empty. And the coal was getting hotter.

Three days later, in group, he told them about Lily.

She had been three years old, and she had died in a way that was medically classified as sudden unexplained death in childhood, which is the medical profession's way of saying we don't know, which is the universe's way of saying there is no reason, which is the cruelest possible answer to the question that every grieving parent asks, which is why.

He had been at work when it happened. Welding. Fusing two pieces of metal into a third thing that was stronger at the joint. His wife had called. He had not heard the phone because he was wearing his welding hood and the arc was loud and the world inside the hood was just light and heat and the precision of the work. When he lifted the hood and saw the missed calls, he knew. He knew the way the body knows things before the mind has time to process them, the way the stomach drops before the brain has finished translating the information, the way the hands go cold and the vision narrows and the world becomes very small and very specific and very, very still.

She had been napping. She had simply stopped breathing. There was no illness. No injury. No explanation. She was there and then she was not there and the distance between those two states was so small, so impossibly, incomprehensibly small, that it broke something in Elijah that could not be unbroken, something that the welding metaphor could not reach, some joint that fire could not fuse.

He told this to the group. He told it slowly, in the halting, uneven cadence of a man pulling a splinter from deep inside himself, feeling it catch on the tissue as it comes, knowing that the removal will hurt more than the embedding did.

When he finished, the room was silent. Curtis sat very still. James sat very still. The nine men in the circle sat very still, holding the weight of what had been placed in the center of the room, a dead child, a father's grief, the terrible arithmetic of a universe that takes three-year-olds in their sleep for no reason anyone can explain.

Curtis spoke first. "Thank you," he said. Just that. Just those two words, spoken with the gravel voice and the sniper's focus and something else now, something underneath the hardness, something that sounded, if you listened carefully, like recognition. Like one broken man acknowledging that another broken man had just done the bravest thing either of them would ever see.

Something shifted in Elijah after that. Not dramatically. Not the cinematic breakthrough where the music swells and the patient walks out of the hospital cured. More like a door opening a crack, not enough to walk through, but enough to let air in, enough to let light in, enough to change the quality of the darkness inside from absolute to something slightly less than absolute, which is, in the geography of recovery, the difference between dying and deciding not to die today.

He began to show up differently. Not perform sharing but actual sharing. He told the group about the welding, about the way the arc fused two broken things into something stronger, and how he had always believed, without being able to articulate it, that this was a metaphor for something larger, something about how the broken places, the joints, the seams, the places where things come apart and are put back together, are the strongest places in any structure.

Curtis nodded at this. "That's it," he said. "That's the thing."

"What thing?"

"The thing you're going to take with you when you leave here. Not the sobriety, although that too. But the knowledge that you broke and the

18

break made you stronger at the joint. That's not a metaphor, brother. That's metallurgy. That's the literal truth about how metal works. And it's the literal truth about how people work if they'll let it be."

The twenty-eight days ended. Elijah packed his small bag. He stood in the doorway of the room where Vernon had sat with him through the worst night of his life and he looked at the bed and the window and the cracked linoleum floor and he felt something he did not expect to feel, which was gratitude. Not the polite, obligatory gratitude of a man who has been helped and knows he should say thank you. Something deeper and more frightening. The gratitude of a man who has been to the very edge of the place where life stops and has been pulled back, not by his own strength, but by a cup of water and a cool cloth and a hand on his shoulder and a gravel-voiced veteran who refused to let him get away with performing recovery instead of doing it.

Grace was at the front desk when he came down. She looked up from her clipboard.

"You leaving?"

"Yes ma'am."

She studied him for a moment. The same level gaze. The same refusal to soften. "You know this is the easy part, right?"

"The easy part?"

"This. The twenty-eight days. The structure. The schedule. The groups and the counselors and the three meals a day. This is the part where someone else holds the scaffolding. Out there, you hold it yourself. And the wind blows harder out there than it does in here."

He nodded.

"You have a plan?"

"I have a meeting tonight. And one tomorrow morning. And one tomorrow night."

"Good. What else?"

"I don't know."

She looked at him for a long time. Then she opened a drawer and pulled out a card. She wrote a phone number on the back.

"That's my number," she said. "Not the facility's number. Mine. You call it when the thing happens."

"What thing?"

"The thing that makes you think you can handle just one. The thing that makes you think you've learned enough to moderate. The thing that sounds so reasonable and so logical that you almost convince yourself it's true. When that thing happens, and it will, you call that number before you do anything else."

He took the card. He put it in his wallet. He walked out of Covenant House and into the sunlight and stood on the sidewalk and breathed the air that did not smell of industrial cleaner and pine-scented surface and he thought, this is the first day. And the first day is not the same as all the days that will follow. But it is the day that makes them possible.

He went to a meeting that night. He sat in a folding chair in a church basement that smelled of coffee and cigarette smoke and the particular brand of honesty that exists only in rooms where people have agreed to stop lying. He listened. When it was his turn, he said his name and he said what he was and he said how long he had been sober, which was twenty-nine days, which was nothing by the standards of the old-timers in the room but which represented, for Elijah, the longest continuous period of sobriety in nine years, the longest he had gone without the chemical barrier between himself and the hot coal in his chest, the longest he had lived in the unmediated company of his own grief.

A man came up to him afterward. Older. Quiet. The kind of quiet that has weight to it, the kind that comes from years of listening rather than years of having nothing to say.

"I'm Daniel," the man said. "I've been sober thirty-one years. If you need a sponsor, I'm available."

Elijah looked at him. "Why me?"

Daniel shrugged. "Because you remind me of me. And because somebody offered when I needed it, and I've been trying to pass that along ever since."

He accepted. Not because he trusted Daniel. Not because he believed that sponsorship would save him. Because Grace had told him to say yes to the things that were offered, because one of the few things he had learned in twenty-eight days was that the scaffolding required other hands, because the alternative was holding it alone, and holding it alone was how he had ended up in a plastic chair in an intake room smelling of industrial cleaner.

This is how the wheat and the weeds grow together. This is the part the parable doesn't tell you: that in the field of recovery, you cannot pull one without disturbing the other. The grief and the sobriety share the same root system. The love of Lily and the need for the needle grew in the same soil. You cannot rip out the addiction without disturbing the grief, and you cannot face the grief without risking the addiction, and the whole field is tangled and messy and nothing grows in neat rows and the farmer who planted the good seed has to watch it grow alongside everything that threatens to choke it.

Elijah learned this. Not all at once. Over months and years, in meetings and in Daniel's kitchen, over coffee that was always too strong, in conversations that started about nothing and ended about everything. He learned that the coal in his chest was not going to cool. That the loss of Lily was not a problem to be solved but a weight to be carried, and that carrying it sober was different from carrying it high, not lighter, not easier, but more honest, more present, more real in a way that made the carrying itself a form of love, because to feel the weight of her absence was to acknowledge the enormity of her presence, and that was something the needle had been stealing from him for nine years.

The weeds did not disappear. They do not disappear. They grew beside the wheat with the same stubbornness, the same refusal to be eradicated, the same deep roots. But the wheat grew too. And the farmer, who in the parable tells his servants to let both grow until the harvest, understood something the servants did not: that the field is not ruined by the presence of weeds. The field is the field. It grows what it grows. And the harvest, when it comes, will sort what needs sorting. But the sorting is not yours to do. Yours is to tend the field. To water the wheat. To show up in the morning and do the work and trust that the field knows things you do not.

The harvest will come. It always does.

But not yet.

For now, the field is growing.

And Elijah Watts, welder, father, addict, survivor, is in it, tending what he can, carrying what he must, pressing his arc against the broken seam and watching the light.

# CHAPTER 3
## THE EYE OF EDNA

*The Parable of the Sower*

*Matthew 13:1–23*

The hurricane did not arrive all at once. That was the first lie it told.

It came in pieces, the way most destruction comes, so gradually that the people standing inside it mistook each individual piece for something manageable. A gust. A shutter banging loose. A palm frond skittering across the yard like a green hand reaching for something it would never grasp. Each piece, taken alone, was survivable. Each piece said: this is not so bad. Each piece lied.

Her name was Edna, and she was a Category 4 storm with sustained winds of 145 miles per hour, and she was heading directly for the coast of southeastern Florida in September of 1968, and in a small apartment three blocks from the beach, a seventeen-year-old boy named Julian Reeves was about to learn the difference between hearing a warning and understanding one.

Julian's mother had left three days earlier. Not because of the hurricane. Because of the dealer.

The dealer's name was Marcus, and he operated out of a house on Oleander Street with the particular entrepreneurial calm of a man who understood that his product sold itself and his only job was to be available. Marcus had been Julian's mother's supplier for two years, which is to say he had been the architect of her disappearance, the engineer of the slow process by which a woman who had once braided her son's hair and sung him to sleep and packed his lunches with notes that said I love you, be brave had been systematically replaced by a woman who could not remember whether she had packed his lunch at all, who could not remember what day it was, who could not remember that the thing she was chasing had stopped being pleasure a long time ago and had become simply the absence of the pain that arrived when she stopped chasing it.

Marcus had gone to Las Vegas. A buying trip, he called it, though what he was buying and from whom existed in a stratum of commerce that did not appear in any ledger. He would be gone for five days. Five days without supply. Five days during which Julian's mother would experience the particular clarity that withdrawal forces upon the addicted, the brutal, unwanted, chemically mandated sobriety that arrives not as a gift but as a punishment, not as freedom but as a prison whose walls are made of the body's own screaming need.

She had left to find another source. She had taken the car, the grocery money, and the last of Julian's faith that the woman who braided his hair still existed somewhere inside the woman who could not remember his name on bad days.

Julian was alone.

The hurricane was coming.

And for three days, in the strange interlude between Marcus's departure and Edna's arrival, the apartment was quiet in a way it had never been quiet before. Not the quiet of peace. The quiet of absence. The quiet of a house from which the chaos has been temporarily removed, leaving behind only the outline of where it used to stand, like the chalk outline of a body on a sidewalk, the shape still visible even after the substance is gone.

Julian moved through this quiet like a boy moving through a museum after hours. He opened the refrigerator: half a carton of milk, a jar of pickles, three slices of American cheese still in their plastic wrappers. He opened the cabinets: a box of saltines, a can of pinto beans, a bag of rice that had been there so long the expiration date had faded to illegibility. He inventoried what he had the way a man inventories his supplies before a siege, counting, measuring, calculating how long each item could be stretched.

He did not call anyone. There was no one to call. His father had been a concept rather than a person for as long as Julian could remember, a name on a birth certificate and nothing more, a ghost who had managed the impressive feat of being absent without ever having been present. His mother's family had stopped calling two years ago, worn out by the particular exhaustion that comes from loving someone who is being consumed by something stronger than your love.

The first bands of rain arrived on Tuesday evening. Julian stood at the window and watched the palm trees begin their slow negotiation with the wind, bending, recovering, bending again, each gust pushing them further from vertical, each recovery a little less complete than the last. The sky had turned the color of a bruise, purple-green, the specific color that means the atmosphere is doing something it should not be doing, that the normal rules have been suspended, that what is coming is not weather but event.

He taped the windows. He had seen his mother do this once, during a tropical storm two years ago, before Marcus, before the pills, when she was still the woman who prepared for things, who thought ahead, who understood that the world required vigilance. He used masking tape because it was all he could find, applying it in the X pattern he remembered, knowing even as he did it that masking tape against a Category 4 hurricane was a gesture of hope rather than a strategy of survival. He did it anyway. Because doing something, even something insufficient, was better than standing at the window and watching the trees bend.

The power went out at 9 PM. The apartment went dark with a finality that was almost physical, as though someone had placed a hand over the world's mouth. Julian lit the candles his mother kept in the kitchen drawer, three of them, scented, lavender and vanilla and something called Ocean Breeze that smelled nothing like the ocean and everything like the idea of the ocean as imagined by someone who had never been to the beach.

He sat on the couch with the candles flickering around him and listened to the wind build. Not the movie version of a hurricane, not the sudden dramatic assault that arrives in the first act and provides the backdrop for heroism. The real version, which is slower and more patient and more terrifying because of its patience. The wind built the way a symphony builds, adding instruments one at a time, the low moan of the bass notes first, then the percussion of rain against glass, then the higher register of things beginning to break loose and fly, shingles and branches and pieces of the world being stripped away and flung into the darkness.

By midnight, the apartment was shaking. Not metaphorically. The walls trembled. The windows bowed inward with each gust, the masking tape stretching, the glass flexing in its frame, and Julian sat on the couch and watched the candles flicker and understood, for the first time in his seventeen years, that he was completely alone and that no one was coming and that the difference between surviving this night and not surviving it was entirely a matter of what he did in the next few hours.

The eye arrived at 2 AM.

He knew it was the eye because the wind stopped. Not gradually. Completely. One moment the world was a roaring chaos of horizontal rain and flying debris and the deep structural groaning of a building trying to hold itself together, and the next moment there was silence. Not the silence of peace. The silence of intermission. The silence that says: this is not over. This is the pause in the middle. The second half is coming, and it will come from the other direction, and everything that survived the first half will be tested again.

Julian opened the door and stepped outside. The air was warm and still and smelled of salt and broken wood and something electrical, ozone maybe, the scent of a sky that had been doing things it should not do. The stars were visible directly overhead, a circle of clear sky surrounded by the towering walls of the eyewall, clouds rising tens of thousands of feet, lit from within by lightning that flickered continuously, turning the walls into something that looked almost architectural, almost deliberate, almost like the walls of a cathedral designed by a god with no interest in human comfort.

He stood there for five minutes. He breathed the still air. He looked at the stars.

Then he went back inside and closed the door and waited for the second half.

The second half was worse. The wind came from the opposite direction, which meant that everything that had been pressed against one side of the building was now being pulled from the other. The physics of reversal. The same force, redirected, finding new weaknesses, new points of failure, new ways to disassemble what the first half had left standing.

A window broke at 3 AM. The one in the bedroom, his mother's bedroom, the room he had not entered since she left because entering it would mean confronting the evidence of her absence, the unmade bed, the empty dresser drawers, the smell of her perfume still faintly present in the fabric of the curtains. The wind came through the broken window like something that had been waiting for admission, filling the room with rain and noise and the particular chaos of the outside world finding its way inside, the boundary between shelter and storm dissolving in a single moment of structural failure.

Julian closed the bedroom door. He pushed the couch against it. He sat on the floor in the living room with his back against the couch and his knees pulled up and the candles burning around him and he waited. He did not pray. He did not make bargains with a god he had no relationship with. He simply waited, with the patience that belongs to people who have been left before and have learned that waiting is sometimes the only thing you can do, that the storm will pass or it won't, that the building will hold or it won't, that morning will come or it won't, and your job is not to control the outcome but to be present for it, whatever it is.

Morning came.

The storm passed.

Julian opened the front door and looked at a world that had been rearranged. Trees down. Power lines draped across the street like black streamers from a party no one had wanted to attend. A car turned upside down in the parking lot of the convenience store across the street, its wheels pointing at the sky in a gesture of surrender. Water everywhere, standing in pools that reflected the gray morning light, turning the neighborhood into a shallow lake dotted with debris.

He walked through it. He walked through the neighborhood and looked at what Edna had done and he thought about the apartment and the masking tape and the candles and the five minutes under the stars in the eye, and he understood something that he would spend the rest of his life trying to articulate: that he had survived not because he was strong, not because he was smart, not because he was brave, but because he had been there. He had not run. He had not hidden. He had stood in the middle of it and waited and the storm had passed over him and he was still here.

His mother came back four days later. She came back the way she always came back, with the particular shame-faced tenderness of someone who knows she has failed and cannot stop failing and wants desperately to make it up to you but does not have the resources, internal or external, to make it up to anyone, least of all herself. She brought groceries. She cleaned the apartment. She fixed the window with plastic sheeting and duct tape. She braided his hair and sang to him and packed his lunch with a note that said I love you, be brave, and for a week, maybe two, the apartment felt like something approximating home.

Then Marcus came back from Las Vegas.

And the supply resumed.

And the woman who braided his hair and sang to him and packed his lunches with notes retreated again into the place where the pills took her, the place Julian could not follow, the place where she went to escape the pain of a life that had become something other than what she had planned, the place that was killing her so slowly that each individual day of dying looked almost like living.

Julian had survived the hurricane. He had stood in the eye and looked at the stars and gone back inside and waited for the second half. He had done this at seventeen, alone, without preparation, without resources, without the infrastructure that makes survival something other than luck.

But he had no infrastructure. No meetings. No sponsor. No counselor named Grace. No gravel-voiced veteran named Curtis to tell him he was holding out. No Daniel to sit with him in a kitchen and drink bad coffee and talk about the difference between carrying weight sober and carrying it high. He had survived the storm, but he had survived it on rocky ground, and the rocky ground had no depth of soil, and when the sun came up it scorched what had sprouted because it had no root.

This is the part of the parable that breaks my heart every time I encounter it. Not the seed that falls on the path and is eaten by birds. Not the seed that falls among thorns and is choked. The seed that falls on rocky ground and springs up immediately because the soil is shallow, and the springing up looks like success, looks like growth, looks like survival, but the root system is not there, the infrastructure is not there, and when the heat comes, when Marcus comes back from Las Vegas, when the supply resumes, when the daily pressure of a life without support begins its slow, patient work of desiccation, the thing that sprouted withers because it has no root.

Julian's sprouting looked like survival. It looked like resilience. It looked, from the outside, like a young man who had weathered a hurricane alone and come out the other side stronger. But strength without root is not strength. It is the appearance of strength, which is a different thing entirely, and the difference becomes visible only when the sun comes out and the heat begins.

He started using at nineteen. The same pills his mother used. The same dealer. The same house on Oleander Street. The progression was textbook, which is another way of saying it was ordinary, which is another way of saying it happened to thousands of people in thousands of apartments in thousands of neighborhoods where the infrastructure of recovery did not exist, where the ground was shallow, where the seed sprouted and the sun scorched and no one noticed because no one was watching.

Years later, many years later, after the progression had run its full course and delivered him to a place that looked remarkably like the intake room at Covenant House, Julian would sit in a circle of folding chairs in a church basement and tell this story. He would tell it to people who understood it not as metaphor but as lived experience, people who had their own hurricanes and their own Marcuses and their own rocky ground. He would tell it because telling it was the root he had never had, because the circle of chairs and the bad coffee and the voices of people saying true things in plain language was the depth of soil that the parable says the rocky ground lacked, because the infrastructure of recovery, the meetings and the sponsors and the phone calls at midnight and the daily unglamorous work of showing up, was the root system that made it possible to survive not just the hurricane but the sun that came after.

The good soil is not good because it is better soil. It is good because it has depth. Because something has been built beneath the surface, a network of root and connection and support that holds the plant in place when the heat comes. The good soil is the meeting at seven in the morning. The good soil is the sponsor who answers the phone at 2 AM. The good soil is the community that says we hear you and we know and keep going. The good soil is the infrastructure of love applied consistently over time, the patient accumulation of small acts of showing up that creates, beneath the surface, a root system deep enough to survive what is coming.

Because something is always coming.

The sun always comes out.

And the question the parable asks, the question it has been asking for two thousand years, is not whether the seed is good. The seed is always good. The question is whether the soil has enough depth to hold it when the scorching begins.

Julian's soil, eventually, had depth. But it took years to build. Years of meetings and sponsors and phone calls and the daily work of putting down roots in ground that had been rocky for so long he had forgotten that depth was possible. The hurricane had taught him survival. The church basement taught him how to live.

The difference is everything.

# CHAPTER 4
## THE FIELD SHE DID NOT KNOW SHE OWNED

### The Hidden Treasure

*Matthew 13:44*

She was born into a house where silence was the loudest sound.

Her name was Miriam Castillo, and she grew up in a neighborhood where the houses were close enough together that you could hear your neighbors' arguments through the walls but far enough apart in every other sense that no one ever intervened. Her father was a presence measured not in words or gestures of affection but in the quality of the silence he carried with him from room to room, a silence that had weight and temperature, that could fill a doorway and make a child press herself against the far wall without understanding why.

Her mother worked double shifts at a textile factory and came home with hands that smelled of machine oil and exhaustion. She loved Miriam in the way that overworked women love their children, fiercely and from a distance, with the constant guilt of someone who knows she is not present enough and cannot figure out how to be more present without losing the income that keeps the lights on and the roof overhead.

What happened to Miriam in that house is not the center of this story. It is the soil from which the story grows. It is the field she did not know she owned.

She was seven when it started and eleven when it stopped, not because anyone intervened but because the person responsible moved away, left the neighborhood, disappeared into the vast American machinery of relocation and reinvention that allows certain people to simply leave their damage behind and start fresh somewhere else, carrying nothing but their appetites and their techniques, leaving their victims to carry everything else.

Miriam carried it. She carried it the way children carry things they have no language for, not in words but in the body, in the flinch that became a posture, in the vigilance that became a personality, in the inability to be touched without a small internal calculation of safety that happened so fast and so automatically that she did not even know she was doing it. She carried it through middle school and high school and into a state university where she declared a major in psychology with the vague sense that she wanted to understand something about human behavior, though she could not yet articulate what that something was or why it mattered so urgently to her.

It was in her sophomore year that she found the camera.

Not literally found. It was sitting on a table in the student union, left behind by someone who had moved on to the next thing, a small 35mm with a scratched lens and a strap that had been repaired with duct tape. She picked it up. She looked through the viewfinder. And something happened that she would spend years trying to describe and never fully succeed: the world, seen through that small rectangular frame, became manageable. Contained. Finite. The viewfinder did what her mind could not do on its own, which was to limit the field of vision to a single, specific thing, to exclude everything that was not that thing, to create a boundary between what she was looking at and everything else.

She started taking photographs. Not artistic photographs, not the kind that get displayed in galleries or published in magazines. Documentary photographs. Images of things as they were, unposed, unlit, unimproved. A crack in a sidewalk. A hand on a doorknob. The shadow of a chain-link fence falling across a concrete wall. The particular angle at which a child holds her body when she is trying to take up as little space as possible.

She recognized that angle. She had held her body at that angle for four years.

The camera became her first language of healing. Not because it cured anything, not because clicking the shutter released her from anything, but because it gave her a way to look at the world, really look at it, from a position of choice rather than helplessness. Behind the camera, she was the one deciding what to see. She was the one creating the frame. She was the one who could look and then look away, who could approach and then retreat, who could be present to what was in front of her without being consumed by it.

She did not understand, at twenty, that she was teaching herself the fundamental skill that would define her life's work. She thought she was just taking pictures.

After college, she applied to a doctoral program in clinical psychology. Her application essay described her interest in intergenerational trauma; in the way damage passes from parent to child like a gene that has not yet been identified but whose effects are visible in every generation. The admissions committee noted the essay's unusual specificity, its personal quality, the way it described the mechanics of inherited pain with the precision of someone who was not theorizing but reporting.

She was admitted. She spent six years in graduate school, studying under a professor named Dr. Abrams who had spent his career mapping the neurological pathways through which trauma rewires the developing brain. She learned the science. She learned the terminology. She learned to speak about amygdala activation and cortisol flooding and the default mode network with the fluency of someone who had mastered a second language. But beneath the science, beneath the terminology, beneath the careful academic apparatus of literature reviews and statistical analyses and peer-reviewed publications, something else was happening. Something that had nothing to do with what she was learning and everything to do with what she already knew.

She was excavating herself.

Each paper she wrote, each study she designed, each case she consulted on brought her closer to the thing she had been carrying since she was seven. Not closer in the therapeutic sense, not closer in the way that a patient moves closer to resolution through the careful guidance of a skilled clinician. Closer in the archaeological sense, the way a dig moves closer to the artifact it is seeking, layer by layer, brushstroke by brushstroke, removing the accumulated sediment of years to reveal the thing that has been there all along, buried but intact, waiting to be found.

Her dissertation was on the photographic self-documentation of trauma survivors. She gave cameras to women who had experienced childhood sexual abuse and asked them to photograph whatever felt important. The results were extraordinary. The women photographed doorways and windows and the spaces between furniture and walls. They photographed their own hands. They photographed their children sleeping, their children's bedrooms, the locks on their children's doors. They photographed the specific architectural details of safety and vulnerability with the precision of people who had spent their entire lives mapping these details without knowing they were doing it.

Miriam looked at these photographs and saw herself in each. She saw the seven-year-old girl who had learned to read a room for danger the way other children learned to read books. She saw the eleven-year-old who had developed an encyclopedic knowledge of every exit in every building she entered. She saw the college student who had picked up a camera and looked through the viewfinder and felt, for the first time, the power of choosing what to see.

She defended her dissertation on a Thursday in May. Her mother came. Sat in the back of the room. Did not fully understand what was happening but understood that her daughter, her quiet, watchful daughter who had carried something through childhood that neither of them had ever named, was standing at the front of a room full of professors and speaking with authority about the thing she had carried, and that the carrying had become something else, something that had weight and purpose and value, something that could help other people who were carrying the same thing.

After the defense, her mother took her to lunch. They sat in a restaurant neither of them would normally have chosen, too expensive, too formal, but the occasion seemed to demand it. Her mother ordered soup. Miriam ordered salad. They sat with their food and their silence, the comfortable silence of two women who had lived through something together and had never discussed it and might never discuss it and were okay with that, or at least had made their peace with it.

Then her mother said, "I knew."

Two words. Dropped into the space between soup and salad like stones into still water.

"I knew something was wrong. I didn't know what. But I knew. And I didn't ask. Because I was afraid of the answer. Because if I asked and you told me, I would have had to do something about it. And I didn't think I could do something about it and keep working and keep the lights on and keep us alive. So I didn't ask."

Miriam looked at her mother. The woman who had worked double shifts. The woman whose hands smelled of machine oil. The woman who had loved her fiercely and from a distance.

"I'm sorry," her mother said.

Miriam reached across the table and took her mother's hand. The hand that had worked so hard. The hand that had not been able to reach her in time.

"I know," Miriam said. "I know you are."

They finished their meal. They drove home. They did not speak about it again. But something had shifted, the way tectonic plates shift, miles below the surface, imperceptible from above but fundamentally altering the geography of everything that follows.

Miriam opened her practice the following year. She specialized in childhood trauma. She worked with children who had been through what she had been through, children who held their bodies at the angle she recognized, children who flinched at sounds she remembered flinching at, children who had developed the same encyclopedic knowledge of exits and the same ability to read a room for danger that she had developed at seven.

She gave them cameras.

Not as therapy, exactly. Not as a clinical intervention with a protocol and a manual and a billing code. As a gift. As a way of saying: here is a tool that will let you choose what to see. Here is a frame you can put around the world. Here is a way of looking that gives you power without requiring you to speak, because speaking is hard and sometimes impossible and the body knows things the mouth cannot yet say.

The children took photographs. They photographed doorways and windows and the spaces between furniture and walls. They photographed their own hands. They photographed the locks on their doors.

And Miriam looked at their photographs and saw the field. The field she had not known she owned. The field that had been there all along, buried beneath the soil of seven years of silence and twenty years of carrying and six years of academic excavation.

The treasure hidden in the field is not the thing you go looking for. It is the thing you find when you are looking for something else. It is the thing that has been there all along, beneath the surface, waiting, patient, undiscovered, valuable beyond any price but invisible until the moment of finding.

Miriam's treasure was this: that the thing that had been done to her, the thing she had carried, the thing that had taught her to read rooms and map exits and hold her body at the angle of minimal space, was not only a wound. It was also, and simultaneously, and without contradiction, a gift. Not a gift she had asked for. Not a gift she would wish on anyone. But a gift nonetheless, because it had given her the specific, precise, irreplaceable knowledge that she now brought to every child who sat in her office and held a camera and photographed the locks on their doors.

She knew. She knew from the inside. She knew the way you can only know things that you have lived, not studied, not read about, not been told about, but lived in the body, carried in the bones, absorbed through the skin during the years when the skin was thin and the world was large and the silence was the loudest sound in the house.

The field she did not know she owned was her own history, and the treasure hidden in it was the capacity to help other people find theirs.

She did not sell everything to buy the field. The field had already been bought; at a price she did not set and did not choose to pay. What she did was recognize it. What she did was stop walking past it. What she did was get down on her knees in the dirt of her own history and start digging, carefully, precisely, with the patience of an archaeologist who knows that what she is looking for is fragile and must be handled with care.

And what she found, buried there, was a treasure that the world had told her was damage, that the world had told her was brokenness, that the world had told her was something to be overcome and moved past and put behind her.

It was not something to be put behind her.

It was something to be brought forward.

Into the light.

Into the work.

Into the hands of the children who needed someone who knew.

# CHAPTER 5
## THE META-MELLOW MEN OF THE SECOND YES

### *The Two Sons*

*Matthew 21:28–32*

Thomas Brennan came home from Vietnam in 1971 with a duffel bag, a set of dress greens he would never wear again, and a silence so heavy it had its own gravitational field. His wife, Catherine, met him at the airport in San Francisco, and when she embraced him she felt the difference immediately, the way you feel the difference when you pick up a piece of furniture that has been hollowed out from the inside, the external shape unchanged but the weight wrong, the substance altered, the thing that had been solid now merely the outline of solidity.

He did not speak about what had happened. This was 1971. Men did not speak about what had happened. They came home and they went to work and they mowed their lawns and they sat in their chairs in the evening and they drank what they drank and they did not speak about what had happened because speaking about it would have required a language that did not exist, a vocabulary for the particular quality of moral injury that belongs to men who have been sent to do things their souls cannot accommodate, and no such vocabulary had been issued along with the dress greens and the discharge papers and the thank you for your service that was already beginning to sound hollow even before the last helicopter lifted off the embassy roof.

Thomas got a job at the post office. He carried mail. He walked his route every day with the methodical precision of a man who had learned that the only way to survive was to keep moving, to maintain forward momentum, to fill each hour with enough activity that the thing living in his chest had no room to expand. He was good at the job. Reliable. Punctual. The people on his route liked him. They left him Christmas tips and bottles of wine and notes thanking him for always getting the mail to the right box. They did not know about the nightmares. They did not know about the three drinks that had become five that had become seven. They did not know about the way he sat in his car in the driveway sometimes for twenty minutes after arriving home, unable to open the door, unable to cross the threshold between the world where he carried mail and the world where Catherine waited with dinner and questions about his day and the patient, terrified love of a woman who could see her husband disappearing and could not find the door behind which he was hiding.

Thomas said yes when it was easy and no when it was hard, and saying no was always easier because no was a wall and walls kept things out and keeping things out was what Thomas had been doing since 1971.

His son, Daniel, was born in 1982. Thomas was thirty-four and had been back from Vietnam for eleven years and had assembled around himself a life that looked, from the outside, like the life of a man who had made it, who had adjusted, who had put the war behind him the way you put a bad chapter behind you by turning the page and reading forward. He had the job. The house. The wife who had stayed despite everything. And now a son, a small perfect human being who arrived in the world with eyes that seemed to see everything and a grip that tightened around Thomas's finger with a force that was inversely proportional to his size.

Thomas looked at his son and felt two things simultaneously: a love so enormous it frightened him, and a terror so deep it had no bottom, because the love meant vulnerability and vulnerability meant that the world now had something it could take from him, and Thomas knew, with the particular knowledge of a man who had seen what the world could take, that having something to lose was the most dangerous condition a human being could occupy.

He said yes to the son. Yes to the love. Yes to the vulnerability. He said the first yes, the easy yes, the yes that every new father says when the nurse places the child in his arms and the weight of it changes everything.

But the first yes is not the yes the parable is about.

Daniel grew up in the shadow of his father's silence. Not a cruel silence. Not the deliberate withholding of a man who wanted to punish. The helpless silence of a man who had something to say and no way to say it, who carried a story he could not tell because telling it would require going back to the place where it happened and he could not go back, could never go back, had built his entire life around the principle of not going back.

Daniel learned to read the silence the way some children learn to read weather. He knew which silences were safe and which were not. He knew the silence that meant his father was tired and would appreciate being left alone and the silence that meant his father was somewhere else entirely, somewhere Daniel could not follow, somewhere that smelled of smoke and fear and the particular quality of darkness that exists in places where young men are sent to do things they will spend the rest of their lives trying to understand.

He did not ask about the war. No one asked about the war. This was the family's unspoken agreement, as binding as any contract, as absolute as any law: we do not ask about the war. We do not name the thing that lives in the house with us. We step around it the way you step around a piece of furniture that has always been there, adjusting our paths, narrowing our movements, making room for the thing that takes up space without ever being acknowledged.

Daniel enlisted in 2004. He was twenty-two. He did not enlist because of September 11th, though September 11th was the occasion. He enlisted because of his father, because of the silence, because somewhere in the inarticulate depths of a young man's need to understand the man who raised him, Daniel had decided that the only way to reach his father was to go where his father had gone, to see what his father had seen, to earn the right to ask the question that had never been asked.

He deployed to Iraq in 2005. He served two tours. He came home in 2007 with a duffel bag and a set of dress greens he would never wear again and a silence so heavy it had its own gravitational field.

Catherine, now sixty-two, watched her son come through the arrivals gate and felt the recognition like a blade between her ribs. She had seen this before. She had watched this walk before. She had embraced this particular quality of emptiness before, thirty-six years ago, in this same airport, holding a man who looked like her husband but wasn't, not entirely, not anymore.

The VA was supposed to help. The VA was always supposed to help. The Veterans Administration, that vast bureaucratic apparatus designed to serve the men and women who had served, existed in a state of permanent overwhelming, a system built for one scale of need perpetually confronted with another, larger scale that exceeded its capacity the way water exceeds a levee during a flood, not because the levee was poorly built but because the water was simply more than anyone had planned for.

Daniel waited six months for his first appointment. Six months during which the silence grew and the drinking started and the nightmares began their nightly rotation through the landscapes of Fallujah and Ramadi and the specific stretch of road outside Baghdad where a thing had happened that he could not speak about, that he would spend years learning to speak about, that would become speakable only when someone who had been there sat across from him and said I know, I know.

Thomas watched his son and recognized everything. The wall. The silence. The drinks that had become more drinks. The car in the driveway. The inability to cross thresholds. The first yes eroding under the weight of everything the first yes had not prepared you for.

And Thomas understood, with a clarity that arrived thirty-six years late but arrived nonetheless, that the first yes was not enough. The first yes, the easy yes, the yes that says I will go, I will serve, I will do what is asked of me, was only the beginning. The second yes, the metamelomai yes, the yes that means I will change my mind at the deepest level of my being, I will turn around, I will go back to the place I have been avoiding, I will open the door I sealed shut in 1971, was the yes that actually mattered.

He went to the garage on a Tuesday evening. Clement Street. Walt's place.

Walt was a Korean War veteran who had been running an informal gathering in his garage every Tuesday night for twenty-three years. There was no sign. No organization. No affiliation with any official body. There were just folding chairs and a coffee pot and a group of men who had been to the places and seen the things and needed a room where speaking about them was possible.

Thomas sat in one of those folding chairs and did not speak for three Tuesdays. He sat and he listened and he drank the bad coffee, and he watched the other men say the things he had never said, and each thing they said was a brick being removed from the wall he had built, not his wall, their wall, but the walls were all made of the same material and removing a brick from one weakened all of them.

On the fourth Tuesday, he spoke.

He said things he had never said. He said them in the halting, uneven cadence of a man using a language he has not spoken in thirty-six years, a language that had atrophied from disuse but had not died, that had been living in him the way seeds live in the desert, dormant, patient, waiting for the rain that would bring them back to life.

He told them about the village. About the order. About what he had done and what he had not done and the difference between the two, which was smaller than he had thought it would be and larger than he could bear. He told them about Catherine's face at the airport. About the silence that had become the architecture of his entire life. About the son who had enlisted to find his father and had found instead the same war in a different country with the same silence waiting at the end of it.

Walt sat and listened. When Thomas finished, Walt said: "Bring him."

Thomas looked at him.

"Your boy. Bring him next Tuesday."

Thomas brought Daniel the following week. Daniel sat in a folding chair in Walt's garage and looked at the circle of old men and young men and middle-aged men, all of them carrying the same weight in different configurations, all of them sitting in the same room doing the same impossible thing, which was speaking the unspeakable.

Daniel did not speak that night. He sat beside his father and drank the bad coffee and listened.

But he came back the next Tuesday. And the next.

On the third Tuesday, he said something to Thomas that he had never said before. Not about the war. Not about Iraq or Fallujah or the road outside Baghdad. He said: "I'm glad you're here, Dad."

Four words. The second yes. Not the easy yes of showing up. The hard yes of being present. The metamelomai yes that reaches down into the gut and changes the direction of everything.

Thomas looked at his son. He put his hand on Daniel's shoulder. The weight of it was intentional, communicating through flesh and bone what thirty-six years of silence had failed to communicate through words.

"Me too," he said.

They sat in Walt's garage, father and son, surrounded by men who had been to the places and seen the things, drinking bad coffee on a Tuesday night on Clement Street, and the silence that had been the loudest sound in the house for thirty-six years began, slowly, imperceptibly, like ice melting at the edge of a frozen lake, to thin.

It did not break. Silence like that does not break. It thins. It becomes, over time and with enough Tuesdays, translucent rather than opaque. You begin to see through it. You begin to hear through it. You begin to reach through it, the way Thomas reached through it to place his hand on his son's shoulder, the way Daniel reached through it to say I'm glad you're here.

The first son said yes and did not go. The second son said no and went.

But the parable does not end with the going. It ends with the metamelomai, the change of mind that is not a change of mind at all but a change of gut, a revolution in the deepest part of the self, the part that decides not what you think but what you do, not what you believe but how you move through the world.

Thomas's first yes was 1971. His second yes was thirty-six years later, in a garage on Clement Street, with bad coffee and folding chairs and a circle of men who had learned that the unspeakable could be spoken if you found the right room.

Daniel's first yes was 2004. His second yes was sitting beside his father in that same garage, learning that the silence he had inherited was not a life sentence but a wall, and that walls could be thinned, if not broken, by the patient accumulation of Tuesdays.

The second yes is always harder. It is always later. It always costs more than the first.

But it is the one that moves the world.

# CHAPTER 6
## *THE PRAYER OF BROKEN SIGHT*

*The Pharisee and the Tax Collector*

*Luke 18:9–14*

Yesterday, pain led me to the hospital, but pain was not the reason I was there.

The emergency room hummed with the low frequency of suffering—a sound you feel more than hear, vibrating through fluorescent lights and linoleum floors. I sat beside my wife, a priest whose presence moves through chaos like a candle carried through wind. My back throbbed. My patience thinned to a wire. And then he entered.

A man. Overweight, disheveled, clutching a large bag as though it contained his last possessions. He looked like someone the world had chewed and spit out. I made my assessment in seconds. Homeless. Addict. Burden. I watched him shuffle to the bathroom repeatedly, and each trip confirmed what I had already decided.

I knew nothing.

But I believed I knew everything. That is the terrible gift of judgment: it arrives fully formed, requiring no evidence, no inquiry, no humility. It is instant. It is efficient. It is poison dressed as discernment.

My wife sat closer to him. She leaned in. She listened. She heard what I had refused to hear: that he was a traveling nurse, far from home, far from help. That the bag held his entire life. That seizures were tearing through his brain because of an inoperable tumor. That he had months—months—and was trying to reach Hawaii to die where the ocean could hold him one last time.

I had already dismissed him. I had looked at his body and decided his worth. I had weighed him on the scales of my comfort and found him wanting.

When I returned from the registration desk, I saw my wife leaning toward him, her voice soft but unshakable. "I don't want to appear that I was eavesdropping, but I couldn't help but hear your story. I'm a priest. Would you like me to lay hands on you and pray?"

He said yes.

And there, in a waiting room that smelled of antiseptic and desperation, the sacred descended. Not through me. Beside me. I stood frozen, a witness to grace I had not earned and could not claim. My wife placed her hands on his shoulders, and her prayer rose like incense—quiet, fierce, unashamed.

I felt the floor tilt beneath me. This man is dying, and I judged him for living.

The pain in my back vanished that night, but the ache in my soul deepened. I lay awake, staring into darkness, and understood: the hospital was never about my body. It was about my blindness. It was about the poverty of my sight. It was about how easily I mistake appearance for truth, surface for depth, the visible for the real.

This was not the first time.

Years ago, I drove a city bus through the gray arteries of morning. One particular day, rain fell like judgment, cold and unrelenting. I arrived at the transit station before it opened and found a man sitting outside the locked doors, soaked to the bone, shivering so hard his teeth rattled.

I needed him to move so I could unlock the gate. I asked. He begged to come inside, out of the storm. I said no. I cited policy. I invoked rules. I shut the door.

When I left the building, he was still there, a monument to my refusal. I said nothing. I drove away.

As the bus filled with passengers, a young woman in the back called out, "Are you just going to leave that poor man outside in the rain?"

I muttered something about not catering to the homeless, about boundaries, about how you can't save everyone. The words tasted like ash even as I spoke them.

She said, "That's pretty heartless."

Her voice was not cruel. It was simply true. And truth, when it names us rightly, is a blade sharper than any accusation.

I prayed then, a desperate, clawing prayer: God, please let him still be there when I return. Not because I was righteous, but because I could not bear the weight of my own cruelty.

And he was.

I ran to him. I apologized. I opened the doors. I listened. He had been robbed. His car stolen. He was trying to reach Spokane, to get home, to find safety. I wept. I promised him food and money. I kept my promise. We embraced. We stood there in the rain, two men holding each other, and for a moment the world felt less broken.

But I did not feel redeemed. I felt late. I felt like a man who arrives at a funeral after the body has been buried, clutching flowers no one needs.

Why does grace always find me after I have failed?

You would think I would have learned. That such moments sear themselves into the soul and remake you. That once you see your own ugliness reflected back, you never make the same mistake again.

But yesterday proved otherwise.

Why am I this way?

It is not ignorance. I know the teachings. I know the parables. I know that the divine wears the face of the stranger, that holiness hides in the margins, that the Kingdom is populated by those the world discards.

It is not cruelty. I do not wish harm. I am not a man who delights in suffering. If anything, I flee from it. I avert my eyes. I cross to the other side of the street.

No, it is something deeper. Something older. A reflex of the soul, a flaw in the architecture of my heart.

Perhaps it is fear. Fear that the suffering of others will demand something of me I do not have the strength to give. Fear that compassion is a door that, once opened, can never be closed. Fear that if I truly see the pain of the world, I will drown in it.

Or perhaps it is pride. The subtle kind. The kind that does not announce itself but whispers in the back of the mind: You are discerning. You are wise. You can tell who is worthy and who is not.

But I cannot. Every time I try, I fail. Every verdict I render is overturned by reality. Every judgment I pass becomes a mirror reflecting my own smallness.

There is a parable Jesus told. You know it. I know it. But knowing is not the same as living.

Two men went to the temple to pray. One stood tall, robed in righteousness, and thanked God that he was not like other men—not a thief, not an adulterer, not a sinner. He recited his credentials: fasting twice a week, tithing all he possessed. He knew the law. He kept the law. He was, by every measure, good.

The other man stood at a distance. He could not even lift his eyes. He beat his chest and whispered the only prayer left to him: God, have mercy on me, a sinner.

Jesus said the second man went home justified. Not the righteous one. Not the one who had earned it. The broken one. The honest one. The one who had nothing to offer but his need.

I have stood in both places. I have been the man who thanks God I am not like the addict, the homeless man, the dying nurse with the bag. I have measured my goodness against the brokenness of others and found comfort in the comparison.

But I have also been the man at a distance, beating my chest, unable to speak anything but the truth of my failure.

I am the Pharisee. I am the tax collector. I am the man with the bag. I am the man in the rain.

And I am the one who still prays: God, have mercy on me, a sinner.

There is no resolution to this story. No triumphant ending where I become the man I want to be. I wish I could tell you that after yesterday, I will never judge again. That my sight has been healed. That I have learned my lesson.

But the truth is darker and more honest: I will fail again. I will look at someone and decide I know who they are. I will measure their worth by their appearance. I will close my heart when it should open.

This is the human condition. We are creatures of sight and blindness, of love and fear, of mercy and judgment. We contain multitudes, and not all of them are holy.

But perhaps—perhaps—the point is not to stop failing. Perhaps the point is to keep returning. To keep praying. To keep asking for the mercy we do not deserve and cannot earn.

Because the Kingdom is not a place where the righteous dwell. It is a place where the broken are gathered up. Where the lost are found. Where the blind are given sight, even if that sight comes slowly, painfully, one failure at a time.

Yesterday, I was blind. Today, I see a little more clearly. Tomorrow, I will likely be blind again.

But I will keep praying. I will keep failing. I will keep asking for mercy.

And maybe—maybe—that is enough.

# CHAPTER 7
## THE ONE WHO STEPPED AWAY

### The Lost Sheep

*Luke 15:3–7*

I walked into the classroom on the first morning of CNA training with a notebook, a pen, and a quiet sense that my life was about to change in ways I couldn't yet name. The room was bright, the tables arranged in a square, and the air carried that mix of nerves and anticipation that always comes when people gather to learn something that matters. I looked around at the others settling into their seats — most of them young enough to be my grandchildren, some of them still carrying the particular exhaustion of people who work two jobs and study on the margins of sleep. I was the oldest person in the room by decades, and I knew it, and I let that knowledge sit beside me without apology.

I took a seat where I could see everything. Years of driving had trained me to read a room the way I read a road — looking for patterns, tension, calm, danger, comfort. I had driven school buses carrying men fresh from incarceration, driven residents of care facilities to appointments and back, driven through weather that had no interest in my schedule. You learn, over that many miles, that the most important skill is not speed. It is attention. I didn't know it then, but that instinct — that practiced, road-worn attention — would become one of the most important tools I brought into this work.

The instructor entered with the calm confidence of someone who had lived this job long enough to know what mattered and what didn't. She didn't need to raise her voice. She didn't need to command the room. Her presence did that for her, the way a river doesn't need to announce itself to shape the land around it. She set her materials down, looked at each of us in turn, and said, "This course is normally eight weeks. You're doing it in three and a half. It will be intense. It will be fast. But you will learn what you need to learn." She paused, letting the weight of that settle. "The people you will care for don't have the luxury of waiting for you to feel ready. So we begin today, and we begin completely."

I believed her. I had been not-ready before — for recovery, for reinvention, for the particular humility of starting over at an age when most people are winding down. Not-ready was familiar territory. I knew how to walk into it anyway.

We started with the basics — handwashing, infection control, body mechanics. Twenty seconds of scrubbing felt almost ceremonial, the soap working between fingers and under nails with a deliberateness that reminded me of something liturgical, something about cleansing before entering a sacred space. I wrote everything down, not because I wanted to impress anyone, but because I had learned long ago that the things you write down are the things you carry with you when fear crowds out memory. I knew that one day someone's safety would depend on whether I had paid attention in this room, and that knowledge made my pen move carefully.

The terminology came next, and it arrived like a foreign country. Words I had never used before filled my notebook in careful columns: tachycardia, systolic, diastolic, apical, radial, Fowler's position, orthostatic hypotension. I practiced saying them quietly under my breath so they would feel natural when I needed them, the way a man practices a prayer until it lives in his mouth without effort. The younger students around me typed notes into phones. I wrote longhand, slowly, the way I had always learned — letting the words move through my hand before they settled into memory.

Every night, I studied four chapters. I read until the words blurred, then read them again. I practiced the steps in my mind before I slept — donning gloves, removing gloves, PPE, transfers, bed making, catheter care, feeding, bathing, dressing. I imagined myself doing them with real people, not mannequins, because the mannequins were only rehearsal and I had no patience for rehearsal that forgot its purpose. I thought about the men I had driven from prison back into the world, the way they sat in the back of the bus carrying everything they owned in a single bag, the way some of them stared out the window as if the landscape itself were astonishing. I had carried them. Now I was learning to tend them. The distance between those two things felt important.

Vitals were the first moment something inside me shifted in a way I couldn't explain with training language.

We paired up, and my partner held out her wrist, and I placed my fingers gently on her radial artery. At first, I felt nothing — just the warmth of her skin, the slight give of flesh over bone. Then, faintly, a tapping. A rhythm. A life, moving beneath my fingertips like a message in a language I was only beginning to read. I counted silently, steadying my breath to match hers, trying not to press too hard, trying to receive rather than demand. When I finished and recorded the number, she smiled at me and said, "You're steady. Most people grip too hard the first time. You just listened."

I didn't tell her that I had spent twenty-six years learning how to listen without gripping. That recovery had taught me, slowly and with great patience for my failures, that the things worth finding cannot be seized. They have to be waited for. They have to be allowed.

Blood pressure was harder. Trying to listen for Korotkoff sounds was like straining to catch a faint whisper, muffled by my own uncertainty.

The first time, I heard nothing but silence. The second time, I heard my own heartbeat, which was not what I was listening for but was perhaps what I needed to hear. The third time, I heard something faint and tentative, like a distant knock on a door I wasn't sure I had the right to open. The instructor came and stood beside me and said quietly, "Slow down. Release the pressure more gradually. Let the sound come to you. You cannot force this." I breathed. I released. I listened with my whole body instead of just my ears. And then — there it was. The first clear tap. Then the next. Then the next, each one a small affirmation, a pulse of confirmation that something was working that had almost stopped.

It felt like learning a new language in the place where all languages begin — not in the mind, but in the listening body.

CPR humbled me in ways I had not anticipated. The mannequin lay on the floor, silent and indifferent the way the dead are always indifferent to our urgency, and the instructor knelt beside it and demonstrated compressions — deep, steady, rhythmic, the heels of her hands finding the sternum with a confidence that came from having done this when it was not a drill. "You are not trying to restart the heart," she said, looking up at us. "You are giving the heart a chance to work again. You are buying time for something larger to arrive. Remember that. You are never the whole story. You are the bridge." When it was my turn, I knelt beside the mannequin and felt the strangeness of kneeling before something that represented a life not yet lost. My hands found the right position. I pressed down. One. Two. Three. Four. The rhythm felt familiar — it moved through me like the steady beat of tires on a long road, mile after mile of presence and forward motion, the discipline of continuing when nothing about the landscape confirms you are going the right direction. I counted out loud, my voice steady, and the instructor nodded and said, "Good. You're strong and you're consistent. In this work, consistent is what saves people."

Clinical days changed everything, and they changed it quietly, the way light changes a room not by arriving dramatically but by making visible what was always there.

The clinical rotation took us to a different facility — not the one I had driven for, but one that felt familiar in the ways all such places feel familiar, carrying the same smell of antiseptic and cafeteria food and something underneath both of those things that was harder to name, the particular atmosphere of lives being tended at their most vulnerable. We arrived in our new scrubs, notebooks in hand, trailing the slightly self-conscious energy of students who know they are being watched and evaluated and found either sufficient or wanting. The instructor pulled us together before we entered and said, "You are going to make mistakes in there. That is not a possibility. That is a certainty. What matters is what you do with them." I wrote that down too, in the margin of my notebook, because I recognized it as a truth that extended well beyond clinical training.

What I did not expect was what my younger classmates did. Several of them had been CNAs before — they had come to the course to refresh their certification, to formalize what their hands already knew. They had the fluid competence of people who have done a thing so many times it has become instinct. And on those clinical days, at a facility where everything was new to me and familiar to them, they stepped aside. Quietly, without ceremony, without making it a gesture that required acknowledgment, they simply let me take the helm. When there was a resident to bathe, they said, "Go ahead." When vitals needed to be taken, they handed me the equipment. When peri care needed to be done — that most intimate and humbling of ministrations, the tending of the body at its most private — they positioned themselves as assistants and let me lead. I have been in rooms where I was the least experienced person present, and I have learned that the most experienced people in such rooms reveal their character in how they treat the least experienced.

These young people, who could have filled every task themselves and been done faster and more efficiently, chose instead to make space for me to become. That is a form of grace I will not forget.

I bathed residents who could not bathe themselves, learning the particular choreography of warmth and modesty and efficiency that the work requires — keeping the person covered except for the area being washed, working quickly enough to prevent chill, slowly enough to communicate care. I took vitals, my fingers finding radial pulses with growing confidence, my ears beginning to trust themselves with the sphygmomanometer. I performed peri care with the focused attention of someone who understands that dignity does not diminish at the boundary of bodily need, that the person receiving this care is still entirely themselves, still deserving of the same regard one extends to anyone. I made beds with residents still in them, turning bodies carefully, tucking sheets with the precision the curriculum demanded. Each task felt less like a procedure and more like a conversation, a form of communication conducted not in words but in the quality of my attention and the steadiness of my hands.

And then there was the woman at breakfast.

The instructor took me aside before the morning meal and said, in the matter-of-fact tone of someone conveying useful weather information, "I'm going to assign you to feed her. Fair warning — she's a hitter. She doesn't always like being helped, and she has a way of making that known." I looked at the woman seated at the table — small, white-haired, her hands folded in her lap with a precision that suggested a lifetime of self-possession. I nodded and said I understood, and I went and sat beside her and introduced myself the way I had been taught, clearly and unhurriedly, giving her my name and my role and the simple fact of my presence.

She looked at me with the careful appraisal of someone who has been failed often enough to make no assumptions about the next person who shows up to help. I held her gaze and didn't rush. I prepared her food, tested the temperature, and offered the first bite without urgency, without the slightly strained cheerfulness that sometimes passes for patience but is actually its opposite. She took it. We found a rhythm — I watched her, she watched me, and between us we developed a small and wordless understanding about the pace she needed and the way she preferred to be approached and the particular angle at which the spoon worked best for her. She did not hit me. Not once, across two days of breakfasts and lunches, did she raise a hand in protest or alarm. I do not say this to claim any special skill. I say it because I think she was simply waiting, as so many people wait, for someone to take the time to learn her language before presuming to speak it.

I fed her and I talked to her quietly, about nothing in particular — the weather outside the window, the food on her tray, small observations about the morning. Whether she understood everything I said I cannot know. But she was present for it, and so was I, and there is a form of communion in that kind of shared presence that requires no confirmation to be real.

I also made mistakes, and I am grateful for every one of them.

One afternoon, I was caught in the hallway wearing gloves that should have come off before I left the resident's room. A cardinal error — gloves carry contamination, and contamination carried into a hallway is contamination spread beyond its source. The instructor appeared beside me with the quiet inevitability of a teacher who has seen this mistake a hundred times and knows exactly what it costs when it matters and precisely how to correct it without crushing the person who made it. "Gloves stay in the room," she said, simply and directly, and I nodded and removed them and threw them away and washed my hands and did not make that mistake again. On another occasion, I emptied a urinary drainage graduate without gloves — another fundamental error, another moment of forgetting in the middle of trying to remember everything at once. Again she was there. Again the correction was clear and without cruelty. "Gloves for that," she said. "Every time. No exceptions." I thanked her, and I meant it, because correction delivered with respect is one of the most valuable gifts a teacher can offer, and I had learned, in twenty-six years of recovery, that the people who care enough to tell you the truth are rarer and more precious than the people who let you go on being wrong to spare your feelings.

I did not make those mistakes again. That is the whole point of being corrected. Not shame, not punishment — correction. The steering of a life back toward its proper lane.

The written exams arrived before I felt ready, which was appropriate, because readiness in this work is not a destination you reach but a direction you keep moving toward. Every day another exam, every night more studying, my brain stretched in ways that felt both uncomfortable and right, the way a muscle feels after work it wasn't sure it could do. I wasn't doing this for a grade. I was doing it for the woman at the breakfast table. For the men I had driven back into the world with a single bag. For everyone I had carried without yet knowing how to tend.

The morning of the State Competency Exam, I stood outside the testing room with my heart steady but alert, the same quality of attention I brought to a road in uncertain weather. I thought of every resident I had transported over the years, every story heard through the thin membrane of a driver's silence. I thought of the young classmates who had stepped aside and let me lead. I thought of the woman at the table, and her patience, and the rhythm we had found together. I thought of the mannequin on the floor, and the instructor who had said, you are never the whole story, you are the bridge. When my name was called, I stepped inside and let training take over the way a road takes over when you stop fighting it and simply drive.

The evaluator nodded when I finished. "Good work," she said, and I thanked her and walked out into the hallway feeling lighter than I had felt in years — not because I had proven something to anyone else, but because I had kept a promise I had made to myself in that classroom on the first morning, when I sat down with a notebook and a pen and a quiet sense that something was about to change.

When the results came — passed — I sat with the word for a long moment before I let myself move. I was not just a driver anymore. I was not just someone who carried people from one place to another across the surface of their lives. I was someone who could care for them, tend them, find them in the silence, sit beside them at the breakfast table and learn the pace at which they needed to be fed. I was a CNA, and the letters felt less like a credential than a covenant.

I returned to the facility, and the staff greeted me with warmth, and one of the seasoned CNAs placed a hand on my shoulder and said, "Welcome to the work." Not the job. The work. The work of tending life. The work of listening with your whole body. The work of being present in the quiet moments that no one else marks or measures or remembers except the person who needed you there. The work of noticing what others walk past. The work of kneeling down so your eyes are level with someone else's. The work of stepping toward the one who has been left by the window, in the silence, in the diminishment, waiting without knowing they are waiting to be found.

I walked down the hallway, past the rooms, past the nurses' station, past the dining room where I had once been only a driver pausing at the threshold. Everything looked the same. Everything felt entirely different.

I had stepped away from who I had been. And I had stepped toward who I was always meant to become.

# CHAPTER 8
## FOUR INCHES DOWN

### The Lost Coin

*Luke 15:8–10*

There are moments in a human life when something moves inside us that has no name. Some call it intuition. Others call it instinct. Some, with trembling caution, call it the whisper of God. Whatever the vocabulary, the experience is older than language and deeper than logic. It rises from a place in the psyche where memory, love, fear, and something beyond all three converge.

Most of the time, we ignore these moments.

Most of the time, they flicker and vanish.

But every so often, maybe twice in seventy years, a hunch arrives with such clarity that it startles the soul awake.

And yet, paradoxically, the first companion of a true hunch is not certainty.

It is doubt.

Because faith, in anything, never begins with belief.

Faith begins with disbelief, and movement anyway.

This is the story of the first time it happened to me.

In the earlier chapter of my life, the one that still echoes like a half-remembered hymn, my daughter was six, living in that fragile age where friendships feel eternal because children haven't yet learned how distance can tear the seams of a small world. Her best friend gave her a mood ring for her birthday, a tiny oracle that promised to translate the weather inside her heart into color.

She guarded it the way a child guards the last warm ember of a campfire.

Then life, in its blunt adult way, cracked open the ground beneath them. Her friend's parents divorced, and the girl was carried three thousand miles away, a migration my daughter could not understand, only feel. Overnight, that little ring became a relic, the final artifact of a friendship that had no farewell ceremony.

One afternoon, I pulled up to the daycare and saw my daughter walking toward the car with the posture of someone who had misplaced the sun. When she climbed in, she collapsed into sobs so fierce they shook the air between us. I sat there, a father with empty hands, trying to decipher grief through tears.

When she finally found enough breath to speak, she told me she had lost the ring. She had searched everywhere. And then she said the sentence that broke something in me:

"It's the only piece of her I have left."

And then, without warning, without logic, without any of the usual scaffolding of thought, something inside me tightened like a compass needle snapping north. A hunch. A premonition. A feeling that arrived so suddenly it startled me. It didn't feel mystical. It didn't feel holy. It felt… impossible.

And the moment it arrived; the doubt arrived right behind it.

No. No, this can't be real. These things don't happen. Not to me. Not in my life.

Up to that moment, I had never experienced anything like it. Not once in seventy years of living. It felt like my own mind was playing tricks on me, offering false hope to a child who needed comfort more than truth.

I didn't want to believe it.

I didn't trust it.

I didn't even like that I was feeling it.

But I got out of the car anyway, not because I believed the hunch, but because to sit there or drive away would have invalidated my daughter's grief. I had to move. I had to try. I had to at least look like a father who would walk into the world and fight for the last thing his daughter cherished.

So I walked through the daycare gate, still arguing with myself, still thinking the whole thing was ridiculous. I wasn't following faith; I was following obligation. I wasn't trusting the feeling, I was resisting it, embarrassed by it, convinced it would lead nowhere.

And yet my feet carried me to the sandbox.

I didn't search. I didn't scan. I walked straight to the center, still doubting every step. I knelt, pushed my hand into the sand, four inches down, and felt something small and circular, with a tiny, raised bump like a heartbeat.

A ring!

A ring!

I pulled it from the sand, blinking at it as if it were a trick of the light. My first thought wasn't triumph, it was shock.

No… no, this can't be…

I wiped it clean, and then the truth hit me like a second heartbeat.

It was her ring.

Her actual ring.

The last bright echo of a friendship already dissolving into memory.

I walked back to the car with a calm that felt borrowed from another world. My daughter looked up, expecting disappointment. I asked her to hold out her hand. When I dropped the ring into her palm, she let out a sound that was part joy, part relief, part resurrection.

"How did you know?" she asked.

And all I could say, the only truth that fit the moment, was:

"I didn't. I just had a feeling."

I have thought about that day for decades. Not because it made me feel powerful, but because it made me feel small in the best possible way. It reminded me that the human psyche is not a closed room. There are windows in us we did not build. There are currents moving through us that do not ask our permission.

Some call it intuition.

Some call it grace.

Some call it the quiet mathematics of love.

Whatever it is, it seems to appear only when the heart is cracked open, when logic has reached its limit, when duty demands movement, when love is the only compass left.

If theology has a word for it, perhaps it is this:

the moment when the human spirit aligns, however briefly, with something larger than itself.

If philosophy has a word for it, perhaps it is this:

the psyche remembering that it is not alone.

And if a father has a word for it, perhaps it is simply this:

a feeling.

# CHAPTER 9
## *THE ONES WHO DID NOT KNOW THEY WERE SACRED*

### *The Growing Seed*

*Mark 4:26–29*

I have become a custodian of the dead.

Not by profession. Not by choice. But by the particular mercy of technology that has learned to do what God alone was supposed to do, stop time, restore light, return the vanished to the visible. I sit in the dark with a screen before me, and the screen opens like a wound in the fabric of the ordinary, and through that wound walks everyone who ever lived.

They do not know I am watching.

They never do.

It is a Saturday in April 1906. Four days before the earth decides it has carried San Francisco long enough and shrugs it into rubble and fire. But the earth has not decided yet. The earth is patient. The earth is keeping its counsel.

The film rolls.

Modern restoration has done something almost criminal to this footage, criminal because it removes every excuse not to feel it fully. The grain is gone. The flicker is gone. The comfortable distance of sepia and shadow that allowed us to say that was then and mean it, gone. What remains is clarity so fierce it becomes accusation. These are not ghosts. These are people. They move at the speed of the living because someone has corrected the frame rate and now they walk the way we walk, turn their heads the way we turn our heads, and exist at the tempo of the present tense.

A man in a wool suit adjusts his collar against the April wind. His shadow trails behind him like an obedient dog. He is thinking about something, you can see it in the slight downward angle of his gaze, the way his jaw is set, something ordinary, something pressing, something that will never be resolved because in four days the ground beneath his feet will become a different kind of ground entirely.

A woman crosses the cobblestones with the stride of someone who is late and knows it and has decided not to care. Her posture is magnificent. Her hat is extraordinary. She carries herself like a person who has made peace with the particular weight of being alive in a body in a city on a Saturday morning when the air is cool and the sky has not yet learned to mourn.

The streetcar glides through the frame. Its bell rings. It is a punctuation mark in the sentence of the city, a comma, a breath, a brief pause before the sentence continues.

None of them look at the camera.

This is what undoes me every time.

Not the knowledge of what is coming. Not the earthquake, not the fire, not the three thousand names that will be carved into the silence of the following week. What undoes me is the ordinary, glorious indifference of their living. They are not performing. They are not aware of being witnessed. They are simply being, which is the most sacred thing a human being can do and the thing we are least aware of doing when we do it.

The seed, scattered. Growing in the dark. The farmer does not know how.

Go back further. Go back to the very beginning of the record.

Lyon, France. December 28, 1895. The Lumière brothers have pointed their new machine at the gates of their father's factory, and at 12 o'clock the gates swing open and the workers pour out into the winter light and become, without knowing it, the first human beings in the history of the world to be recorded on film.

They are going home for lunch.

That is all. They are tired and hungry, and the morning shift is done and they want bread and warmth and the company of people who know their names. Some of them are laughing. A dog runs through the frame, and someone reaches down to pet it without breaking stride, the gesture so unremarkable, so perfectly human, that it reaches through one hundred and thirty years and lands in the chest like a fist.

They do not know they are making history.

They do not know that every film ever shot, every frame ever captured, every moving image that will exist until the end of time begins with them, with this moment, with these workers in their dark coats walking into the winter light of a December afternoon in Lyon.

Modern restoration has returned the color to this footage, warm stone, gray sky, the brown of wool coats, the pale faces turning briefly toward the camera with expressions that say what is that machine before they decide it is not their concern and continue toward home.

They are the first.

They do not know they are the first.

The seed does not know it is the seed.

Berlin. 1930.

This footage exists in multiple archives, restored now to a clarity that
is almost unbearable. A Saturday market. Flowers being sold from
wooden carts. Children chasing each other between the legs of adults
who do not notice because children have always chased each other and
always will. A man eating something wrapped in paper, standing at the
corner, watching the traffic with the comfortable expression of
someone who has nowhere particular to be and is enjoying the luxury
of that.

I know what is coming.

They do not.

This is the particular cruelty of the time traveler, not that you cannot
warn them, but that warning was never the point. The point is witness.
The point is to see them as they were before the world rearranged itself
around them, to hold in the mind simultaneously the man eating his
lunch in the autumn sunshine and the world that is three years from
arriving, to feel the full unbearable weight of the distance between
what was and what came.

And yet.

Even here. Even knowing. Even with the full catastrophic weight of
history pressing down on every frame, they are beautiful.

The woman arranging flowers at her cart. The child who stops chasing
and looks directly at the camera for one full second with an expression
of complete and uncomplicated curiosity before running away. The old

man on the bench who has seen enough of the world to simply sit in it, unhurried, present, sufficient.

They are beautiful because they are alive in the way that only the unaware can be truly alive, without the performance of significance, without the burden of knowing they are being watched, without anything between them and the simple animal fact of their existence.

The seed grows and the farmer sleeps and rises and sleeps again and does not know how the growing happens.

It happens anyway.

Coney Island. 1903.

Someone has aimed their camera at the beach and what pours through the lens is joy so unguarded it feels almost transgressive to watch. People in the water, the women in their extraordinary bathing costumes, the men in their striped wool suits that would be agony to swim in and yet here they are, swimming, laughing, being knocked down by waves and standing up laughing harder. Children building things in the sand that the tide will erase. A couple sitting at the water's edge doing nothing at all except existing near each other, which is its own form of grace.

The restored color gives the water a blue that feels almost too beautiful. The restored frame rate gives the waves their true rhythm. And the effect is not that this looks like yesterday. The effect is that yesterday looks like this, that the present and the past are the same gesture repeated, the same wave breaking, the same child running toward the water and being pulled back by a mother's hand, the same laughter that sounds exactly like laughter always sounds, which is to say like proof that being alive is sometimes, against all odds, enough.

They are evidence.

Every one of them. Evidence that the world was inhabited by people who felt the cold water and laughed anyway, who built things knowing the tide was coming, who sat near the ones they loved and let that nearness be sufficient.

We are not promised longevity.

We are promised now.

And so I arrive, finally, at the question that all this footage has been quietly asking from the beginning.

If they are evidence, those men in their wool suits, those workers going home to lunch, those children on the Berlin street, those people laughing in the cold Atlantic waves, if their gestures and their glances and their ordinary unremarkable living constitutes a kind of scripture that we are still reading more than a century later, then what are we?

Right now. This moment. Whatever Saturday or Tuesday or unremarkable Thursday this happens to be.

We are being recorded.

Not necessarily by cameras, though cameras are everywhere now, more eyes than the ancient world could have imagined, more witnesses than any life has ever had. But recorded in the deeper sense. Recorded by the ones who will come after. By the children who will find the footage, by the grandchildren who will restore it, by the strangers not yet born who will sit in their own dark rooms with their own screens and watch us move through our ordinary days and feel the same thing we feel watching the man in San Francisco adjust his collar against the April wind.

They did not know they were sacred.

And they will be right.

This is what the parable has always known.

A man scatters seed on the ground. He sleeps and rises, night and day. The seed sprouts and grows and he does not know how. The earth produces of itself, first the blade, then the ear, then the full grain in the ear. And when the grain is ripe, at once he puts in the sickle, because the harvest has come.

The workers leaving the Lumière factory did not know they were planting anything.

The woman crossing the San Francisco cobblestones did not know she was leaving something behind.

The child on the Berlin street who looked directly into the camera for one full second did not know that look would travel one hundred years and land in a stranger's chest like a seed finding soil.

They scattered themselves into time simply by living. By being present in their bodies on their particular streets on their particular Saturdays. By adjusting collars and arranging flowers and eating lunch in the autumn sunshine and laughing in cold water.

And the harvest came.

Is coming.

Will come.

For them. For us. For the ones not yet born who will restore our footage to a clarity we never imagined, who will correct our frame rate and return our colors and watch us move through our days at the tempo of the present tense, who will lean toward their screens the way we lean toward ours and feel the full unbearable weight of our ordinary beauty.

They will say: look at the way she carries that. Look at the way he turns his head. Look at how they did not know.

And they will be right.

We do not know.

We are the seed that does not know it is growing.

We are the grain that does not know the harvest is coming.

We are the footage, already shot, already sacred, already on its way to becoming the thing that someone not yet born will watch in a dark room and feel, in the chest, like a hand resting gently on the back of the neck.

Like breath on the shoulder.

Like someone saying: I'm here. I see you. You were real.

So walk carefully on your cobblestones.

Speak as though your words will be studied by the unborn, because they will.

Carry your sorrow without spilling it, the way the woman on the San Francisco street carried hers, with the grace of someone who understands that grace is not proclaimed but practiced, one ordinary gesture at a time.

Build your sand castles knowing the tide is coming, because the building is the point, not the keeping.

And when you see someone adjust their collar against the wind, when you see a child look directly at you with that expression of complete and uncomplicated curiosity, stop.

Bear witness.

Because the camera is always rolling.

The seed is always growing.

And the harvest, when it comes, will be more beautiful than anything we planted.

We just won't know how it happened.

We never do.

That is the grace.

That has always been the grace.

*CHAPTER 10*
*THE ROAD BETWEEN REALMS*

*The Good Samaritan*

*Luke 10:25–37*

The sky had begun its slow unraveling, gray silk fraying into white like the lie Elias Cormier had been telling himself for six months, that he could keep walking, keep moving, keep the cold at bay through sheer forward momentum, as though distance were the same as escape, as though you could outrun what you carried in your chest like a second heart, black and beating, pumping shame through every vein until even your fingertips throbbed with it, until the cold was a mercy because it numbed everything, froze the guilt solid so you could carry it without feeling its weight.

Snowflakes drifted from the heavens not in the chaotic swirl of a proper blizzard but with the deliberate patience of something that knew it had all night, all week, all winter to bury the world beneath its cold communion. They settled on Elias's shoulders like the hands of the dead, accumulating, patient, inevitable. He stood on a street corner in Warsaw, Missouri, population 2,127, a town so small it barely warranted a dot on most maps, a place where highways intersected and people passed through but rarely stayed, a place where being forgotten was easier than being remembered, which was why Elias had chosen it, or why the road had delivered him here, he was no longer sure which.

His name was Elias Cormier, though no one had spoken it aloud in eleven days. He had not eaten since Tuesday, three days ago, or was it four? Time had become elastic, unreliable, a thing that stretched and

81

compressed without pattern, marked not by clocks but by the intensity of his hunger, the depth of the cold that had settled into his bones like a second skeleton made of ice, the way his thoughts circled and circled the same dark center, like water spiraling down a drain. He had not slept in a bed since Christmas Eve, which felt like a memory from someone else's life, from the person he had been before the highway, before the wallet, before he learned that you could kill someone without meaning to and then kill yourself slowly afterward, one frozen step at a time, walking until your body gave out or your conscience did, whichever came first.

He stood before a brick building whose façade bore the faded remnants of what had once been a Salvation Army thrift store, the logo barely visible, the paint peeling like old skin, the windows dark except for a single amber light on the second floor that glowed with the soft constancy of a vigil candle, a light that suggested someone was awake, someone was present, someone might answer if he knocked.

But Elias did not knock.

He had tried three churches that afternoon, and three churches had failed him in three different ways, each failure a small education in how mercy worked in America, which was to say: carefully, selectively, within business hours and according to policy, never spontaneously, never impulsively, never in a way that might create liability or precedent or the uncomfortable obligation to see a stranger as fully human.

The first church had been a white clapboard Methodist building with a red door and a sign that read All Are Welcome in letters that had once been gold but had faded to the color of old brass, tarnished, dull, more promise than truth. The door had been locked. Elias had pulled the handle, had knocked, had waited in the cold while snow began to accumulate on his shoulders like judgment taking physical form. No one came. Through the stained glass window, Jesus with the children, rendered in blues and golds that caught what little light the gray afternoon offered, he could see the empty pews, the altar draped in purple for Advent, the cross catching light from somewhere unseen. The building was beautiful in the way abandoned things sometimes are, full of the ghost of what it had been meant for, what it had promised, what it had failed to deliver.

He had stood there for twenty minutes, knocking periodically, his knuckles raw from the cold and the futile percussion of need against indifference. Finally, a man in a heavy coat had walked past on the sidewalk, glanced at Elias, glanced at the locked door, and kept walking without breaking stride, as though Elias were not there at all, as though he had already become what he feared he was becoming: invisible, insubstantial, a ghost haunting the margins of a world that no longer had room for him.

The second church had been larger, modern, with a parking lot that could hold two hundred cars and a digital sign that scrolled inspirational messages in bright red LED: Jesus Loves You and Wednesday Night Bible Study 7 PM and Food Pantry Open Thursdays 10-2. The building had the institutional feel of a school or a hospital, all clean lines and efficiency, designed not for transcendence but for function, for the smooth processing of souls through programs and services and the carefully managed distribution of grace according to approved protocols.

A woman sat in the office behind a desk of blonde wood, her workspace organized with the precision of someone who valued order above all things, who believed that chaos could be held at bay through proper filing systems and clear signage and the rigorous enforcement of policy. She had looked up when Elias entered, her smile freezing when she registered his appearance, the unwashed smell that preceded him like an announcement, the hollowness of his cheeks, the way he held himself like a man bracing for a blow he knew was coming but could not avoid.

"Can I help you?" she had asked, though her tone suggested she already knew the answer was no, that she was simply following the script, performing the ritual of hospitality without any intention of actually providing it.

"I'm hungry," Elias had said. His voice sounded strange to him, hoarse, unused, the voice of someone who had spent too many days alone, who had forgotten how to shape words for another person's hearing. "And I need a place to stay. Just for tonight. The storm they're saying it's going to be bad."

"The food pantry is only open Thursdays," she interrupted, her words arriving before he had finished speaking, as though she had heard this request so many times that she no longer needed to listen to know what was being asked. "Ten to two. And we don't have overnight facilities. You'll need to contact the county social services office. They have a list of shelters."

"I called," he said. "They're full."

She had looked at him with something that might have been pity or might have been fear, he could no longer tell the difference, had learned that the two emotions wore the same face, produced the same result, which was distance, the careful maintenance of boundaries, the preservation of one's own comfort at the expense of another's need. "I'm sorry," she said, and perhaps she even meant it in some abstract way, in the way you might be sorry about suffering that happened far away, in other countries, to people whose names you would never know. "I wish I could help, but we don't have the resources. Our insurance doesn't cover… Have you tried the Salvation Army?"

He had not answered. Had simply turned and walked back into the cold, understanding that "we don't have the resources" was code, was the language institutions used when what they really meant was "we have resources but we're saving them for people who look like they deserve them, who smell better, who won't make the other members uncomfortable, who fit the demographic we're trying to serve."

The third church, Catholic, stone, ancient by Missouri standards, with stations of the cross carved into the exterior walls like a catechism written in granite, had offered him the cruelest rejection of all, which was the rejection of proximity, of near-mercy, of help that was almost offered and then retracted at the last possible moment.

A priest had been leaving just as Elias approached, descending the steps in a long black coat, breath visible in the cold, keys jingling as he walked toward a car idling at the curb, a nice car, Elias noticed, German, well-maintained, the kind of car that spoke of stability and comfort and a life lived at a sufficient distance from desperation that you could afford to ignore it when it appeared before you asking for help.

The priest had glanced at Elias. Their eyes had met. For one moment, one terrible, crystalline moment—Elias had seen recognition flash across the man's face, had seen the priest understand exactly what Elias needed, had seen him calculate the cost of stopping, of helping, of opening the church and disrupting his evening, of inviting this stranger with his smell and his need into the warm sanctuary of a building that existed, theoretically, to provide exactly this kind of mercy.

And then the priest had quickened his pace. Had climbed into the car without a word. Had driven away, red taillights disappearing into the thickening snow like the eyes of some animal retreating into the forest, choosing survival over engagement, self-preservation over service.

Elias had stood in the empty parking lot and felt something inside him crack, not loudly, not dramatically, but with the quiet finality of ice on a pond in early spring, a sound only he could hear, a fracture that would widen slowly, inevitably, until there was nothing left to hold, until the self he had been, the young man who had believed in fairness and work and the basic decency of the world—collapsed entirely and what remained was only this: a body, walking, animated by nothing more than the dumb biological imperative to keep moving, to seek shelter, to postpone the final reckoning as long as possible even though you knew it was coming, knew it was inevitable, knew that every step forward was also a step toward the moment when the walking would stop and the accounting would begin.

And now he stood before this fourth building, this place that was not quite a church and not quite abandoned, this window with its amber light that suggested the possibility, only the possibility, nothing promised, nothing guaranteed—that someone inside might see him not as a problem to be managed or a liability to be avoided but as a human being in need of the simplest, oldest form of love: the kind that says come in from the cold.

He did not know how long he stood there. The snow continued its patient work, covering his shoulders, his hair, the tops of his boots that had holes in them he'd tried to patch with duct tape but which still let in water, still let in cold, still reminded him with every step that he was breaking down, falling apart, becoming the kind of person whose shoes don't work anymore, whose body is failing, whose presence in the world grows more tenuous with each passing day.

Then the door opened.

Not the front door of the building, that remained closed, dark, forbidding. But a side door, wooden, set into the brick like an afterthought, a door he had not noticed before. And from this door stepped a man who looked like he had been awake too long, who carried the weariness of someone who knew what it meant to stay up through the night bearing witness to other people's suffering.

He wore a long black coat, worn at the cuffs. A crimson scarf tucked at his throat. His hair was silver, swept back from a face deeply lined, the kind of face that earned its texture through years of listening to confessions, to grief, to the endless catalog of human failure and human hope. He was perhaps seventy, perhaps older, age being less a number than a quality, a depth, the weight of decades visible in the way he moved, slowly, deliberately, like someone who had learned that haste solved nothing, that mercy required patience, that the work of healing happened at its own pace and could not be rushed.

He looked at Elias with eyes that were neither kind nor unkind but simply present, eyes that saw without flinching, without the small calibrations of disgust or pity that Elias had learned to recognize in the faces of strangers, eyes that looked and did not turn away.

"You're not dressed for this kind of storm," the man said. His voice was low, warm, textured like old wood that had been handled by many hands, worn smooth by use. Not the voice of authority but of experience, of someone who had stood where Elias was standing, not literally perhaps but spiritually, in the cold place where help is needed and help is not certain.

Elias shrugged, a gesture that cost him. His shoulders screamed. His muscles had frozen into positions of defense, of hunching against the cold, and every movement required conscious effort, required the override of a body that wanted to stop, to lie down, to let the snow do its work. "Didn't know there was one coming."

"The weathermen have been talking about nothing else for three days."

"I don't watch the news."

The man nodded, as though this were a perfectly reasonable answer, as though walking endlessly through a Missouri winter without checking the forecast were something he encountered regularly, which perhaps he did. "Where have you been?"

"Walking."

"For how long?"

"A while."

"Would you like to come in from the cold?"

The question hung in the air between them, simple, direct, free of conditions or qualifications, free of the institutional language that always came with help in America, the forms to be filled, the eligibility to be established, the worthiness to be demonstrated. Just the question: would you like to come in?

Elias hesitated. Not because he distrusted the invitation but because accepting it required a small act of will, a decision to step from one state into another, and he was so tired, so profoundly exhausted, that even small decisions felt monumental, felt like they required reserves of strength he no longer possessed. He had been walking for so long that walking had become not a choice but a condition, and stopping, truly stopping, accepting shelter, admitting need, felt dangerous in a way he could not articulate, as though to stop moving was to allow the thing he was running from to catch up, to allow the truth he was carrying to finally announce itself.

Snowflakes melted on his lashes. He blinked them away. Looked past the man into the building where the soft amber light promised warmth, dryness, a temporary reprieve from the cold that had become his only constant companion.

"Sure," he said finally. The word came out hoarse, barely audible over the whisper of falling snow.

The man stepped aside. Elias crossed the threshold. The door closed behind them with a sound like a covenant being sealed, like the world outside agreeing to wait, to suspend its verdict, to give him one more night before the reckoning resumed.

Inside, the air was thick with the scent of old wood and brewed coffee and something faintly medicinal—eucalyptus, maybe, or camphor, the kind of smell that clung to churches and nursing homes and places where the sick came to be tended, where bodies and souls in various states of disrepair sought refuge. A narrow hallway stretched ahead, illuminated by a single bulb in a glass fixture overhead, the light weak, yellow, casting shadows that made the walls seem to breathe.

The walls themselves were lined with framed photographs, black and white images of people Elias did not recognize: men in work clothes standing before factories whose smokestacks had long since gone cold, women in aprons holding children whose lives had already been lived and finished, groups gathered for church picnics or union meetings or weddings, faces turned toward the camera with expressions that suggested they believed the future held promise, that their children would have it better, that the arc of history bent toward something good. They had been wrong, mostly, but they had not known that yet, and there was something heartbreaking about their optimism, their faith, their willingness to smile for a camera that would outlive them, that would bear witness to their hope long after the hope itself had proven unfounded.

The man led him to a staircase at the end of the hall. The steps were narrow, wooden, each one groaning under their weight like a psalm sung in a minor key, like the voice of the building itself acknowledging their presence, acknowledging that something was happening here that mattered, that two people were climbing stairs in a snowstorm while everyone else in the world was safe at home, and that this small act of mercy, a door opened, a stranger invited in, was significant in ways that could not be measured but only felt.

At the top, the man opened a door into a small office. The room was modest but dignified: a desk of dark oak scarred with the rings of a thousand coffee cups, surfaces that bore the history of long nights and difficult work, brass lamp with a green shade that cast a circle of warm light across papers stacked in careful piles, bookshelves lined with volumes on theology and philosophy and the occasional novel, Elias glimpsed Tolstoy, Dostoevsky, Camus, names that stirred something in him, some memory of a life before this one, a life where he had been a student, a reader, a person who believed that books held answers to questions that mattered. A crucifix hung above the desk, simple, unadorned, no corpus, just the crossed beams, stark and absolute.

"Sit," the man said gently, gesturing to a chair upholstered in faded green fabric.

Elias sat. The chair exhaled beneath him, springs creaking, fabric sighing, as though it too had been waiting for someone to need it. He could feel heat beginning to return to his fingers, a sensation that bordered on pain, the nerves waking up, reporting their damage, informing him of all the small ways he had been destroying himself one frozen step at a time.

The man moved behind the desk but did not sit. He stood at the window, looking out at the snow, hands clasped behind his back, shoulders slightly hunched, the posture of someone carrying weight, someone who knew what it meant to bear other people's suffering, to take it into yourself, to hold it because no one else would.

When he spoke, his voice was quiet, almost conversational, as though they were old friends catching up rather than strangers meeting for the first time in circumstances of desperation.

"My name is Father Anselm," he said. "I've been in this building for forty-two years. Started as a young priest full of certainty about how the world worked, how God worked, how people worked. Took me about twenty years to unlearn most of that. To realize that certainty is just fear wearing a nice suit. That the work isn't about having answers but about sitting with questions. About being present when people are falling apart."

He turned from the window. Looked at Elias with eyes that had seen this before, that knew the shape of what Elias was carrying even if they didn't know the specifics.

"You have the look of someone carrying a great weight," he continued. "Something you've been carrying alone for a long time. The kind of thing that gets heavier the further you walk. The kind of thing that makes you think if you can just keep moving, you won't have to face it. But eventually you get too tired. Eventually you have to set it down."

The words pierced something in Elias's chest, something he had kept carefully sealed for months, wrapped in layers of denial and forward motion and the desperate belief that if he never stopped moving, never stopped walking, the thing behind him would never catch up.

He felt his throat tighten. Looked away.

"I don't know if I can," he managed, his voice barely above a whisper.

"Can, or will?"

Elias met the priest's eyes. "Does it matter?"

"Yes," Father Anselm said simply. "One is about capacity. The other is about choice. One says, 'I'm not strong enough.' The other says 'I'm not ready.' Very different things."

Silence settled between them, not uncomfortable but weighted, full, the kind of silence that forms when something true is about to be spoken, when the air itself seems to hold its breath in anticipation.

Outside, the wind picked up, rattling the window in its frame, the storm announcing itself, claiming the night.

Father Anselm sat down behind the desk. Folded his hands. Waited.

And Elias understood, in that moment, that this man would not push, would not demand, would simply wait with the infinite patience of someone who had learned that people spoke when they were ready, that confession could not be forced, that the only way to the other side of shame was through it, and that the journey had to be undertaken freely or it meant nothing.

"What did you do?" the priest asked finally. Not accusatory. Not even particularly curious. Just… there. The question sitting in the room like a third presence.

Elias exhaled slowly. The truth sat in his mouth like a stone, heavy, sharp edged, the kind of thing that would cut on the way out. He had not spoken it aloud to anyone. Had barely allowed himself to think it in full sentences, in complete thoughts, preferring instead to let it exist as fragments, as images that flashed and disappeared before they could coalesce into meaning.

But he was so tired.

So tired of carrying it alone.

So tired of walking.

"I killed someone," he said.

The words fell into the room like objects dropped from a great height, like stones into still water, the ripples moving outward, touching everything.

Father Anselm did not move. Did not recoil. Did not reach for a phone or cross himself or make any of the gestures Elias had imagined a thousand times in his mind when he played out this confession in the dark hours before dawn when sleep would not come and the past would not stop presenting itself for review.

The priest simply nodded. Once. Slowly.

"Tell me," he said.

And so Elias told him.

It had been six months ago. Late August. The tail end of summer when the heat had not yet broken but the light had already begun to change, to take on that particular quality of late afternoon in the Midwest where everything looks golden and temporary, beautiful and sad at the same time, as though the world knows something you don't, knows that change is coming, that loss is inevitable, that nothing gold can stay.

Elias had been driving home from his job at a warehouse in Kansas City, third shift, the graveyard hours, the shift for people who couldn't get better work or who had reasons for wanting to be awake when everyone else was asleep. He had been loading trucks, moving boxes, doing the kind of physical labor that exhausted you so completely that you couldn't think, couldn't feel, could only move from task to task until the shift ended and you drove home and collapsed and woke up and did it again.

He had been exhausted that night. Bone-tired. His eyes burning from the fluorescent lights and the dust that hung in the warehouse air and the simple accumulated weariness of working sixty hours a week at a job that paid barely enough to cover rent on a studio apartment in a part of Kansas City where gunshots at 2 AM were background noise, where the heat didn't work in winter and the AC didn't work in summer and the landlord never answered the phone unless you were calling to say you'd pay late, in which case he answered immediately and threatened eviction.

The highway had been empty at 3 AM. Just Elias and the occasional semi hauling goods cross-country, the big trucks passing him with a blast of wind and diesel exhaust, their taillights disappearing into the darkness ahead like red eyes watching, judging, bearing witness.

He had been sober. He needed that understood. Needed whoever heard this story to know that he had not been drinking, had not been high, had not been texting or distracted or doing any of the things people did that made accidents explicable, that made them fit into categories, that allowed you to say, "well of course that happened, he was drunk/high/stupid, he deserved what he got."

He had simply been tired. Tired in the way you get tired when you work too much and sleep too little and exist in a state of low-level desperation that never quite resolves, that becomes the baseline of your life, that makes you forget what it felt like to not be tired, to not be scared, to not wake up every morning calculating whether you had enough gas to get to work, enough food to make it to payday, enough of yourself left to keep going.

He had not seen the man until it was too late.

The figure had appeared in his headlights like an apparition, a man, middle aged, wearing dark clothes, standing in the right lane of the highway, not moving, not waving, just standing there as though he had materialized from nowhere, as though the darkness itself had taken shape and stepped into Elias's path.

Elias had swerved. Had slammed the brakes. But the road was slick from an earlier rain, light rain, barely more than mist, the kind that makes pavement treacherous without seeming dangerous, and the car had hydroplaned, had spun, the world tilting and rotating in a way that made no sense, the headlights sweeping across empty fields and highway barriers and finally, terribly, the man.

The sound of impact was a sound Elias would carry with him for the rest of his life, would hear in moments of quiet, would wake to in the middle of the night, a sound like breaking wood, like something fundamental giving way, like the noise the world makes when it cracks open and reveals what's underneath, which is nothing, just emptiness, just the void that we paper over with laws and meaning and the desperate fiction that any of this matters, that there's some order, some justice, some reason things happen the way they do.

He had stopped. Had pulled over. Had sat in his car for thirty seconds that felt like thirty years, his hands shaking so badly he could barely turn off the engine, his heart hammering in his chest like something trying to escape, like it knew what was coming and wanted no part of it.

Then he had gotten out. Had run back.

The man was lying in the road, his body at an angle that was wrong, that spoke of things shattered and displaced, bones in configurations they were never meant to hold. Blood pooled beneath him, black in the yellow glow of Elias's hazard lights, spreading slowly across the pavement like oil, like something the earth was rejecting, refusing to absorb.

His eyes were open.

He was trying to speak.

His lips were moving soundlessly, forming words that never became sound, and Elias had knelt beside him, had pulled out his phone with fingers that felt thick and clumsy, had begun to dial 911, had started to press the numbers that would summon help, that would bring ambulances and police and questions and the machinery of the state that would process this event, would categorize it, would determine fault and assign consequences,

And then he saw the wallet.

It was lying a few feet away, knocked from the man's pocket in the impact, brown leather worn soft from years of use, and in the moment that Elias's eyes registered its presence, in the split second between seeing it and understanding what it meant, he also saw the corner of bills protruding from it, green paper visible even in the dim light, money, currency, the thing that made the difference between surviving and drowning in the America he lived in.

And in that moment, in that terrible, crystalline, eternal moment that would define every moment that came after—Elias understood that he had a choice.

He could call 911. Could stay. Could face the questions: Why were you driving at 3 AM? Were you tired? Were you impaired? How fast were you going? Could you have stopped sooner? Could you have seen him earlier? Could you have swerved differently? The questions that would come even though he had not been at fault, even though the man had been standing in the road like he wanted to be hit, because that was how America worked, someone had to be blamed, someone had to be held accountable, someone had to pay, and Elias was young and poor and exhausted and driving an uninsured car with expired registration because he couldn't afford to do otherwise, and even if he wasn't charged with a crime he would still lose his license, his job, his ability to survive in a country with no safety net, no mercy, no second chances for people who fell through the cracks.

Or.

Or he could take the wallet. Could leave. Could tell himself that the man was dying anyway, look at him, look at the angle of his body, look at how much blood there was, he was dying, nothing Elias did or didn't do would change that, could tell himself that survival required ugly choices, that he had not asked for this, had not wanted this, but here it was and he had thirty seconds before another car came, before witnesses appeared, before the choice was taken from him.

His hand had been shaking as it reached for the wallet.

The man's eyes had found him.

Their gazes locked.

The man's lips formed a word. Not sound. Just the shape. A question.

Why?

Or maybe: Please.

Or maybe: Stay.

Elias would never know. Would spend the rest of his life trying to decode that final word, that last message from a dying man to the person who would take his money and leave him to die alone on a highway at 3 AM in a country that had failed them both.

He had taken the wallet.

Had stood.

Had walked back to his car.

Had driven away.

In the rearview mirror, he had seen the man still lying there, had seen the hazard lights still flashing, had seen the blood still spreading, and he had driven faster, had pressed the accelerator down, had put distance between himself and what he had done, between himself and the man whose name he didn't know, whose face he would never forget, whose death would be recorded as a hit-and-run, a tragedy, a statistic, one more person who died alone because someone chose not to stop.

When Elias finished speaking, the room was silent except for the wind outside and the soft tick of a clock he had not noticed before, time marking itself, indifferent to confession, to shame, to the small human dramas that played out beneath its steady progress.

Father Anselm sat very still. His face showed nothing, not judgment, not disgust, not pity. Just attention. Witness.

Finally, he spoke.

"You did not kill Gerald Pritchard," he said. "He killed himself."

"I left him," Elias said. His voice broke. "I took his money. I let him die alone."

"Yes."

"So what does that make me?"

"Human," Father Anselm said. "Fallible. Someone who made a terrible choice in a terrible moment. Someone who has been punishing himself ever since."

"I don't deserve mercy."

"None of us do," the priest said quietly. "That's why it's called mercy. If we deserved it, it would just be payment. Transaction. But mercy is what happens when you don't deserve it and you get it anyway. When the universe decides, against all evidence, against all logic, to offer you another chance. Not because you've earned it. But because grace doesn't work that way. Because love doesn't work that way."

Elias shook his head. "I can't forgive myself for this."

"No," Father Anselm agreed. "You can't. Not yet. Maybe not ever. But you can do something. You can make a choice right now, tonight, about who you're going to be from this moment forward. You can't undo what you did. Can't bring Gerald Pritchard back. Can't give him the minutes you took from him. But you can decide whether his death will mean something or nothing. Whether it will break you permanently or whether it will break you open. Make you more human. More awake. More capable of seeing other people's suffering and stopping. Stopping when you could keep driving. Stopping when it would be easier not to. Stopping because someone stopped for you."

He opened a drawer. Pulled out a small card. Wrote something on it. Handed it to Elias.

It was a phone number. Beneath it, a name: Linda Pritchard.

"Gerald's widow," Father Anselm said. "When you're ready, not tonight, not tomorrow, but when you're ready—you call her. You tell her what happened. You tell her you're sorry. It won't fix anything. Won't bring him back. But it will be true. And truth is where healing starts. Not comfort. Not forgetting. Truth."

Elias took the card. His hands were shaking. "How did you know his name?"

"I read the papers," Father Anselm said. "I've been reading them for forty-two years. I read about Gerald Pritchard. I read about the hit-and-run. I wondered who did it. Wondered if they were suffering. Wondered if they would ever find their way to somewhere like this office, to a moment like this one. And here you are."

"What if I can't do it? What if I call her and it makes everything worse?"

"It probably will make everything worse," the priest said. "For a while. And then, maybe, it will start to get better. That's how these things work. They get worse before they get better. The wound has to be opened before it can be cleaned. The truth has to be spoken before forgiveness becomes possible. Not guaranteed. Just possible."

Elias folded the card. Put it in his pocket next to the last ten dollars he had in the world, money he had been saving for food but which now felt like blood money, like everything he owned was tainted by that night, by that choice.

"There's a hotel across the street," Father Anselm said, standing. "Called The Wayfarer. I've arranged a room for you tonight and tomorrow night. The storm is going to get worse before it gets better. Stay off the roads. Rest. Eat. Think. And when you're ready to leave, when you're ready to take the next step toward your grandmother, toward Linda Pritchard, toward whatever comes next, you take it. But take it from a place of strength. Not this." He gestured at Elias's body, at the exhaustion, the hunger, the cold. "You can't walk toward redemption if you're dying. So first: live. Then: atone. In that order."

The hotel was small, modest, the kind of family-owned place that had somehow survived the chain motels, the Marriotts and Holiday Inns that had killed most of the independent operators. The clerk at the desk—a woman in her sixties with kind eyes and reading glasses on a chain, nodded when Elias entered, snow falling from his coat in clumps, melting on the worn carpet.

"Room 203," she said, handing him a key. An actual key, metal, attached to a plastic tag, with the room number embossed in fading gold. "Father Anselm called ahead. You're all set. Breakfast is included—continental, nothing fancy, but there's coffee and pastries. And there's a diner next door if you want something hot. He covered dinner too."

"How much do I owe—"

"Nothing," she said firmly, cutting him off before he could finish the question. "Just take care of yourself. That's all the payment needed."

Room 203 was on the second floor. He climbed the stairs slowly, each step an effort, his body protesting, demanding rest. The room was small, clean, furnished with the anonymous efficiency of hotels everywhere: a double bed with a floral comforter, a nightstand with a lamp and a Gideon Bible, a bathroom with a tub. A window overlooked the street where snow continued to fall, the world outside disappearing beneath white, becoming abstract, unreal.

He turned on the faucet in the bathroom. Water roared into the tub, hot, steaming, the sound so loud in the small space that it drowned out thought, drowned out everything except the simple physical reality of heat and water and the promise of being clean, of washing away the grime of weeks on the road even if he couldn't wash away what he'd done.

He undressed slowly. His clothes were stiff with dirt and sweat and the accumulated shame of homelessness, the way you started to smell when you couldn't shower, when you slept in your clothes, when your body became a burden you carried without relief. He looked at himself in the mirror. Barely recognized the person staring back. Hollow-eyed. Gaunt. Beard grown patchy and unkempt. Skin gray.

He looked like a ghost.

Maybe that was accurate.

He lowered himself into the bath. The heat was almost painful, his frozen skin protesting the sudden warmth, nerves screaming as they woke up, as blood returned to places it had abandoned. He made a sound that was half sigh, half sob, a sound that came from somewhere so deep he had not known it existed, some place in him that still wanted to live, that still believed survival was possible, that still hoped mercy might be real.

He stayed in the water until it cooled. Drained it. Refilled it. Stayed until it cooled again. On the third refill, he finally felt warm all the way through, felt the cold leave his bones, felt something in him begin to thaw that had been frozen for longer than just these weeks on the road.

The diner was called Rosie's. The waitress, Rosie herself, maybe, though he didn't ask, smiled when he entered, really smiled, not the professional smile service workers give but something genuine, something that suggested she saw him not as a problem but as a person.

"You must be Father Anselm's friend," she said. "He called. Said to feed you well. Sit anywhere you like."

He chose a booth by the window where he could watch the snow, where he could see the world outside continuing despite everything, despite his failures, despite Gerald Pritchard dying alone on a highway, despite all of it.

He ordered meatloaf, mashed potatoes, green beans, and coffee. The food came fast, hot, generous. He ate slowly, tasting each bite, aware that this might be the last real meal he had for a while, aware that tomorrow or the next day the road would resume, the hunger would return, the precarity that was his life would reassert itself.

But for now, for this moment, he had food. Had warmth. Had a bed waiting.

Had Linda Pritchard's phone number in his pocket.

Had a choice to make.

When Rosie brought him pie, "on the house," she said, "everyone needs pie on a night like this," he felt tears prick his eyes, felt something in his chest crack open, felt the weight of months of isolation and shame press down on him until he could barely breathe.

"You okay, honey?" Rosie asked, concern creasing her face.

He nodded. Couldn't speak.

She patted his shoulder. Didn't press. Just left him with his pie and his tears and the snow falling outside like the world being remade.

Back in the room, he sat on the edge of the bed. Pulled out the card with Linda Pritchard's number. Stared at it until the numbers blurred.

Not tonight. He wasn't ready. Wasn't strong enough.

But soon.

He pulled out his phone. Battery at 4%. Enough for one call.

He dialed the number he hadn't called in six months. The number he'd been too ashamed to call, too afraid of what he'd become to let anyone who'd known him before see what he'd turned into.

His grandmother answered on the second ring.

"Hello?"

Her voice. After all this time. After all these miles.

"Grandma." His voice broke. "It's Elias."

Silence on the other end. Then: "Baby? Is that really you?"

"Yes ma'am."

"Where are you? I've been so worried, I've called everyone, I filed a missing persons report with the police in Kansas City, I thought you were dead, I thought…"

"I'm in Missouri. Warsaw. I'm okay. I just… I needed to hear your voice."

"You come here," she said immediately, no hesitation, no questions, just the command born from love, from family, from the kind of bond that doesn't break even when you've been gone six months without a word. "Right now. You come to me."

"I will," he said. "I promise. I just need a few days. To figure some things out. To… to make some things right."

"What things, baby?"

He couldn't tell her. Not yet. "I made some mistakes. I need to fix them. Or at least try."

"Whatever it is, we'll fix it together."

"I need to do this part alone."

Silence. Then, quietly: "Are you in trouble?"

"I was," he said. "I'm trying not to be anymore."

They talked for twenty minutes, until his phone died mid-sentence, until the battery finally gave up and the screen went black. But it was enough. She knew he was alive. Knew he was trying. Knew he was coming home.

He plugged the phone in to charge. Lay down on the bed fully clothed. Closed his eyes.

For the first time in months, he slept without nightmares.

In the morning, the storm had passed. The world outside was buried under two feet of snow, pristine, unmarked, white silence as far as he could see. He ate breakfast in the hotel lobby, coffee, danish, orange juice from concentrate—then packed the few things he had, which was nothing really, just the clothes on his back and a phone that worked and a card with a phone number and a heart that felt slightly less broken than it had yesterday.

He left a note at the front desk:

Please give this to Father Anselm: Thank you. I don't know what last night was, but I think it saved me. I'm going to my grandmother's in Sikeston. I'll find my way. I'll make things right. I promise. —E

He stepped outside. The street was empty. No plows yet. No cars. Just white silence and cold air that hurt to breathe.

And then he heard it: an engine, distant but growing closer.

A truck emerged from the whiteness, a panel semi, the kind used for commercial deliveries. White cab streaked with road salt. On the side panel, painted in fading green letters: PLANTS - Wholesale Nursery Supplies.

The truck stopped. The driver rolled down the window. He was older, maybe sixty five with a weathered face that suggested years on the road, eyes that crinkled at the corners, a flannel shirt and a wool cap and the look of someone who knew what it meant to work hard, to get up early, to haul goods across the country for wages that barely covered the fuel.

"What the hell are you doing out here?" he asked. Not unkindly. Just genuinely curious why anyone would be standing on an empty street in two feet of snow.

"Walking," Elias said.

"Walking where?"

"Sikeston. My grandmother lives there."

The man laughed. Not meanly. Just at the absurdity. "Son, that's over three hundred miles. In this snow? You'll be dead by tomorrow."

"I don't have another choice."

The driver studied him for a long moment. "You running from something or toward something?"

Elias thought about it. About Gerald Pritchard. About Linda's phone number. About his grandmother's voice on the phone. About Father Anselm and this empty street and the long road ahead.

"Both," he said.

The driver nodded. "Get in. I'm headed to St. Louis, picking up plants, then swinging back south. I can get you to Sikeston. It's not far out of my way."

Elias stared. "Are you serious?"

"Do I look like I'm joking? It's ten below out here. Get in the damn truck before we both freeze."

Elias climbed into the cab. Heat enveloped him like an embrace. The driver handed him a thermos.

"Coffee," he said. "Real stuff. Not gas station sludge."

"Thank you."

"Name's Ray."

"Elias."

They shook hands. Ray put the truck in gear. They pulled away from the curb, the tires cutting through snow that had not yet been touched by other vehicles, leaving twin tracks that would fill in within the hour, that would disappear as though they had never been there at all.

They drove in silence for the first hour, Ray concentrating on the road, Elias staring out the window at the white landscape, at the world transformed, made unfamiliar, everything he knew buried beneath snow, hidden, waiting to be rediscovered.

Finally, Ray spoke.

"You look like someone who's been through something."

Elias nodded. "I have."

"Want to talk about it?"

"Not really."

Ray nodded. "Fair enough. Just so you know: I've picked up a lot of people over the years. Hitchhikers. Runaways. People down on their luck. And I can tell the difference between someone running from the law and someone running from themselves. You don't look like a criminal. You look like someone who made a mistake and is trying to figure out how to live with it."

Elias glanced at him. "You a therapist or a truck driver?"

Ray smiled. "Both, apparently. Comes with the job. You spend enough time alone on the road, you start to see patterns. Start to understand people. Or at least I like to think so. Maybe I'm full of shit. Wouldn't be the first time."

"Why do you pick people up? Most drivers don't."

"Most drivers are smart," Ray said. "It's dangerous. You never know who you're letting into your truck. Could be anyone. Could be trouble."

"Then why?"

Ray was quiet for a moment. "Because someone picked me up once. Long time ago. I was in a bad place. Worse than bad. And this old guy in a Ford pickup stopped on a highway outside Amarillo, middle of nowhere, 110 degrees, and he said, 'You look like you need a ride.' Took me three hundred miles. Didn't ask questions. Didn't judge. Just drove. And when he dropped me off, he gave me fifty bucks and said, 'Pass it on someday.' So I do. When I can. When it feels right."

"Did you ever see him again?"

Ray shook his head. "Never got his name. Never got his number. He just… helped. And then he was gone."

They drove on.

At a truck stop in Columbia, Ray bought breakfast. Eggs, bacon, hash browns, toast, coffee. They sat in a booth that looked out at the parking lot where other trucks idled, their engines running to keep the cabs warm, drivers sleeping or eating or checking their phones, the transient population of America's highways, the people who kept goods moving, who kept the country running, who rarely got thanked and frequently got blamed when things went wrong.

"You're rebuilding," Ray said, watching Elias eat. "I can see it. You're trying to put yourself back together. That takes fuel. Body fuel, soul fuel. Can't do it on empty."

After they ate, Elias asked, "Can I see the plants?"

Ray's face lit up. "Sure. Come on."

They walked around to the back of the truck. Ray unlocked the rear doors. Swung them open.

Inside was Eden.

Or something close to it. A green oasis contained in metal: ferns cascading from hanging baskets, ivy climbing makeshift trellises, orchids blooming in impossible shades of purple and white and yellow, succulents clustered on shelves like small green galaxies. The air inside was warm, humid, smelled of soil and growth and the complex chemistry of photosynthesis, of life making more life, of things that had been dormant coming back, blooming, proving that death was not final, that with enough water and light and patience, even things that looked finished could start again.

Golden grow lights bathed everything in soft radiance, artificial suns keeping the plants alive through a Missouri winter.

"It's like Eden," Elias whispered.

Ray nodded. "Funny, isn't it? Driving through a frozen world with this behind me. Taking life from one place to another. Keeping things alive that shouldn't survive. That's the whole business, really. Defying winter. Saying 'not yet' to the cold."

"Why plants?"

"Because they grow," Ray said simply. "Because you can take something that looks dead—a dried-up bulb, a bare stick, a seed the size of a pinhead, and with enough water and light and patience, it comes back. It blooms. It makes something beautiful out of nothing."

Elias looked at him. "You think that's true for people too?"

"I know it is," Ray said. "I've seen it. Hell, I've lived it. You just need the right conditions. Water, light, patience. For people, that translates to: basic needs met, someone who gives a damn, and time. Time to heal. Time to grow. Time to become something other than what you were."

They stood there in the green warmth, in the truck full of Eden, listening to the distant sound of the highway, the wind outside, the constant hum of America moving goods and people and hope from one place to another, endlessly, relentlessly, the great machine of commerce and survival grinding on.

"Life is always growing somewhere," Ray said quietly. "Even when everything looks dead. You just have to find where. Or make it yourself. Create the conditions. Be the light for someone else's growth. That's the whole game, really."

As dusk fell, the truck rolled into Sikeston. Elias directed Ray through streets he half-remembered from childhood visits, past schools and parks and gas stations, until they reached a modest house on a quiet street, the kind of house with a porch swing and flower beds buried under snow and a mailbox shaped like a cardinal.

Ray put the truck in park. Looked at Elias.

"You've got a good heart, kid," he said. "It's bruised. It's been through hell. But it's still beating in the right direction. That matters. That's what makes the difference between someone who stays broken and someone who heals."

"I don't know how to thank you," Elias said.

"You already did," Ray said. "You got in the truck. You accepted help. That's harder than it sounds. A lot of people would rather freeze than admit they need saving. The fact that you got in—that tells me you're going to be okay. Maybe not today. Maybe not for a while. But eventually."

"I'll pay you back somehow."

"No need," Ray said. "But if you want to square the account: someday, when you see someone standing in the cold, someone who looks lost, someone who looks like you looked this morning—you stop. You offer a ride. You pass it on. That's the payment. That's how this works."

Elias nodded. Opened the door. Climbed down from the cab. Stood in the snow, the cold biting, the dusk turning everything blue and purple and gold.

He turned to wave.

Ray waved back. The truck idled, its engine a low rumble, exhaust visible in the cold air, the word PLANTS barely legible in the fading light.

Elias walked toward the house. He could see lights on inside. Could see shadows moving behind curtains. His grandmother.

Home.

He was halfway up the walk when the front door opened.

His grandmother stepped onto the porch, no coat, just her cardigan, her slippers, her arms already open.

"Baby," she said. "Oh, baby."

He ran the last few steps. Fell into her arms. Let her hold him while he cried, great heaving sobs that came from somewhere so deep he hadn't known it existed, six months of walking and shame and cold and fear all pouring out at once.

"How did you get here so fast?" she asked when he could finally speak. "I thought you were days away."

"A truck driver picked me up," he said, his voice muffled against her shoulder. "Outside Warsaw. Guy named Ray. He brought me all the way here."

She pulled back, and looked over his shoulder toward the street. "Where is he? I want to thank him."

Elias turned.

The street was empty.

No truck. No idling engine. No exhaust. Just the quiet suburban evening, snow covering everything, a few porch lights coming on as neighbors settled in for dinner.

He walked back down to the curb. Looked both ways. The snow in the street was undisturbed except for tire tracks from the morning's plow, tracks that came from the main road and continued past the house, no place where a large truck had pulled over, no place where someone had stopped.

"What was his name again?" his grandmother called from the porch.

"Ray," Elias said automatically. Then stopped. Tried to remember his last name. Tried to picture the business card he surely would have gotten, the phone number he would have exchanged, the way you do when someone helps you that much, when you want to thank them properly, want to send them something, want to—

Nothing came.

Just Ray. Just a truck full of plants. Just a man who had stopped.

"I…" Elias frowned. Walked back up to the porch. "I don't actually know his last name. I didn't get his number. I don't even know the name of the nursery company. It just said 'PLANTS' on the side."

His grandmother looked at him for a long moment. Then took his hand.

"Come inside, sweetheart," she said gently. "You're safe now. That's what matters."

But Elias stood there a moment longer, staring at the empty street, at the snow that showed no evidence of the truck that had carried him three hundred miles, at the world that suddenly felt less solid than he had believed, more mysterious, a place where the distance between one kind of life and another was shorter than it appeared, where mercy could arrive from nowhere and disappear just as quickly, leaving you changed but with no way to prove it had ever happened at all.

He followed his grandmother inside.

The house smelled like something cooking, something warm, something that meant safety and love and the kind of care that didn't ask questions, that just opened its arms and said you're home now, we'll figure out the rest later.

She sat him at the kitchen table. Poured him tea. Sat across from him and held his hands and looked at him with eyes that had seen a lot of life, a lot of mistakes, a lot of people trying to find their way back from places they never should have gone.

"You want to tell me what happened?" she asked.

He pulled out the card. Set it on the table between them. Linda Pritchard's phone number in Father Anselm's careful handwriting.

"I did something terrible," he said. "And I need to make it right. Or at least try."

She picked up the card. Read it. Set it back down.

"Okay," she said simply. "When you're ready, we'll do it together. But first: food. Rest. Being human again. You can't atone for anything if you're half dead."

They ate dinner. She told him about the neighbors, about her book club, about the leak in the roof that the landlord still hadn't fixed, about ordinary things, normal things, the texture of a life that continued despite everything, that kept going because that's what life did, it kept going, it grew around the wounds, it found ways to bloom even in winter.

After dinner, she showed him to the spare room. His old room from when he used to visit as a child, still decorated with the same faded wallpaper, the same quilt on the bed, the same small desk where he used to do homework during summer breaks when his parents couldn't take care of him, when this house had been refuge, safety, the place where someone loved him without conditions.

He lay down. Closed his eyes.

Tomorrow, he would call Linda Pritchard.

Tomorrow, he would begin the work of atonement, of trying to make right what could never be fully righted, of living with what he'd done while also trying to become someone who wouldn't do it again.

Tomorrow.

But tonight, he slept.

And in his dreams, he walked through a truck full of Eden, through green abundance impossible in winter, through a space that should not exist but did, and a man whose face he could no longer quite remember said: Life is always growing somewhere. You just have to find it. Or make it.

He woke at dawn.

The card with Linda Pritchard's number sat on the nightstand.

He picked it up.

His finger hovered over his phone.

The call that would change everything.

The call he wasn't sure he could make.

The call he knew he had to make.

Outside, the sun rose over snow-covered Sikeston, golden light touching the white world, making it shine, making it new, making it possible, just possible, to believe that winter didn't last forever, that spring eventually came, that things frozen could thaw, that things broken could mend.

He dialed.

The phone rang.

Once.

Twice.

Three times.

Then a woman's voice: "Hello?"

Elias took a breath.

And began.

# CHAPTER 11
## THE WINDOW BETWEEN STORMS

### The Pearl of Great Price

*Matthew 13:45–46*

The sun baked the New Guinea airstrip with the weight of memory, its heat pressing into the earth like something that had been buried and refused to stay dead. Jack Dunley stood beside the plane, boots sinking into dust that smelled of rubber, rust, and a fear so old it had calcified into the ground itself.

He lit a cigarette with trembling fingers. "You still dreaming in black and white, Charlie?"

Lieutenant Charles Dunley chuckled as he slung his duffel across one shoulder, the canvas worn thin by years of carrying what could not be left behind. "No," he said. "Nowadays it's infrared. And flames."

The brothers hadn't seen each other in four years—not in person. Just letters. Tattered, censored, ink smudged by rain and hands that shook when they held pens. Stories half-told because truth in war becomes a kind of poison if not diluted.

"I still see him," Charlie said suddenly.

Jack frowned. "Who?"

"The young man. One of the first missions. Cologne. Three floors up. I photographed the building before the B-17s came. His face in the window. Like he knew."

Jack didn't speak.

Charlie went on, his voice flat, rehearsed, as though he'd told this story to himself a thousand times in the dark. "When I flew back days later for post-strike photos, the window was gone. No wall. Just ash and glass, stuck to snow."

Jack dropped his cigarette. "I'm sorry."

"You ever name the ones you shot down?" Charlie asked quietly.

"No," Jack said. "But I remember their wings."

They stood in silence, two men whose hands had been instruments of precision and death, whose eyes had measured distance in seconds and lives in fractions.

"I still hear the palms," Jack added. "When they rot in the rain, they peel like skin. I spent three nights in a ditch outside Buna, waiting for a Zero to swing low. It never came. Just malaria and the sound of dying trees."

"And we're the lucky ones?" Charlie asked.

Jack nodded. "We are."

The plane rumbled to life behind them, propellers spinning with the kind of purpose that makes men believe in destinations. The air shimmered. Soldiers called out. Laughter danced across the tarmac like it wanted to be real.

Jack elbowed Charlie. "You still play piano?"

Charlie smiled faintly. "Not since Dresden. My hands shake too much."

They walked toward the boarding steps. For a moment, they were just boys again—Sunday pies cooling on windowsills, fishing lines tangled in cottonwood roots, a mother's singing voice behind closed windows.

Then the General arrived.

What makes a man willing to give everything for something he cannot name?

The sages ask this, and the answer is terrible, holy, unbearably simple: Because he has seen it. And having seen, he cannot unsee.

It started with a pie.

Apricot, speckled with cinnamon, resting on a windowsill that overlooked a field of waving wheat. The Dunley farmhouse sat just outside Cedar Grove, Iowa, bordered by cottonwoods and stories that never quite ended but circled back on themselves like prayers.

Jack and Charlie used to race barefoot through those rows, shouting secret codes they'd invented—"Black Raven to Red Fox!"—ducking under branches like spies in some invisible war. Their mother, Evelyn, sang hymns as she baked, but her laughter always had a rebellious note, as though holiness and mischief had once kissed and left her changed.

Every Sunday, Jack was the crust man. Charlie stirred the filling. They'd argue about ratios, call each other "Chef General" and "Sous Commander." Flour dusted their eyelashes like snow. It wasn't just ritual—it was covenant. When Jack turned ten, he declared the pie sacred.

"If you're ever lost," he told Charlie, "eat pie. It'll guide you home."

And somehow, that made sense.

Twenty years later, Jack stood in the same kitchen, looking at an oven that hadn't been touched in months. His hands were clean. Too clean.

A knock at the door.

Roger, neighbor, lifelong friend, Sunday church usher.

"You going to service this morning?" Roger asked.

Jack didn't answer.

"Pastor's preaching on restoration."

Jack's face twitched. "Restoration doesn't come by sermon."

Roger hesitated. "There's still pie at the gathering after."

Jack opened the door wider but didn't invite him in.

Roger stepped back. "You hear anything from Charlie? I mean… the Army hasn't released the full list yet."

Jack's eyes turned sharp. "The plane vanished. That's all that matters."

Roger looked down. "He was the best of us."

"No," Jack whispered. "He was better."

Later that week, Jack sat alone in the church pew after hours. The sanctuary was dim, lit by late sunlight slanting through stained glass, casting colors like bruises across the floor.

The chaplain, Father Jonah, entered quietly, holding a small book. "You came back."

Jack didn't respond.

"I read your brother's letters," Jonah said softly. "He used to write about you."

Jack turned slowly. "Letters mean nothing."

Jonah sat beside him. "He said you once chased a tornado to protect a stray dog."

Jack snorted. "Wasn't brave. Just stupid."

"Still," Jonah said, "he saw love in it."

Silence.

Jonah opened the book. "Do you want to pray?"

Jack laughed, bitter and sudden. "I did, Father. The day before he flew out."

Jonah waited.

"And guess what I said?" Jack continued, voice cracking. "I asked God to let us fly home together. I said we'd bake pies again. I said we'd sit in Mom's garden like nothing ever happened."

Jonah listened.

Jack's eyes welled. "Then a man with medals stole his seat."

"You think God abandoned you?" Jonah asked.

Jack didn't hesitate. "No. I think He chose that General. Which means He chose to break me."

Jonah closed the book. "Then let me say something Charlie might have wanted you to hear."

Jack looked at him.

"Some storms don't pass. They settle in. You don't have to forgive the thunder. But maybe, someday, you'll bake again—not for memory, but for miracle."

Jack stood.

"I don't believe in miracles anymore."

And he walked out.

What does a man do when the treasure he spent his whole life protecting is taken from him?

Does he curse the thief? Does he close his hands forever? Or does he—against all reason, against all fairness—open his palms again and ask: What else might I hold?

The adoption paperwork smelled faintly of bureaucracy and hand sanitizer. Jack sat at a small desk in the American Services office in Frankfurt, his thumb tracing the edge of a signature line as though the ink might burn him.

A thin man named Gruber adjusted his glasses and said, "He is five. Mother unknown. Records suggest abuse, but we… we do not discuss that." He gestured to a file, closed tightly as if grief were contagious.

Jack nodded once.

"He does not speak," Gruber added. "But he listens. We think."

Jack didn't flinch. "That's fine."

The boy was led in, flanked by two women in gray skirts. He was small. Palms clenched. Hair too neat, as though someone had tried to make him presentable for a transaction. His eyes were dark—not empty, but layered, like a well that had been filled with stones.

Jack knelt.

"I'm Jack," he said, voice soft but firm. "I'm not asking you to smile."

The boy looked at him.

"I'm just here to remember you."

Still silence.

The boy turned and walked to the corner, sat down, and began folding a scrap of paper into a shape that vaguely resembled a boat.

Gruber raised a brow.

"I'll take him," Jack said.

The merchant knows pearls. He has handled hundreds—smooth, flawless, priced and cataloged. But when he sees THE pearl, something shifts. It is not more beautiful. It is not larger. It simply is. And in that moment, he understands: everything he owns is worthless compared to this.

Six weeks later, they lived in an apartment above a bakery near Rue Saint-Paul in Paris. Helen, Jack's wife, kept mostly to her room—a quiet woman whose body had betrayed her dream of motherhood but whose kindness glowed in small gestures: folded shirts, warm soups, blankets tucked in without words.

Jack and the boy walked every morning. Past Notre-Dame, past bridges tangled with lovers' locks, past old men playing chess in the Jardin du Luxembourg. Once, near the Seine, the boy pointed at a crumbling pigeon wing and then at his own shoe.

Jack said, "You're not broken."

The boy didn't respond, but that night, he slept without the light on.

There was a woman named Sylvie who ran the bakery below. She loved the boy instantly. "He sees the world like a poet," she said one morning. "Does he speak?"

"Not yet," Jack replied.

"He will," she said, handing them two croissants. "When words feel safe."

One afternoon, Jack took the boy to a small toy shop. The boy stared at a wooden fighter plane hanging from the ceiling, suspended by invisible wire, frozen mid-flight.

Jack reached up and bought it. "This one flew in New Guinea," he said.

The boy held it gently, as though it might shatter.

Jack knelt beside him. "I had a brother. We flew different skies. He never came home."

The boy looked at Jack, then pointed at the plane and folded his arms like wings.

It wasn't language. But it was understanding.

Paris began as a hush—a season of quiet rituals: cracked baguettes shared at dawn, walks beneath balconies strung with drying linen, and the kind of stillness where even a child afraid to speak could begin to breathe differently.

But Jack Dunley, having spent years airborne, knew movement could be healing. So he chose pilgrimage—not the kind done on knees, but with open eyes and good shoes.

The boy's silence remained untouched. Yet within it, Jack heard every syllable that hadn't been spoken. And so they journeyed.

The boy walked beside Jack down the gravel path to Château de Versailles, his small hand tucked in Jack's coat pocket—not for fear, but anchoring.

In the Hall of Mirrors, they paused. Gilded chandeliers flickered above, casting their reflections like spirits waiting for names. The boy stared at the dozens of selves shining back at him.

Jack leaned in and whispered, "Sometimes, you have to see yourself multiplied before you remember who you are."

The boy didn't speak, but he pointed—at his reflection standing beside Jack's.

He'd chosen a mirrored version with the faintest smile.

They stood beneath the Arc de Triomphe, watching tourists mill like ants beneath stone. Jack told the story of soldiers marching beneath it, broken men returning with dignity stitched into their uniforms.

"They built this for those who came home," Jack said.

The boy looked up, then down, then took a slow, deliberate step forward, beneath the arch.

Jack followed.

On the Champs-Élysées, the boy stopped at a toy shop window. Another fighter plane sat suspended, identical to the one Jack had bought him.

Jack knelt. "Want to see how far it can fly?"

The boy touched the glass. Then his own heart.

No words. Just alignment.

In Monaco, it rained softly. The boy sat on one of the fort cannons, legs swinging, eyes on the glinting sea.

Jack told him about pirates, princes, and how sometimes peace lives behind walls meant for war.

Nearby, a girl sang in Italian. The boy turned toward the music but didn't speak.

Jack asked, "Do you ever sing in your head?"

The boy traced the barrel of the cannon with his finger, then tapped it softly—once, twice—like the rhythm of a lullaby.

Jack smiled.

The Leaning Tower of Pisa stood like a question never fully answered, tilting toward the earth as though gravity and grace were locked in eternal negotiation.

Jack adjusted his camera. "Hold up your hand like this," he said, positioning the boy just right.

The boy complied, carefully straightening his arm. For a moment, it looked as if his small hand held the tower in place.

Jack clicked the photo.

"This one's going on the mantle."

The boy tilted his head. Then pointed toward the sky.

"You think it's going to fall?" Jack teased.

The boy gave a small shrug, then—without warning—reached up and placed his hand gently on Jack's cheek.

It was the first gesture of comfort he'd ever offered.

Jack didn't speak. But he knew.

The merchant sells everything. Not because he is reckless, but because he has learned the terrible mathematics of the Kingdom: nothing you possess is worth keeping if it stands between you and the pearl.

In the waning summer of 1960, a final offering took form.

Jack, Helen, and the boy drove their car onto a boxcar in France, where steel chains locked it to the rails like a memory fastened to time. The train lurched forward. And then: blackness.

The tunnel swallowed them whole—not violently, but completely, the way night swallows day without apology. For what felt like hours, there was nothing but the rhythmic clatter of steel on steel, the boy's breath small and steady beside Jack, and the weight of mountains pressing down from above.

Jack stared into the dark and thought of Charlie. Of the plane that vanished. Of the window that was there one day and gone the next. Is this what it felt like for you, brother? This silence? This waiting?

Then—a speck. No larger than a pinprick.

It grew. Slowly at first, then faster, swelling like hope that had been held underwater and was finally allowed to surface.

The light widened. The walls of the tunnel peeled back. And then—

Boom.

The Swiss Alps erupted into view like the first morning of creation, snowfields blazing white as revelation, valleys spreading their arms wide as mercy. The peaks tore through clouds, jagged and holy, and the train burst into light so fierce it felt like waking from a long, cold dream.

Jack gasped. Helen laughed. And the boy—

The boy laughed.

Not a giggle. Not a chuckle. A full, bright, unguarded sound that filled the cabin and spilled into the mountains, where it echoed and multiplied, as though the world itself had been waiting to hear it.

Jack looked at the boy, and in that moment, he understood: This is resurrection. This is what it means to be found.

The brother who'd been lost was not forgotten. But he was no longer alone. This boy—this miracle—had stepped into the grief like a lit match in a cavern. Not to replace, but to illuminate.

Jack reached over and rested his hand on the boy's shoulder. Beneath that thin coat, he felt something stronger than flesh—a future unspooled and waiting, bright as the snow that stretched to the horizon.

This, he thought, is the pearl I sold everything to find.

The Atlantic was not kind.

It began on the second day. The sea turned gray as regret, then green as stomach bile, then black.

Waves towered like old gods reawakened, heaving themselves skyward only to collapse upon the deck with a roar that sounded far too personal. You dared to be joyful? You thought healing came without cost?

Jack held the boy close—not tightly, he didn't want to trap him, only tether him. They both wore orange life vests, bloated and absurd-looking, like sacrificial lambs in carnival clothing. The ship's crew conducted drills each morning with military precision. "If we go down," one barked, "you hold your breath until heaven calls."

But for seven days they didn't die. They just suffered.

Jack vomited until his throat bled. The boy watched him, then curled beside him and began to mirror every motion, as if love required mimicry. He, too, began to retch. They lay side by side in their cabin, eyes hollowed, souls echoing the sway of the sea. Even the walls seemed to sweat.

The other passengers disappeared into their sickness. Ninety-five percent heaved in corners, clutching railings like prayer beads.

Except for her.

Helen did not flinch. She danced in the lounge with a spritz in one hand and rum in the other. "We're only crossing the ocean!" she sang once. "Not the River Styx!" She toasted with two Belgian women who had come aboard with false eyelashes and three husbands between them. She seemed immune to the sermon the storm preached.

Jack loved her for it—not resentfully, not bitterly, but as one loves a lighthouse they'll never reach. She had no lesson to learn. Her faith was the kind you're born with, the kind that floats.

But Jack and the boy—they were being taught.

On the fifth night, the boy pointed at the ceiling and whimpered—not from fear, but from some unnamable understanding. His eyes had begun to change: they no longer darted, they dwelt.

Jack whispered, "You feel it, don't you? The ocean's not angry. It's just awake."

The boy nodded. Barely.

By the seventh night, the storm broke.

Not all at once, but like a curtain reluctant to rise. The wind stilled. The decks dried. And the ship began to hum again, as if someone had offered it forgiveness.

In the quiet, Jack held the boy's hand and said, "We've crossed something bigger than water."

And the boy, still weak, still silent, reached up and pressed his hand to Jack's heart.

The pearl is not found in calm seas. It is formed in darkness, beneath pressure, in the hidden places where suffering becomes beauty.

The ocean had calmed, yet Jack still felt its ghost beneath the deck, like sorrow remembered in bone. The ship carved a patient path through waters gray and glinting, the fog lifting in fragile ribbons, like a veil the world was finally ready to part.

Jack stood beside the boy at the porthole. The child's face was drawn, hollow with hunger, with silence, and yet—his eyes were clearer now. No longer drowning, but surfacing.

There was something sacred in the stillness.

Then, out of the softened light, rose a shape:

The Statue of Liberty.

Tall and pale, her flame raised not in triumph, but in invitation. Around her, gulls wheeled like echoes. Her silhouette stood against the sky like a hymn cast in copper.

The boy pressed his small hand to the glass.

His breath bloomed on the pane, then faded.

He whispered,

"This is America?"

Jack blinked hard.

The words—so simple, so heavy—pierced a place inside him he hadn't named since the war, since the letter arrived with his brother's name misspelled and no apology enclosed.

That letter had drilled a hole through him. A quiet crater. No blast. Just absence.

The boy said it again, louder now.

"This is America?"

Jack knelt beside him—not because grief demanded it, but because hope deserved it.

He reached up and rested his hand on the boy's shoulder. Beneath that thin coat, Jack could feel something stronger than flesh—a flicker of future, of stories unspooled and waiting.

"Yes," he said. "Welcome home."

A gull passed the window just then, its wings wide as mercy, its cry brief and wild.

Jack looked at the boy and saw it clearly now:

The child, once seasick and wordless, carried something forward—a future bright enough to light the hollow Jack had carried for years.

The boy kept looking out, silent again. But this time, his silence shimmered.

Somewhere in the harbor, behind the boy's brightening gaze, a continent opened its arms.

In the Kingdom, the merchant does not regret what he sold. He stands in the marketplace, empty-handed, and smiles. Because the pearl is not something he owns. It is something that owns him.

And in being owned, he is free.

Jack Dunley did not bake another pie for three years.

But when he did—when the boy was eight and laughing in the kitchen, flour dusting his eyelashes like snow—Jack understood:

Grace is not the restoration of what was lost.

Grace is the gift of what was never expected.

The boy was not Charlie. He would never be Charlie.

But he was the pearl—hidden, overlooked, formed in darkness and pressure—that Jack had sold everything to find.

And in finding him, Jack had found the Kingdom.

# CHAPTER 12
## THE UNFORGIVING SERVANT

*The Unforgiving Servant*

*Matthew 18:21–35*

He had forgotten the sound of his own heartbeat.

That was the first thing he noticed in the hospital hallway, long before the diagnosis, long before the bill, long before the moment that would divide his life into before and after. He sat in a plastic chair molded to the shape of a thousand other frightened bodies, and he realized he could not hear himself. Not the pulse in his ears. Not the thrum in his chest. Not the quiet rhythm that had carried him through fifty-three years of living.

It was as though the machinery of the hospital had swallowed it, the beeping monitors, the rolling carts, the overhead announcements calling for rapid response teams, the soft squeak of nurses' shoes on polished floors. Everything hummed with purpose. Everything moved with urgency. Everything had a place.

Except him.

His name was Daniel Mercer, and he had spent twenty seven years working for the largest health insurance company in the state. He had been good at his job. Efficient. Precise. He knew the codes, the clauses, the exclusions, the loopholes. He could read a claim the way a musician reads a score, seeing the structure beneath the surface, the patterns, the places where the melody would break.

He had denied thousands of claims in his career. Not out of cruelty. Out of duty. Out of the belief that systems only worked when someone enforced the rules. He had told himself he was protecting the many from the few. He had told himself he was keeping premiums stable. He had told himself he was doing what was necessary.

He had never imagined he would become one of the people on the other side of the desk.

But here he was, sitting in a hallway that smelled of antiseptic and fear, waiting for a doctor to tell him whether the pain in his abdomen was something simple or something fatal.

A nurse paused beside him. Young. Dark circles under her eyes. She had the look of someone three hours past the end of a twelve hour shift.

"You doing okay over here?" she asked.

"Fine," he said.

She studied him for a moment. Not clinically. Just as a human being looking at another human being.

"You don't look fine," she said. "You look like a man who hasn't taken a breath in an hour."

He almost laughed. He couldn't remember the last time someone had looked at him that carefully.

"First time in the ER?" she asked.

"First time as a patient," he said.

She nodded, as if that explained everything. "It's different on this side of it." She handed him a cup of water he hadn't asked for. "The doctor will be right with you."

When the doctor finally came, her face was calm, practiced, unreadable.

"Mr. Mercer," she said, "we found a mass."

The world tilted. Not dramatically. Not like in the movies. Just a small shift, like a floorboard giving way beneath his feet.

"We need to run more tests," she continued. "But we're concerned."

Concerned. A word that meant everything and nothing.

He nodded. He didn't trust his voice.

She placed a hand on his shoulder, a gesture so gentle it nearly undid him.

"We'll take care of you," she said.

He wanted to believe her. He wanted to believe someone would.

The diagnosis came two days later. Stage three. Aggressive. Treatable, but only with a combination therapy so new it wasn't yet standard. The kind of treatment that lived in the gray zone between hope and policy.

He knew what that meant. He had denied this exact therapy before.

He sat in the consultation room, staring at the printout the oncologist had handed him. The words blurred. Not because he was crying, he wasn't, but because his mind was already racing ahead, calculating, assessing, predicting. He knew the cost. He knew the coverage limits.

He knew the likelihood of approval. He knew the answer before anyone said it.

But the oncologist said it anyway.

"We've submitted the request to your insurance," she said. "We're hopeful."

Hopeful. Another word that meant nothing.

He nodded again. He had become good at nodding.

She set down her pen and looked at him directly. "Mr. Mercer, I want to ask you something, and I need you to answer honestly."

He waited.

"Do you understand what this treatment can do for you? Not statistically. For you, specifically, right now?"

He looked at the printout. He looked at the numbers. He thought of the claims he had reviewed in rooms just like this one, lives reduced to line items, to codes, to the language of exclusion.

"I understand what it costs," he said finally.

She was quiet for a moment. "I know you do. But that's not what I asked."

The denial arrived forty eight hours later. He didn't need to open the envelope to know what it said. He recognized the weight of the paper, the thickness of the packet, and the way his name was printed in the window. He had sent thousands of these.

He opened it anyway.

The language was familiar. Too familiar. While we recognize the potential benefits of this therapy, it remains investigational under current guidelines and therefore falls outside the scope of covered benefits as outlined in Section 12.4(c) of your policy.

He had written those words. He had crafted that sentence. He had believed in it.

Now it was a blade pressed against his own throat.

He sat at his kitchen table; the denial letter spread before him like a verdict. The house was silent. His wife had died three years earlier. His daughter lived two states away. He had no one to show the letter to. No one to ask for help. No one to witness the moment when the system he had served turned on him.

He folded the letter. He placed it back in the envelope. He set it aside. Then he went to work.

His supervisor looked surprised to see him.

"Daniel," she said, "shouldn't you be resting?"

He shrugged. "I need the hours."

She hesitated. "I heard about the diagnosis."

He stiffened. "I'm fine."

She didn't believe him. But she didn't press.

He sat at his desk, logged into the system, and began reviewing claims. The screen glowed with familiar codes, familiar language, and familiar decisions. Approve. Deny. Deny. Approve. Deny. He moved through them with mechanical precision, his fingers typing the same phrases he had typed for decades. Not medically necessary. Experimental. Out of network. Excluded under policy terms.

At lunch, his colleague Marcus pulled a chair up beside him. Marcus had been in the department for twelve years, a quiet man who kept a photograph of his granddaughter taped to the corner of his monitor.

"Heard you were back," Marcus said. "Didn't expect you so soon."

"Nothing to do at home," Daniel said.

Marcus unwrapped a sandwich. Didn't look at him. "You know what gets me sometimes?" he said. "The ones with kids. When I see a pediatric claim, I just, I try not to look at the name. Just the codes." He took a bite. "Otherwise you can't do it."

"That's how it works," Daniel said.

"Yeah," Marcus said. He didn't sound convinced. "That's how it works."

He denied a claim for a woman with lupus. He denied a claim for a man with a rare heart condition. He denied a claim for a child whose parents had begged for an exception. He told himself he was doing his job. He told himself he had no choice. He told himself the rules were the rules.

But something inside him had begun to crack.

Three weeks later, he collapsed in the break room.

He woke in the hospital, surrounded by machines that beeped in steady rhythms. His daughter was sitting beside him, her face pale, her eyes red.

"Dad," she whispered, "why didn't you tell me?"

He looked away. He didn't have an answer.

She took his hand. Her voice was controlled but barely. "You have people, Dad. You have me. You don't have to disappear into this."

"I didn't want to worry you."

"Worry me," she said. "That's my job. That's what I'm here for."

He stared at the ceiling. He had spent twenty seven years processing other people's emergencies from a safe and distant remove. He had not understood, until now, what it meant to be the emergency.

The oncologist entered the room. She looked tired. Determined. Human.

"We appealed the denial," she said. "We pushed it through medical review. We argued compassionate grounds."

He braced himself.

"They approved it," she said.

He stared at her.

"They approved it," she repeated. "You're getting the treatment."

He felt something loosen in his chest. Not relief. Not joy. Something quieter. Something like breath.

"Thank you," he whispered.

She smiled. "Everyone deserves a chance."

Everyone. He didn't know how to respond.

The treatment was brutal. It left him weak, nauseated, hollowed out. His hair thinned. His appetite vanished. His skin turned sallow. But the scans showed progress. The tumors were shrinking. The therapy was working.

He was alive because someone had fought for him. He was alive because someone had bent the rules. He was alive because someone had shown him mercy.

On his fourth infusion, a woman sat beside him in the treatment bay. Sixty, maybe sixty-five. A scarf wrapped around her head. She was knitting, the needles clicking in a small steady rhythm.

She glanced over at him. "First time?"

"Fourth," he said.

"It gets easier," she said. "Not the treatment. The sitting with it."

He didn't answer. She returned to her knitting.

After a while he asked, "How long have you been coming?"

"Fourteen months," she said. "Insurance denied my first protocol. By the time we got the appeal through, I was at stage four." She said it without bitterness, as a fact. "They said it was experimental. Now it's standard of care." She held up her knitting, checked the row. "Funny how that works."

He looked at the IV line running into his arm. He said nothing for a long time. Then: "I'm sorry."

She looked at him. "Do you have something to be sorry for?"

He couldn't answer that.

He told himself he would remember that. He told himself it mattered. He told himself it would change him. He believed it. For a while.

He returned to work six months later. The office looked the same. The desks. The screens. The people. Everything was unchanged. Except him.

He sat at his desk, opened the first claim, and felt a strange heaviness settle over him. It was a request for the same therapy he had received. Same diagnosis. Same stage. Same urgency. He read the oncologist's letter. He read the clinical notes. He read the plea. He knew what the policy said. He knew what the guidelines required. He knew what the system expected. He also knew what mercy felt like.

He hovered over the approval button. His hand trembled. Then he clicked deny.

He told himself he had no choice. He told himself he was protecting the system. He told himself he was doing what was necessary. But something inside him recoiled. He ignored it. He moved to the next claim.

Two weeks later, he received an email from his supervisor. We need to discuss your recent decisions.

He felt a chill.

He entered her office. She gestured for him to sit.

"Daniel," she said, "your denial rate has dropped."

He blinked. "Dropped?"

She nodded. "Significantly."

He frowned. "I've been following policy."

She tapped her screen. "You approved three claims last week that should have been denied."

He stiffened. "They were borderline."

"They were outside guidelines."

He said nothing.

She leaned forward. "We value your experience. But we need consistency. We need discipline. We need you to remember the role you play."

He swallowed. "I understand."

"Good," she said. "We can't afford exceptions."

He nodded. But something in him had begun to fracture.

The next day, he denied a claim for a man with the same cancer he had survived. He denied a claim for a woman whose daughter had written a letter begging for help. He denied a claim for a veteran who had already lost everything. He denied them all. He told himself he was doing his job. He told himself he had no choice. He told himself mercy was dangerous. But the words tasted like ash.

Marcus stopped by his desk late in the afternoon. He stood there for a moment, hands in his pockets.

"Hey," Marcus said. "You alright?"

"Fine."

Marcus looked at his screen. Then looked away. "I saw the Reyes file on your queue. Little girl, six years old. Rare enzyme deficiency." He paused. "Her mother called three times today. They put her through to general review each time."

Daniel kept his eyes on his screen.

"I just thought you should know," Marcus said. "In case it mattered."

He walked away.

Daniel sat very still. He thought of the woman in the treatment bay. Fourteen months. Stage four. Funny how that works. He opened the Reyes file. He read it. He closed it. He clicked deny. He went home. He did not sleep.

The call came on a Thursday. A woman's voice, trembling.

"Mr. Mercer," she said, "you denied my husband's treatment."

He closed his eyes. "I'm sorry."

"He's dying," she whispered.

He said nothing.

"You got the same treatment," she said. "I looked it up. You got the same therapy. Why would you deny it to him?"

He felt the question like a blow.

"I don't make the rules," he said.

"You lived," she said. "He won't."

He opened his mouth. No words came.

She exhaled, a sound full of grief and fury.

"I hope you never forget this," she said.

Then she hung up.

He sat in silence; the phone still pressed to his ear. He didn't move. He didn't breathe. He didn't hear his heartbeat.

The letter arrived three days later. Not a denial. A bill. A clerical error, they said. A coding mistake. A misfiled authorization. His treatment, the one that had saved his life — had been approved under the wrong category. The insurance company was reversing the approval. The cost was now his responsibility.

Three hundred and twelve thousand dollars.

He stared at the number. He read it again. And again. And again.

His hands began to shake. He called the number on the letter. He waited on hold for forty-seven minutes.

When someone finally answered, a young man's voice, scripted, apologetic in a rehearsed way that meant nothing, he explained the situation.

"I understand your frustration, Mr. Mercer," the young man said. "I really do. But this has been reviewed by our billing team and the determination stands. I'm sorry."

"I'm an employee," Daniel said. "I've been with this company twenty-seven years."

A pause. The sound of typing.

"I can see that, sir. And I appreciate your service to the company. But the billing determination is separate from employment status. There's nothing I can do at this level."

He felt something inside him collapse. Not break. Collapse. Like a building whose foundation had been quietly eroding for years.

He appealed. He wrote letters. He called supervisors. He begged. He pleaded. He used every trick he had learned in twenty-seven years. Nothing worked. The system he had served did not recognize him. The mercy he had received was revoked. The debt was reinstated. The torturer had arrived. Not as a person. As a consequence.

He lost his savings. He lost his house. He lost his job. He lost the quiet certainty that the world made sense. He moved into a small apartment with peeling paint and thin walls. He slept on a mattress on the floor. He ate canned soup. He avoided mirrors. He stopped answering the phone. He stopped opening the mail. He stopped hearing his heartbeat.

His daughter drove twelve hours to see him. She stood in the doorway of the apartment and looked at the mattress on the floor and the stack of unopened envelopes on the kitchen counter, and she didn't say anything for a long moment.

Then she said, "Dad." Just that. Just his name, the way it can hold a whole world of grief when someone loves you.

She sat on the floor beside the mattress. She did not try to fix it. She just sat there.

After a while she said, "Tell me what happened. All of it."

And he did. He told her everything. The denials. The woman in the treatment bay. The Reyes file. The phone call. The letter. He told her things he had never said aloud, things he had kept folded inside himself like the denial letters, pressed flat and set aside.

She listened without interrupting.

When he finished, she was quiet. Then: "You already know what you did wrong."

"Yes," he said.

"And you can't undo it."

"No."

She took his hand. "So what are you going to do with the rest of it?"

He didn't have an answer. But for the first time in months, the question felt like something other than a condemnation.

One night, unable to sleep, he walked to the hospital where his treatment had begun. He wandered the halls like a ghost, passing nurses who didn't notice him, patients who didn't see him, families who didn't know he existed. He found the consultation room where the oncologist had first told him he had a chance. He sat in the same chair. He placed his hands on the same table. He closed his eyes.

The night nurse found him there. The same young woman from his first night, the one with the dark circles, the one who had handed him a cup of water he hadn't asked for.

She looked at him for a moment. She looked at the chair, the table, the way he was sitting.

"You were here before," she said. "A while back."

"Yes."

She leaned against the doorframe. "You look different."

"Different how?"

She considered. "Like someone who finally let go of something heavy. Or maybe like someone who's finally picking it up. I can never tell which is which at three in the morning."

He almost smiled.

She pushed off the doorframe. "You need anything?"

"No," he said. "I'm just, sitting with it."

She nodded. "That's good," she said. "That's actually the hardest part."

She left him there.

He remembered the oncologist's words. Everyone deserves a chance. He whispered them aloud. "Everyone deserves a chance." The words trembled. He felt something rise in his chest, not anger, not grief, something older, something raw.

He began to weep. Not quietly. Not politely. He wept like a man who had finally understood the cost of the life he had lived. He wept for the people he had denied. He wept for the mercy he had withheld. He wept for the debt he had carried and the debts he had enforced. He wept for the little girl in the Reyes file. For the man whose wife had called. For the veteran who had already lost everything. For the woman with fourteen months and stage four and needles clicking in a treatment bay.

He wept until his body shook. He wept until he could breathe again. He wept until he could hear his heartbeat.

When he finally stood, the hallway was silent. He walked out of the hospital and into the cold night air. He did not know what would come next. He did not know how to repay what he owed. He did not know how to undo what he had done.

But he knew this: the system had taken everything from him. And he had helped build it. He could not change the past. But he could refuse to be its servant.

He walked into the darkness, the sound of his heartbeat steady, fragile, real.

And for the first time in his life, he understood the parable. Not as a warning from outside him. As a mirror he had been holding face-down for twenty-seven years.

He turned it over.

He looked.

## CHAPTER 13
### THE GLASS OVER THE RUINS

*The Barren Fig Tree*

*Luke 13:6–9*

The five objects always came first, laid out in whatever room I landed in like the stripped-down vocabulary of a life that had forgotten every other word. The drugs. The paraphernalia. The RC car. The Stratocaster. The Crate amplifier. They sat there on the carpet of the Hollywood Holiday Inn as if they had been waiting for me, as if they were the only things that still recognized me. I never explained them to myself. I didn't need to. They were the last five nouns left in a language I had burned down to its roots. The RC car sat closest to the door, its antenna bent slightly from being shoved into backpacks and duffel bags, its plastic wheels still carrying the dust of a dozen motel lobbies. I picked up the controller and squeezed the trigger, listening to the faint electric whine. "You ready?" I asked it, as if it could answer. It didn't need to. It always was.

I drove it out into the hallway, the little wheels buzzing over the industrial carpet, and then into the elevator. A couple stepped in behind me, the woman laughing softly as the car spun in a circle at her feet. "That yours?" she asked. "Yeah," I said, as if it were the most natural thing in the world for a grown man to be escorting a toy car through a hotel. "It goes everywhere with me." The man nodded politely, the way people nod when they're not sure what they're looking at. The doors opened into the lobby, and I let the car shoot forward, weaving between suitcases and ankles. People smiled. Or at least I thought they did. In my mind, they were charmed, delighted, entertained by the strange man with the toy. Years later I would understand the difference between smiling at someone and smiling about someone, but at the time the distinction didn't exist. The world was full of approval. The RC car was my passport.

I drove it through the dining room, past the buffet where a cook in a white hat said, "Hey buddy, watch your little racer there." I grinned. "He's got a mind of his own." The cook shook his head, amused or confused or both. The RC car bumped gently into a chair leg, reversed, and darted away. I followed it like a parent chasing a toddler, except toddlers grow up and RC cars don't. They stay exactly what they are, which is maybe why I kept mine so close. It was the last piece of childhood I hadn't managed to destroy.

From the window of my room, the Capitol Records building rose in the distance, round and iconic, a stack of vinyl records turned into architecture. A monument to music, to achievement, to the kind of life people imagine when they come to Hollywood. I stood there holding a guitar I couldn't play, looking at a building full of people who could. The contrast didn't sting. It didn't even register. I wasn't a barren tree. I was just a tree. I didn't know I wasn't producing anything. I didn't know I was taking up soil and water and light without giving anything back. I thought I was doing what trees do.

That night the warmth came first. Hollywood rarely gets hot, not really, not the way the Valley does, but the air felt thick and soft, like it had been warmed from the inside. I stepped out onto the roof with the Strat slung over my shoulder and the Crate amp under my arm. The RC car stayed behind this time, parked neatly by the bed like a loyal dog waiting for its master. The roof was quiet, the city humming below like a distant engine. I set the amp down, plugged it in, and then felt the heat settle on my skin in a way that made clothing feel unnecessary, almost insulting. I pulled my shirt over my head, dropped my pants, stepped out of everything until I was just a body in warm air. It didn't feel reckless. It felt right. Like the night itself had asked for it.

I walked across the roof, the concrete warm under my bare feet, and sat on the edge. Twenty stories up. The parking lot below looked like a map someone had drawn with tiny toy cars. People moved like insects, small and slow and unaware of the naked man swinging his legs above them. I leaned back on my hands and let my legs dangle, kicking them out and pulling them back with more force than made sense. Normally a step ladder made my stomach flip. Normally I couldn't look over a balcony without feeling the ground tilt. But that night the height felt like nothing. I looked down and thought, I could jump and it wouldn't even be scary. The thought didn't frighten me. It didn't thrill me. It just existed, like a cloud passing overhead.

And then, just as quietly, something else existed too. Something that said not yet. Not in words. Not in any language I knew. Just a presence, a pause, a hand on the back of the neck that wasn't a hand at all. The tree stood at the edge of the cutting. And the cutting did not come.

I stood up and walked back to the amp. The guitar cable clicked into place. The amp hummed. I turned the volume knob until it couldn't turn anymore. One hundred and ten decibels. The Strat hung awkwardly against my hip, the strap too long, the body too light. I didn't know a single chord. Not one. But I strummed anyway, dragging the pick across the strings in a jagged, chaotic rhythm that felt like music to me. The sound tore across the roof, bounced off the walls, spilled into the night like a siren. I closed my eyes and imagined myself on a stage, imagined the crowd roaring, imagined the Capitol Records building turning its full attention toward me.

When I opened my eyes, I saw them. A group of people on a hill far away, silhouetted against the night sky, waving their arms. I grinned. They liked me. They were cheering. I lifted the guitar and played harder, the strings buzzing, the amp screaming. The people waved more frantically. I thought they were encouraging me.

They were shaking their fists.

The helicopter arrived like a divine interruption. The thump of the blades cut through the night, and then the floodlight hit, bright and merciless, illuminating the entire roof. For one second — just one — I felt like a rock star. The light was my spotlight. The roof was my stage. The city was my audience. I lifted the guitar triumphantly, ready to play the greatest solo in the history of music, even though I didn't know how to play anything at all.

Then the paranoia hit. I yanked the cable from the amp, grabbed the guitar, scooped up the amp, and ran barefoot across the roof to the stairwell. The metal door clanged behind me. I reached my floor, burst through the door, and sprinted to my room. Clothes flew onto my body in whatever order they landed. I grabbed the RC car, the guitar, and the amp. The drugs stayed on the nightstand, forgotten in the panic.

The elevator doors opened into a lobby full of police. Not one or two. A crowd. Officers talking into radios, standing in clusters, scanning the room. I froze for half a second, then forced myself to walk. The RC car hung from my hand by its antenna. The guitar strap dug into my shoulder. The amp banged against my leg. I walked past the officers, waiting for a hand on my arm, waiting for someone to say, that's him. But nothing happened. They didn't look at me. They didn't see me. I moved through them like a ghost, like someone the world had decided, for reasons it would never explain, to let pass.

Outside, the parking lot was full of police cars, lights turning silently. Officers stood in small groups, pointing at the roof, talking in urgent clusters. I walked through all of it, unlocked my car, and got in. The engine started. I drove away. No one stopped me. No one glanced in my direction.

The axe had been raised. It had not fallen.

That night was like every other night on those drugs. Euphoric one minute, scattered and fractured the next. The chemicals didn't distinguish between a rooftop and a parking lot, between a helicopter floodlight and a bedroom ceiling. They just kept doing what they did, which was make the world feel manageable right up until it didn't. The paranoia came and went in waves. The euphoria came back. Then the paranoia again. This was the rhythm. This was the only rhythm I knew. As long as the drugs were there, I was in a good place. Never mind what that good place looked like from the outside. Never mind that my definition of a good place had somehow come to include standing naked on the roof of a twenty-story hotel at 110 decibels, convinced a crowd of strangers on a distant hill were cheering for me. That was fine. That was Tuesday. The chemicals kept their promise, which was not happiness exactly, not peace exactly, but the absence of the thing underneath, the thing that waited whenever the supply ran low, the thing I had no language for and no interest in meeting. So I drove. And the night passed the way those nights passed, loud inside, quiet outside, the city moving around me like a river moves around a stone, indifferent, continuous, unaware that anything had happened at all.

It wasn't until I was halfway home that I realized the drugs were still in the room. I gripped the steering wheel. I knew what I would do. I would go back in the morning. I would check into the same hotel. I would ask for the same room. And if the drugs were gone, then they were gone.

But if they weren't.

The next morning I walked into the lobby, the RC car tucked under my arm. The clerk smiled. "Back again?" "Same room as last night, if it's open." She typed. "It is," she said. "Lucky you."

Lucky. That was one word for it.

The elevator ride felt longer than it had the night before. The hallway brighter. The door heavier. I opened it slowly. The room was immaculate. The bed made. The carpet vacuumed. The bathroom shining. My heart sank. Of course the drugs were gone. A cleaning person would have found them, thrown them away, perhaps reported them. That was the logical outcome. The expected outcome.

I stepped further into the room, letting the door close behind me.

And then I saw it.

On the nightstand, next to the bed, sat a glass. Upside down. Beneath it, visible through the clear surface, was a pile of drugs. Neatly heaped. Preserved. Protected. As if someone had found them, paused, and then decided — without knowing why, without any obligation to do so — to cover them instead of discarding them. A gesture so small it barely qualified as a decision. A gesture so enormous it rearranged the entire meaning of the night before.

I walked toward it slowly, as if approaching something I didn't have a name for. The glass caught the morning light, casting a faint circle on the nightstand. I lifted it. The drugs were untouched. Waiting. As if someone had said, in the quiet language of ordinary mercy, these belong to someone.

I sat on the edge of the bed and stared at the pile. The room smelled of bleach and clean linens. The world had been reset. The consequences erased. The axe raised again, and again laid down.

I reached for the drugs. Of course I did. The tree did not suddenly bear fruit. The roots did not suddenly deepen. The one more year was not a triumph. It was a chance. And I used it the way a man uses chances when he doesn't yet know they are chances at all. The gardener does not guarantee the harvest. The gardener only asks for the time to work the soil. What grows inside that time belongs entirely to the tree.

Later — much later — I would understand what the upside down glass was. Not grace in the triumphant sense. Not rescue dressed in light. The vinedresser doesn't always arrive with a remedy. Sometimes the vinedresser arrives with a glass, placed quietly over the very thing that is killing the tree, because the tree is not ready yet. Because the fruit has not come yet. Because the cutting would end something that still has a year left in it, maybe more, maybe everything. The gardener gets down in the dirt around the roots. The dirt is real. The roots are real. And the one more year is not clean. It smells like bleach and drugs and a warm Hollywood night and a rooftop at 110 decibels and a lobby full of police who somehow did not see what was standing right in front of them.

The parable ends without a verdict. Luke doesn't tell us whether the tree eventually bore fruit. He leaves us in the intercession, in the not yet, in the one more year suspended between the axe and whatever comes after. I think he knew what he was doing. Because the people who most need this parable are still inside their one more year. They are not ready for the ending. They need the space between.

I set the glass back on the nightstand. Upside down again, as if returning it to its rightful place. Then I picked up the RC car and squeezed the trigger. The wheels spun. The little car darted forward, bumped gently into the wall, reversed, and came back toward me.

The tree was still alive. Still taking up soil. Still reaching in all the wrong directions. Still, somehow, not cut down.

The gardener was still in the dirt.

Give it one more year.

*CHAPTER 14*<br>*THE LAST HOUR*

*The Workers in the Vineyard*<br>*Matthew 20:1–16*

He drove across the LA basin with the director of the sober living house on the phone and he did not hang up once. Not for a red light. Not for a freeway merge. Not for the forty five minutes it took to cross from one side of that sprawling broken beautiful city to the other. Twenty eight days of treatment behind him and he was still so spun he could barely tie his shoes. He knew what he was doing and why he was doing it. Without that voice in his ear, without that thin wire of human connection stretched across the basin, he might have made the wrong turn. He knew exactly which turn that was. He knew exactly where it led. So he kept the director on the phone and kept driving and when he finally pulled into the parking lot the director said, "I'll see you in a minute," and he said, "Yes sir," and he sat there for a moment with the engine running and his hands on the wheel and the phone silent in his lap.

Twenty eight days. And here he was at the only door still open.

He went inside.

The director was a compact man with steady eyes and the particular calm of someone who had seen everything and been surprised by none of it. He shook hands without ceremony, showed him his room, introduced him to the five other men who would share it. Six beds. Six dressers. Six men at various distances from the bottom. He sat on the edge of his assigned bed and looked at his hands and thought, this is what is left. These hands. This bed. This room. He had nothing else that could be carried or counted.

In the morning the director handed him a sheet of paper.

"These are your chores," he said.

Toilet patrol. Ashtrays. Laundry. Dishes.

He looked at the list for a long moment. Then he folded it and put it in his pocket. There was nothing left in him to flinch with. The dawn workers in the vineyard take the worst jobs because the worst jobs are the only jobs being offered at dawn. He took the mop. He took the bucket. He filled the bucket at the utility sink, the water steaming, the smell of industrial cleaner sharp in the back of his throat, and he carried it down the hall to the first bathroom and he got down on his knees on the cold tile floor and he cleaned what needed cleaning. Not quickly. Not resentfully. Not with the performance of a man demonstrating his willingness to be humbled. Just carefully. Thoroughly. The way a man cleans something when he understands that the cleaning is not beneath him. That nothing is beneath him. That the floor he is kneeling on is exactly the floor he belongs on right now and that is not a punishment. That is a beginning.

The house had its rhythm and he learned it the way you learn the rhythm of any place that is trying to keep people alive. Morning meeting at seven. The folding chairs arranged in a circle in the common room. The burned coffee that nobody complained about because the coffee was not the point. The voices of men saying true things in plain language, which is one of the hardest things a human being can do and also one of the most necessary. He sat in those meetings and listened. When it was his turn he said what was real. The room received it without drama, without excessive comfort, without the particular cruelty of false reassurance. Just, we hear you. Just, we know. Just, keep going.

After thirty days the director called him into the office.

"You've earned a twenty four hour furlough," he said. "You can leave after dinner tonight and be back by dinner tomorrow."

He sat with that for a moment.

"I'll pass," he said.

The director looked at him. "You sure?"

"Yes sir."

He didn't explain. There was nothing to explain that the director didn't already understand. No family waiting with an open door. No friend whose couch would feel like anything other than a reminder of everything he had lost. The furlough was a gift with nowhere to be delivered. He left it on the table and went back to the toilets and the ashtrays and the laundry and the dishes and showed up the next morning and did it again.

Some of the other men thought this was strange. He heard them talking about it once, quietly, the way men in close quarters talk about each other when they think no one is listening.

"He never takes his day off."

"Maybe he's got nowhere to go."

"That's sad, man."

He didn't think it was sad. He thought it was clarity. The marketplace is not the place you leave when the work gets hard. The marketplace is the place you stay until someone comes for you. And no one was coming if he wasn't there.

He had been in the house about six weeks when his roommate came to him in the dark.

It was past eleven. The house had settled into its nighttime quiet, that specific institutional silence made of men trying not to disturb each other's fragile sleep. He was lying on his back looking at the ceiling when he heard his roommate sit up. Then the sound of bare feet on the floor. Then his roommate's voice, low and careful, like a man stepping onto ice he isn't sure will hold.

"You awake?"

"Yeah."

A long pause. The kind of pause that has weight in it.

"I need to tell you something."

He sat up. In the dark he could see the outline of his roommate on the edge of the bed across from him, shoulders hunched, head down, the posture of a man carrying something he can no longer carry alone.

"I used on my furlough."

The words landed in the silence and stayed there.

"How much?"

"Enough."

He didn't say anything for a moment. He didn't reach for judgment and he didn't reach for comfort. He just let the confession exist in the room between them the way it needed to exist before anything else could happen.

"You have to tell the director," he finally said.

"He'll kick me out."

"Maybe. But you have to tell him."

"I can't—"

"I'll go with you." He said it quietly, without drama, the way you say something when you mean it completely. "Tomorrow morning. I'll stand right next to you and I'll tell him what I see. Which is a man who made a mistake and came back and told the truth about it instead of hiding it. That counts for something. That counts for a lot."

His roommate was quiet for a long time. Then: "Why would you do that?"

He thought about it. "Because somebody would have done it for me," he said. "If I'd asked."

They went together in the morning. He stood beside his roommate in the director's office and said what he had said he would say. The director listened without interrupting, his steady eyes moving between the two of them, measuring something that wasn't guilt or innocence but something more complicated than either. When they were finished he leaned back in his chair and looked at the ceiling for a moment.

"You understand what a contract means," he said to the roommate. It wasn't a question.

"Yes sir."

"One more. That's it. One more and the door closes."

"Yes sir."

"All right." He looked at both of them. "Get back to work."

In the hallway afterward his roommate stopped and turned to him. His eyes were red. He looked like a man who had just set down something very heavy and wasn't sure yet whether his legs would hold without it.

"Thank you," he said.

"Don't thank me," he said. "Just stay."

His roommate stayed. He never tested positive again. He never relapsed again. Whatever seed had been planted in that dark room at eleven o'clock at night took root in his roommate's life and grew into something he would never fully see and was not meant to see. He went back to the toilets and the ashtrays and the dishes and the laundry and did not think of himself as having done anything worth noting. He had simply refused to let a man face his worst moment alone. It seemed to him the minimum requirement of being human.

The rooms changed as the months accumulated. Six men became four. Four became two. Two became one. The day the director walked him down the hall to the private room and opened the door he stopped in the doorway and stood there for a long moment without going in. It was not a large room. It was not a remarkable room. But it had a fireplace. A small one, modest, the kind that exists more as a gesture toward warmth than an actual source of it. He looked at that fireplace for a long time. He thought about the parking lots and the motel rooms and the years of living in spaces that held him the way a container holds something it doesn't care about. And then he walked in, set his few things down, and sat in the chair by the fireplace and put his face in his hands and stayed that way for a while. Not crying exactly. Just being still. Just letting the room be a room that was his.

He understood that he had not earned this by being exceptional. He had earned it by being consistent. Exceptional requires talent. Consistent requires only the willingness to return. He had returned every morning. That was all. That was everything.

The chores changed with the rooms. The indoor work gave way to outdoor work. The director handed him the key to the equipment shed.

"Lawn and leaves," he said. "Yours now."

He took the key. He liked the outdoor work in a way he hadn't expected. There was something clarifying about it, about being outside in the morning air with a specific piece of ground to tend and a machine in his hands that asked nothing of him except that he point it in the right direction. The cut grass. The cleared leaves. The visible evidence of effort applied to a specific patch of earth. The work simple enough that the hands could do it without the mind's supervision. The mind therefore almost quiet. Not healed. Not resolved. Not anything so clean as that. But quiet enough that something underneath the noise could occasionally be heard. Something that sounded, on the best mornings, almost like the future. He would stop sometimes and just stand there with the leaf blower idling at his side and look at the cleared ground and think, I did that. That is a thing I did today that was not there before I did it. And then he would pull the trigger and keep going.

He was operating the leaf blower on a morning indistinguishable from the mornings before it when the car turned into the driveway.

He knew it before it stopped. He knew it the way a man knows the outline of something that once held everything he loved — the particular color, the particular make, the way it sat on its wheels, the specific geometry of a life he had destroyed and grieved and was still in the process of learning to live without. His hands went still on the machine. The leaf blower fell silent. The engine of the car died. The driver's door opened. And then the second door. And then the back doors.

Two little girls.

Eight months. He had not seen them in eight months and the last time he saw them the ground was coming apart beneath everyone's feet and everything was ending and he had not known, standing in that rubble, whether he would ever again stand in the same space as these two faces. His oldest. His youngest. Their particular faces that were his face and their mother's face and something that belonged entirely to themselves. The leaf blower dropped from his hands onto the grass. His knees followed it. The sound that came out of him was not crying in the way that word is usually meant. It was something larger than crying, something that had been compressed for eight months under the weight of all that waiting and was now releasing all at once in the middle of a sober living front lawn on an ordinary morning with the smell of cut grass in the air and two little girls standing by a car watching their father come apart and come together at the same time.

He didn't know how long he stayed on his knees. Long enough for his oldest to take a step toward him and then stop. Long enough for his youngest to say, softly, the word that had no business being as devastating as it was:

"Daddy."

He pulled himself upright from the grass. He wiped his face with the back of his hand. He walked to them and held them and for a moment the world was nothing but the specific weight of two children in his arms who were still willing to be held.

His ex-wife stood at the edge of the driveway. She had been watching. Not just today. For months. She had people who knew people who knew the director of the house and the reports had been consistent. A man doing the work. Honestly. Without shortcuts. Without the performance of recovery that she had seen before and learned to recognize and knew better than to trust. Just the work, done every day, in the particular unglamorous way that real work gets done. She had brought the girls because the girls needed a father.

That was the whole of her reasoning and it was enough.

He looked at her over the tops of their daughters' heads.

"Why?" he asked. It was all he could manage.

"They need their father," she said.

He held that for a moment. Then: "Do you still need a husband?"

She looked at him for a long time. The particular look of a woman who has been burned and has not forgotten the burning but has decided, for reasons that are her own, to stand near the fire one more time.

"No guarantees," she said.

"I'll take it," he said.

He said yes. Without conditions. Without negotiation. Without asking what yes would cost him in the years ahead or what it would look like from the inside of a house where two people sleep on opposite sides because the love has been used up but the commitment to the children has not. Just yes. The way the last hour worker says yes when the landowner finally pulls up at five o'clock. You don't negotiate when you've been standing on the curb since dawn. You get in the truck.

Fourteen years.

Not fourteen years of reconciliation. Not fourteen years of a marriage restored to what it was before the drugs took it apart, because that marriage was gone and both of them knew it and the honest acknowledgment of that fact was one of the few courtesies they consistently extended to each other. They were two people raising children in the same house and they did it with a kind of careful respect that asked nothing of either of them except decency and consistency and the shared refusal to let their daughters grow up in a broken home. On most days that was enough. On some days it was everything.

What there was instead of love was presence. The particular irreplaceable presence of a father in the daily life of his daughters. School mornings with lunches to be packed and hair to be brushed and permission slips to be found on the kitchen counter at seven in the morning. He was good at the school mornings. He liked them. The particular chaos of getting two children out the door by eight, the missing shoe, the forgotten library book, the argument about whether a certain shirt was appropriate for picture day. He liked being the one who found the shoe. He liked being the one who remembered the library book. He liked being needed in the ordinary daily way that children need their parents, which is the most sustaining form of being needed that exists.

Parent helper afternoons where he sat in a small chair designed for a body a third of his size in a classroom full of children learning to read and he helped with the reading groups and listened to small voices sound out syllables with the concentration of people doing the most important work in the world, which they were. He felt something in his chest during those afternoons that had no name in any language he knew. Something that had nothing to do with the drugs or the parking lots or the motel rooms or any of the years he had spent making himself smaller and smaller until there was barely enough of him left to fill a car seat in a sober living driveway. Something that was simply the feeling of being exactly where he was supposed to be.

The Indian Princess program where he and his oldest daughter sat at a table with other fathers and daughters and made things with their hands. He was not a crafts man. He had never pretended to be. He glued things crooked and cut things uneven and his daughter would look at his work and then look at him with an expression of patient affection that made him feel like the luckiest man in the room, which he was.

"Daddy, that's not straight," she would say.

"I know," he would say.

"Here," she would say, and she would take it from him and fix it, her small hands precise and certain, and he would watch her and think, where did you come from, how did something this good come from anything I was a part of, how is it possible that I get to sit at this table with you.

Father daughter dances where his youngest put on a dress and he put on a tie and she inspected him carefully before they left the house, straightening the tie with the seriousness of someone performing a sacred duty.

"You look nice, Daddy," she would say, and the words would land in his chest like something he had been waiting to hear his whole life without knowing he was waiting.

They went out into the world together, father and daughter, and the world received them as exactly that, two people who belonged to each other, and he thought each time, this is the wage. This is the full day's wage being paid out in real time and I am holding it in my hands and it weighs nothing and it weighs everything.

Walking them to school. Watching their faces in the morning light. The particular way his youngest laughed, sudden and total, her whole body involved. The particular way his oldest thought before she spoke, a small pause, a gathering, that reminded him of no one so much as himself on his best days. Being there. Just being there. The ordinary unremarkable sacred daily work of fatherhood that he had almost not gotten to do and had been given anyway at the last possible hour.

His friends watched from the outside and called it sacrifice.

"Man, I don't know how you do it," one of them said once, over coffee, shaking his head. "Fourteen years in that house. Sleeping on opposite sides. No intimacy. That's not a life."

He looked at his friend for a moment. He thought about the right way to say what he wanted to say.

"You're counting the wrong thing," he said.

"What do you mean?"

"You're counting what I didn't have. I'm counting what I did."

His friend looked at him the way the dawn workers looked at the landowner. The look of a man who has done the math correctly and cannot understand why the answer is wrong.

"Same wage," he said quietly.

"What?"

"Nothing." He picked up his coffee. "Never mind."

He listened to his friends without anger because they were not wrong by the mathematics they were using and their concern for him was genuine. But they were measuring the wrong currency. They were standing at the end of the day counting denarii when the actual wage had been paid in a different form entirely, in the form of two little girls who had a father present for the years when a father's presence leaves its deepest mark, in the form of mornings and evenings and ordinary Tuesdays that added up to a childhood that contained him. He had not sacrificed fourteen years. He had been paid fourteen years. The last hour worker does not sacrifice the afternoon just because he arrived late. He receives the same wage as the ones who came at dawn. The wage is not diminished by the lateness of the hour. The wage is the wage.

The youngest turned eighteen. The oldest was twenty three with a job and a life building itself in the way that young lives build themselves, forward and outward and away from the house that made them. The time had come the way time always comes, not as a dramatic conclusion but as the quiet arrival of what was always going to be inevitable. He left. He took what was his and left what wasn't and drove away from a house he had lived in for fourteen years as a father and a ghost simultaneously, which is a particular kind of haunting that leaves marks on everyone it touches.

What happened after he left belongs to a silence this chapter will not fill. There are things that silence contains that are too close to the bone for the page and too unresolved for any ending that could be offered honestly. What can be said is this. The fourteen years happened. They are permanent in the way that all real things are permanent — not in the sense that they continue, but in the sense that they cannot be made not to have occurred. The Indian Princess afternoons happened. The father daughter dances happened. The school mornings and the parent helper afternoons and the homework at the kitchen table and the particular way his youngest laughed and the particular pause before his oldest spoke — all of it happened and is therefore always happening in the permanent record of what was real.

Seeds planted do not disappear when the farmer walks away. They grow in the dark without his knowledge and without his presence and without his being consulted about the timing of the harvest. He scattered himself into their lives simply by being there. By being present in his body in their house on their ordinary mornings on their particular Tuesdays. By finding the shoe. By remembering the library book. By sitting in the small chair and listening to small voices sound out syllables. By straightening the tie and going to the dance. By saying yes at the edge of a sober living driveway when every reasonable calculation said the day was already over.

The last will be first.

Not because they worked less. Because they understood, in the way that only the ones who have lost everything can understand, what the wage actually was. Not the hours. The presence. Not the denarius. The daughters. Not the vineyard. The driveway. The car he recognized before it stopped. The knees finding the grass. The word that his youngest said in a voice so soft it should not have been able to reach him from that distance and yet did.

Daddy.

He had been hired at the last hour.

He had been paid everything.

And no subsequent silence reaches back far enough to take it from him.

# CHAPTER 15
## THE FORGOTTEN MELODY

### *The Talents*

*Matthew 25:14–30*

Reinhardt Vogler was not merely Vienna's preeminent composer. He was a man who had made a religion of order, and like all devoted priests, he had long since forgotten what first drove him to the altar.

His father had been a horologist, a maker of clocks, and Reinhardt had grown up inside the theology of precision. He spent his boyhood afternoons in his father's workshop, watching the tiny gears mesh and turn, learning that the universe rewarded those who refused to tolerate slippage. His father's hands never trembled. His father's pronouncements never wavered. "Perfection isn't a luxury, Reinhardt. It's necessity." The boy had received those words the way a sapling receives a stake driven into the earth beside it. He grew toward them. Eventually he could not tell where they ended and he began.

By the time Reinhardt reached his seventieth year, he had composed forty-three works of celebrated precision. Critics spoke of his music the way astronomers speak of mathematical proofs, not merely beautiful, but correct. His symphonies moved through their appointed measures like the gears of his father's finest clock, each note arriving exactly where it was expected, the silence between movements calibrated to the millisecond. Audiences left his performances feeling not so much moved as confirmed, as though the universe had been briefly audited and found to be in order.

But in the deepest chamber of Reinhardt's memory, behind the locked doors of his most vigilant self-discipline, something lived that he had never managed to kill. Only to silence.

He had composed it at nineteen, in a single feverish night, the kind of night that arrives once in a life and never announces itself as extraordinary until it is already gone. The melody had poured out of him the way floodwater pours through a breach, not guided, not shaped, simply released. It was raw and asymmetrical and stubbornly, almost embarrassingly alive. It frightened him in the way that a mirror frightens a man who does not recognize the face looking back. He had written it out by hand, stared at it for three days, and then buried it in a leather satchel he carried to a secondhand bookstore on the edge of the Naschmarkt, where he sold it along with a bundle of student manuscripts for a few coins, telling himself it was refuse, telling himself he was being disciplined, telling himself his father would have approved.

He had spent fifty years almost believing it.

Emil Roth had grown up in Salzburg's working-class Lehen district, in an apartment where the walls were thin enough to hear the neighbors' arguments and the ceiling leaked in three places when it rained. His mother stitched garments late into the night, her needle moving with the same quiet persistence as water finding its level. His father repaired bicycles in the narrow corridor that served as both hallway and workshop, his hands perpetually darkened with grease, his laughter perpetually ready. They were people who knew how to find warmth in small things, who understood that beauty did not require a frame.

Emil saw beauty where others saw chaos.

He had taught himself to play on a piano salvaged from a demolition site when he was seven years old, three of its keys permanently silenced, its soundboard cracked along a diagonal that gave certain notes a ghostly second voice. He learned to play around the dead keys the way a river learns to move around stone, not despite the obstacle but somehow because of it, the detour becoming the music. Teachers who heard him marveled and then retreated into uncertainty. He was talented in a way they had no category for, his playing unorthodox as a conversation between old friends, unpredictable as weather, lacking every refinement their pedagogy demanded and possessing something their pedagogy could not name.

By his late twenties, Emil had made himself the custodian of forgotten things. He haunted the secondhand bookstores and estate sales of Salzburg and Vienna, rescuing abandoned scores from the indignity of dusty shelves, bringing them home to his small studio where a better piano now stood, its keys worn smooth as river stones by the passage of his hands. He did not do this for recognition. He did it because he believed that every unheard melody was a small tragedy, a light extinguished before it could illuminate anything.

It was during one of these pilgrimages, on a grey Thursday in November, that Emil found the manuscript.

It was tucked between two volumes of student exercises, water-stained and fragmentary; its pages soft with age. There was no name on the cover, only a date, fifty years prior, and the ghost of a title partially obscured by a water stain. Emil carried it to the window and held it in the thin afternoon light. Then, because he could not help himself, he hummed the opening measures aloud.

The melody entered him like a key turning in a lock he had not known was there.

He worked on it for three weeks, alone in his studio with the flickering overhead light and the worn piano and the peculiar sensation of completing someone else's dream. The original fragment was skeletal, all impulse and no architecture, but its emotional grammar was so precise, so nakedly human, that Emil felt less like a composer than an archaeologist, brushing dirt from something that had always been whole. He filled the missing measures not by imposing his own ideas but by listening to what the fragment itself seemed to be reaching toward. Where the original composer had stopped, Emil heard the next note waiting in the silence like a held breath.

He did not know whose manuscript it was. He did not think to investigate. He only knew that it deserved to be heard.

The gala at Schönbrunn Palace was Reinhardt's apotheosis, or so the invitation had promised. Forty years of Vienna's most discerning critics, scholars, and patrons had gathered beneath the chandeliers to witness the debut of his magnum opus, "Celestial Architectures," a symphony in four movements that Reinhardt had spent six years constructing with the methodical devotion of a man building a cathedral. The program notes described it as the culmination of a lifetime's pursuit of perfection. Reinhardt had approved those notes himself.

But standing in the wings, listening to the murmur of the crowd, he felt the familiar hollowness open beneath his ribs. It was a sensation he had learned to outrun through work, through rehearsal, through the management of ten thousand details, but it always returned in these moments before performance, when the machinery of preparation finally stilled and there was nothing between him and the silence but his own reflection.

He was thinking about his father's clocks. About the way they kept perfect time but could not tell you what the time meant.

Emil had spent the last of his savings on the tuxedo. It was rented, not owned, he would return it tomorrow, but it fit him well enough, and more importantly it fit the occasion. He had arranged everything with meticulous care, presenting himself to the palace's head of stage management three hours before the gala as a piano technician, hired to oversee the final preparation of the Bösendorfer Imperial that would carry the evening's music. The man had glanced at Emil's formal attire, at the worn leather satchel under his arm, and nodded without further inquiry. The aristocracy, Emil had long understood, rendered certain people invisible. He intended to make use of that invisibility for exactly as long as it served him.

He spent two hours in genuine service, tuning the upper register, adjusting the bench, polishing the fallboard until it reflected the chandelier's light like dark water. He touched the instrument with the reverence of a man who understood what it meant to have been made for something. And when the hall began to fill, when the murmur of the gathering crowd reached him through the heavy curtains, Emil straightened his jacket, tucked the manuscript under his arm, and walked to the piano bench as though he had always been expected there.

Reinhardt ascended the stage to a swell of anticipation, the chandeliers catching the moment with their gilded arms of bronze and teardrop prisms that gleamed like frozen constellations above the gathered faithful. He stood at the podium and felt the hollowness again, wider now, a room inside him that applause had never managed to furnish.

The room's reaction to Emil moved through the crowd the way cold moves through an old building, finding every crack, settling into every corner. A ripple of incredulous murmurs. A critic near the front leaned to whisper in his neighbor's ear. Two security men at the door took a step forward and then hesitated, uncertain of the protocol for a man in a tuxedo seated at the piano with the composed stillness of someone who belonged there absolutely.

Reinhardt, frozen at the edge of the stage, watched with his mouth slightly open.

Emil did not look up. He placed the manuscript on the music stand, smoothed it gently with one hand the way his mother had smoothed fabric before cutting it, and began to play.

The melody emerged from the piano the way dawn emerges from darkness, not announced, not sudden, but inevitable. It was hesitant at first, skeletal, the original fragment exactly as its composer had abandoned it fifty years ago. And then Emil's additions began to unfold, the measures he had spent three weeks coaxing from the silence, and the piece opened outward like a hand releasing something it had held too long.

Reinhardt heard three notes and felt the floor shift beneath him.

He knew it. He knew it the way you know the face of someone you loved before you remember their name, in the body first, in the sudden alteration of the heartbeat, in the inexplicable pricking behind the eyes. He stood perfectly still while fifty years collapsed around him like a building whose foundations had been quietly dissolving for decades.

The room had grown uncertain. Several critics exchanged glances of professional skepticism. An elderly countess near the window closed her eyes, though whether in disapproval or something else was impossible to say. But a young woman in the third row had stopped pretending to consult her program and was simply listening, her hands folded in her lap, her face open in a way that faces rarely are in rooms like this.

Emil played through the dissonances Reinhardt had never dared attempt, the unresolved harmonies, the measures that refused the comfort of return. He played the flaws not as apologies but as declarations. Where the music broke, he let it break fully, and in the breaking it became something that Reinhardt's forty-three perfect compositions had never managed to be.

It became true.

When the last note dissolved into the air of the palace hall, the silence that followed was a different quality of silence than the room had known before. Not the polished silence of an audience observing protocol, but the raw silence of people who have been briefly ambushed by something they were not prepared to feel.

Emil rose from the bench. He crossed the stage to where Reinhardt stood, and held out the manuscript with both hands, the gesture of someone returning a lost child.

"Maestro Vogler." His voice was steady. "This belongs to you. I found it in an old shop. I thought it deserved more than silence."

Reinhardt looked at the manuscript for a long moment before taking it. His fingers found the faded ink, the water stains, the ghost of his own nineteen-year-old handwriting. "You shouldn't have played this," he began, and then stopped. Because the sentence was true in every way except the one that mattered.

"It wasn't about being ready," Emil said quietly. "It was about being heard."

They spoke briefly, and then the gala reassembled itself around its original purpose, and "Celestial Architectures" was performed to its anticipated acclaim, and the critics wrote what they had come prepared to write. Emil slipped away before the reception, his rented tuxedo still perfectly pressed, the leather satchel empty now.

Reinhardt did not sleep that night.

He sat in his study until the city outside his window moved through its dark hours and began, reluctantly, to lighten. The manuscript lay open before him on the desk, and beside it his own handwritten score for "Celestial Architectures," forty years of disciplined labor spread across two hundred pages of perfect notation. He looked at them for a long time, the abandoned and the celebrated, the wild and the controlled, the thing he had been and the thing he had made himself become.

Then, slowly, he pulled the manuscript toward him. He sat at the small upright piano in the corner of his study, the one he had owned since conservatory, its keys yellowed and familiar as old friends. He placed the manuscript on the stand. He looked at it for another long moment, feeling the weight of fifty years in his hands, in his shoulders, in the slight tremor of his fingers that had not been there at nineteen.

He began to play.

He played it badly at first, rustily, haltingly, his trained hands resisting the music's refusal to resolve where they expected resolution. He played through the measures he had written and into the measures Emil had added, and something in the juncture between them, the seam where one man's abandoned dream met another man's faithful completion, undid something in his chest that he had not known was fastened.

He did not stop when he made mistakes. He played through them, and then he played them again deliberately, holding the dissonant notes until they stopped sounding like errors and started sounding like weather, like truth, like the particular cry of a thing that has survived its own burial.

He played it a second time, and a third. And somewhere in the third playing, something shifted. The flaws were not wounds in the music. They were windows. Each imperfection opened onto a view that his forty-three perfect compositions, for all their celebrated architecture, had kept carefully obscured, the view of a man who had felt something once, something enormous and ungovernable, and had spent a lifetime building walls tall enough to forget it.

Dawn came through the study window and found him still playing, his face wet in a way he did not bother to acknowledge, the manuscript before him soft with age and somehow luminous, the way very old things sometimes are when they have finally been returned to the light.

His father's clocks kept perfect time on the wall behind him. Reinhardt did not hear them. He was listening to something older, the sound of a melody that had waited half a century in the dark and emerged not diminished but deepened, the way rivers emerge from underground passages carrying the memory of stone, of darkness, of the long patient journey toward open air.

He played it until he knew it by heart. Until it was no longer a fragment but a homecoming. Until perfection, that old merciless god, finally stepped aside and let the music through.

*The Rich Fool*

*Luke 12:13–21*

Walter Ames had spent thirty years inside the machinery, and the machinery had rewarded him for his precision.

He joined Meridian Health Assurance fresh out of state college at twenty-five, a young man with a business degree that hung on his wall like a passport to legitimacy, a pressed white shirt that still held the creases from the package, and a new briefcase his father had given him with the words Make something of yourself unspoken but understood in the weight of the leather. He believed then—with the uncomplicated certainty of someone who has never been crushed by circumstances beyond his control—that systems, when followed correctly, kept the world from falling into chaos. That rules existed not to punish but to protect. That fairness was a matter of applying policy consistently, without sentiment, without the dangerous intrusions of emotion that bent judgment and broke budgets and left everyone worse off in the long run.

He rose quickly through the ranks of claims adjustment. He had a gift for reading policy language the way some men read music, seeing patterns and progressions where others saw only dense paragraphs of legal prose. Exclusions, sub-clauses, limitations, discretionary review procedures—he could spot a denial pathway in a forty-page policy document before most adjusters finished the intake summary. His supervisors noticed. Within five years, he was senior adjuster. Within ten, he was the man they called when a claim looked "borderline," when the medical necessity was ambiguous, when the treatment requested lived in that gray territory between standard care and experimental intervention, between coverage and exclusion, between yes and no and the thousand gradations of maybe that required someone with judgment, with experience, with the fortitude to make difficult decisions without flinching.

By fifty-five, Walter Ames had become the institutional memory of denial. He had reviewed more than eighteen thousand claims. He had approved perhaps twelve thousand. He had denied six thousand. He kept no count—the numbers came from an HR review he'd glimpsed once—but they did not surprise him. Denial was not failure. Denial was discipline. It was the necessary function that kept premiums stable, that prevented abuse, that ensured the system remained solvent for the many rather than bankrupted by the few who wanted everything covered, every treatment pursued regardless of evidence or cost, every experimental protocol funded as though insurance were charity rather than contract.

He never thought of it as cruelty. He thought of it as stewardship.

"Without discipline," he would say in quarterly meetings, his voice calm and measured, the voice of a man who has thought deeply about his work and arrived at conclusions he can defend, "the whole system collapses. We're not denying care. We're ensuring that care remains available to everyone by preventing unsustainable expenditures on unproven treatments."

And people nodded, because Walter was good at his job, and efficient, and he saved the company millions of dollars every year, and his denial rate was exactly where actuarial models predicted it should be— high enough to maintain profitability, low enough to avoid regulatory scrutiny. He received commendations. Bonuses. A corner cubicle with a window that looked out over the parking lot, which was not much of a view but was better than the interior cubes where fluorescent light never changed and you could forget what time of day it was, what season, whether the sun still rose and set or whether the world had become this eternal gray present tense of ringing phones and claim forms and the quiet hum of systems processing human need into data points and risk assessments.

He saved for himself, too. The bonuses went into index funds, into a 401(k) that grew with mechanical regularity, into a money market account earmarked for a specific dream he had nurtured for twenty years: a cabin upstate, on a lake whose name he had memorized from a real estate listing he kept in his desk drawer—Lake Serenity, though he suspected the name had been invented by developers and the lake itself probably had some older, harder name that the Iroquois had given it centuries ago. He imagined the cabin often, especially on the long drives home through traffic that never seemed to thin, past strip malls and fast food restaurants and the sameness of suburban sprawl that made every exit look identical. He imagined a small dock, a rowboat, mornings with coffee and mist rising off the water, grandchildren someday visiting in summer, learning to fish, learning that there was a world beyond screens and noise and the frantic pace of a culture that had forgotten how to be still.

The cabin was his reward. His proof that discipline paid dividends. That a man who followed the rules and did his job well and saved carefully could, at the end of it all, step away from the machinery and live simply, quietly, in the kind of peace that only comes when you have earned it.

He planned to retire at sixty. He had the number calculated down to the dollar—the amount he needed to maintain a modest standard of living, to pay property taxes on the cabin, to cover healthcare premiums for himself and his wife until Medicare kicked in, to leave something for his daughter.

His daughter.

Lydia.

She had been born when Walter was twenty-four, before Meridian, before he understood what it meant to carry another person's future in your wallet, in your decisions, in the trade-offs you made between security and risk. Her mother—his wife, Joan—had wanted to name her something classical, something with weight, and Walter had agreed because he was young and in love and had not yet learned that love was not enough, that the world required money and insurance and the kind of relentless planning that turned romance into spreadsheets and hope into contingency funds.

Lydia grew up quiet and thoughtful, the kind of child who brought home stray animals and cried over news reports about refugees and asked questions at dinner that made Walter uncomfortable because they had no clear answers, no policy to reference, no procedure to follow. Why do some people have houses and some people sleep outside? Why does Grandma's medicine cost so much if she needs it to live? If we have enough food, why doesn't everyone?

Walter gave the answers he knew: the world was complicated, resources were finite, systems distributed goods according to contribution and merit, charity was important but couldn't replace personal responsibility. Joan would touch his hand under the table, a silent signal that maybe these answers were not sufficient, that their daughter was asking something deeper than economics, but Walter didn't know how to answer the deeper questions. He knew how to read policies. He knew how to assess risk. He knew how to say no when the numbers didn't work.

Lydia became a school counselor. She worked at an underfunded middle school in a district where half the kids qualified for free lunch, where teachers bought supplies with their own money, where the guidance office was a converted storage closet with one desk and a poster of a kitten hanging from a branch with the caption Hang In There! that someone had donated and that Lydia kept up because the kids liked it, even though she found it vaguely depressing.

She was thirty-one. She lived in a small apartment with a roommate, drove a used Honda with a bumper sticker that said Be Kind, and called Walter every Sunday evening, a ritual she had maintained since college. The calls were brief—twenty minutes, sometimes less—but they were consistent, and Walter appreciated consistency. They talked about weather, about her work, about small repairs he needed to make to the house, about Joan's book club and the neighbor's dog that wouldn't stop barking. They did not talk about politics or religion or anything that might create friction. They did not talk about whether Walter's work was ethical or whether Lydia thought the healthcare system was broken or whether the fact that her students couldn't afford to see a dentist represented a moral failure of the society they both inhabited.

They kept it light. They kept it safe.

Until the call came on a Tuesday in October, at 9:47 PM, which Walter remembered because he was watching the news and the time was displayed in the corner of the screen when his phone buzzed and he saw Lydia's name and felt a small spike of alarm because she never called this late, never deviated from the Sunday schedule.

Her voice was thin when he answered. Not panicked, but stretched, like a wire pulled too tight.

"Dad," she said. "I need to tell you something."

The doctors had found a mass in her abdomen during a routine exam she'd delayed for two years because her deductible was high and she kept thinking she'd wait until she really needed it, until something was actually wrong, and then something was actually wrong and the exam led to an ultrasound and the ultrasound led to a CT scan and the CT scan led to a biopsy and the biopsy came back with words like malignant and aggressive and rare, a cancer so uncommon it didn't have a colloquial name, just a string of medical terminology that Walter wrote down on a notepad as Lydia recited it, her voice steady in the way people sound when they've rehearsed difficult news, when they've practiced staying calm.

"It's treatable," she said. "The oncologist says there's a protocol. It's newer, but it works. They've had good results."

Walter asked the questions he knew to ask: What stage? What's the prognosis? What does the treatment involve?

Stage three, she said. Prognosis good if treated aggressively. The treatment was a combination of targeted therapy and immunotherapy— two drugs used in tandem, administered intravenously every three weeks for six months, with follow-up scans to monitor response. The oncologist was optimistic. The clinical trials showed a seventy-eight percent remission rate for her specific cancer subtype.

"That's good," Walter said, and he meant it. Seventy-eight percent. Those were odds you could work with.

"There's one thing," Lydia said, and the thinness in her voice pulled tighter. "The insurance is giving me trouble."

Walter felt something shift in his chest. Not fear. Not yet. Just attention, the way a mechanic hears a sound in an engine that doesn't belong.

"What kind of trouble?"

"They're saying it's experimental. That it's not covered under my plan."

Walter wrote that down too. Experimental. Not covered.

"What's your plan?" he asked.

She told him. It was a Meridian plan. The mid-tier option her school district offered. The one with the manageable premium and the reasonable deductible and the coverage that looked adequate on paper.

His company. His plan.

"I'll take care of it," Walter said.

He took a personal day. Drove to the office. Sat in his cubicle with Lydia's claim file open on his center monitor, the one he used for detailed policy review.

The request was straightforward: pre-authorization for six months of combination immunotherapy—Drug A plus Drug B—at a specialty oncology center ninety miles from where Lydia lived. The oncologist had submitted a comprehensive letter of medical necessity, citing peer-reviewed studies, survival statistics, the specific genetic markers in Lydia's tumor that made her a candidate for this protocol. The documentation was thorough. Persuasive, even.

Walter knew before he finished reading that it would be denied.

He knew because he had written the guidelines.

Not personally—he wasn't a policy author, wasn't senior leadership—but he had contributed. Five years ago, when Meridian was tightening approval criteria for high-cost oncology drugs, Walter had been part of the review committee. They'd been tasked with identifying treatments that fell into gray areas: effective but expensive, promising but not yet standard-of-care, supported by evidence but not yet codified in national treatment guidelines. The goal was to create clear language that would allow adjusters to deny these treatments without protracted appeals, without the company looking heartless, without exposure to lawsuits.

Walter had been good at this work. He had a gift for finding the clause that justified denial while sounding reasonable, even compassionate. While we recognize the potential benefits of this therapy, it remains investigational under current guidelines and therefore falls outside the scope of covered benefits as outlined in Section 12.4(c) of your policy.

He had crafted language like that dozens of times. Had used it hundreds of times in his own denial letters. It was elegant, really—a way of saying no that sounded like regret, that positioned the company as bound by rules rather than making choices, that shifted responsibility onto the policy itself, as though the policy were a natural law rather than a document written by people in a conference room who'd been told to reduce expenses by fifteen percent without increasing member complaints.

Lydia's drugs—Drug A and Drug B—were on the list. The list Walter had helped create.

He read the oncologist's letter again. It was compelling. The evidence was strong. If this were anyone else's daughter, if Walter were reviewing this claim dispassionately, he would still deny it. Because the policy said to deny it. Because the treatment, however effective, had not yet been adopted widely enough to be considered standard-of-care. Because someone had to hold the line, had to prevent costs from spiraling, had to make the hard decisions that kept the system functioning.

But this was Lydia.

His daughter.

Who called every Sunday.

Who had cried when their dog died when she was nine.

Who worked in a storage closet helping kids who had nothing.

Who had a seventy-eight percent chance if she got this treatment.

And no chance if she didn't.

Walter picked up his phone. Called the head of medical review.

"Tom," he said. "I need a favor."

He tried everything.

He submitted an appeal, writing it himself, using every argument, every precedent, every internal memo he'd ever seen that created exceptions. He cited the oncologist's letter. He cited the clinical trial data. He cited compassionate use provisions that technically didn't apply but that he framed in language designed to make the reviewer hesitate, to create just enough ambiguity that they might approve it to avoid the hassle of further appeals.

The denial came back in forty-eight hours.

He called Tom again. Called his own supervisor. Called a director in another division who owed him a favor from a case three years ago when Walter had expedited an approval for the director's friend.

"I can't," the director said. "You know I can't. It's not my call. It's policy."

"I wrote the policy," Walter said.

"Then you know why I can't."

He escalated to external review, the process that sent the claim to an independent physician reviewer who was supposed to evaluate it without bias, without consideration of cost. The external reviewer upheld the denial. Treatment does not meet criteria for medical necessity as defined by recognized standards of care.

Walter read that phrase and felt something crack inside him. Not loudly. Just a small fracture, like ice on a pond in early spring.

He had written similar phrases a thousand times.

They had always seemed reasonable before.

Lydia started a GoFundMe. Her friends shared it. Her coworkers contributed. Strangers on the internet donated five dollars, ten dollars, twenty dollars, each contribution accompanied by messages: Praying for you. Stay strong. Fuck cancer.

The fund raised forty-three thousand dollars in three weeks.

The treatment cost three hundred and twenty thousand.

Her oncologist tried to get her into a clinical trial, but the trial had specific eligibility requirements and Lydia didn't meet them—her cancer subtype was close but not exact, and trials required exact.

They tried a different protocol, one that was covered, one that used older drugs with worse outcomes. Fifty-two percent remission rate instead of seventy-eight. It was something. It was better than nothing.

It didn't work.

The scans at three months showed progression. The tumors were growing.

Lydia called Walter on a Sunday, their usual time, and told him.

"We could try the original protocol now," she said. "Pay out of pocket. I could take out loans."

Walter did the math in his head. Three hundred twenty thousand. Her salary was forty-six thousand a year. The loans would bury her. Even if the treatment worked, even if she went into remission, she'd spend the rest of her life paying it off, working a second job, never buying a house, never having the security that Walter had spent his whole life building.

"Let me think about it," he said.

He thought about it.

He had four hundred thousand in retirement savings. He could withdraw it. Pay the penalties. Pay the taxes. It would cost him the cabin. The retirement. The quiet mornings on the dock.

But Lydia would live.

Seventy-eight percent chance.

He called her back.

"I'll cover it," he said.

There was silence on the line.

Then: "Dad, no. That's your retirement."

"I don't care."

"I can't let you do that."

"Lydia—"

"I can't."

Her voice was firm. The voice of someone who had decided something and would not be moved.

"I'm not taking your future," she said. "You've worked your whole life for that."

"You're my daughter."

"And you're my father. And I won't let you destroy everything you built."

"Lydia—"

"I have to go," she said. "I love you."

She hung up.

She died in early spring, when the snow was melting in uneven patches and the world looked like it couldn't decide whether to live or not.

The funeral was small. Her friends from the school came. Her roommate. A few cousins. Walter stood at the grave and watched them lower the casket and felt nothing, which frightened him more than grief would have. He should feel something. Rage. Sorrow. Guilt. But there was only a vast blankness, as though someone had turned off a switch inside him and now he was just machinery running on residual power, performing functions out of habit, waiting for the system to recognize that he was no longer operational.

Joan cried. Her friends held her. Someone said something about God's plan, and Joan nodded, and Walter wanted to ask what kind of plan included children dying while their fathers had four hundred thousand dollars in index funds, but he didn't ask because he knew there was no answer, or the answer was that there was no plan, just systems, just policies, just the machinery grinding forward and sometimes you were on the side that got ground up.

After the funeral, after the people left, after Joan went to stay with her sister because she couldn't bear to be in the house, Walter drove to HR and submitted his retirement paperwork.

"Effective when?" the HR rep asked.

"Now," Walter said.

"You don't want to give notice? Transition your cases?"

"No."

She printed the forms. He signed them. Thirty years reduced to signatures on six pages.

He cleaned out his cubicle. Threw away the files. Threw away the commendation letters. Kept only the mug that said World's Okay-est Dad because throwing it away felt like erasing her, and he couldn't do that, not yet.

He drove north.

The cabin had been listed for three years. The price had dropped twice. The realtor sounded surprised when Walter called and said he wanted it, said he'd pay cash, said he wanted to close within a week.

"Don't you want to see it first?" the realtor asked.

"No," Walter said.

He drove up the day after closing. The cabin was smaller than the photos suggested. The dock was rotting in places. The lake was still half-frozen, the ice breaking into geometric shards that looked like the pieces of something that had shattered.

He sat on the dock anyway.

He didn't fish.

He didn't unpack.

He didn't call Joan.

He just sat, staring at the water, as the days passed and the ice melted and the loons returned, their calls echoing across the lake in the early mornings, a sound both mournful and indifferent, the sound of a world that continued without regard for what had been lost.

Spring became summer.

Neighbors stopped by occasionally. Introduced themselves. Invited him to a barbecue, a fish fry, a Fourth of July gathering. He declined politely. They stopped asking.

He sat on the dock and thought about the eighteen thousand claims he had reviewed.

He thought about the six thousand he had denied.

He thought about the letters he had written, the language he had crafted, the policies he had enforced.

He thought about a woman named Catherine Mora, whose claim had crossed his desk four years ago, whose request for immunotherapy he had denied because it was experimental, because the policy said so, because someone had to hold the line.

He thought about a man named David Chen, whose claim for a cardiac procedure he had denied because it was performed out-of-network, because the patient should have known better, because the policy was clear.

He thought about a child—he couldn't remember the name, just the case number—whose parents had requested a treatment for a genetic disorder so rare there were only three hundred cases documented worldwide, whose claim he had denied because rarity was not grounds for exception, because the treatment's effectiveness was unproven, because the cost was staggering and someone had to make the difficult decision.

He thought about all of them.

And he thought about Lydia, who had refused his money because she didn't want to take his future, who had died so he could sit on this dock and stare at this water and live in this cabin he had saved thirty years to buy.

The system had worked exactly as designed.

He had followed the rules.

He had been disciplined.

And his daughter was dead.

One morning in late July, a man appeared on the neighboring dock. Older, maybe seventy, wearing waders and a fishing vest covered in flies. He cast his line with the easy rhythm of someone who had done this ten thousand times.

After an hour, he walked over.

"You fish?" he asked.

Walter shook his head.

The man nodded. "You just sit."

"Yes."

"That's alright too."

He stood there a moment, not leaving, not intruding, just present.

"Lost someone?" he asked.

Walter looked up. "How did you know?"

"You got the look."

"What look?"

"The look of a man who's trying to figure out if he's haunted or if he's the ghost."

Walter said nothing.

The man sat down beside him. Didn't ask permission. Just sat.

"I lost my son," the man said. "Fifteen years ago. Car accident. He was seventeen."

"I'm sorry," Walter said.

"Me too." The man stared at the water. "Spent two years sitting here, just like you. Thinking if I sat long enough, I'd figure out what I did wrong. What I could've done different."

"Did you?"

"Figure it out?"

"Yes."

The man shook his head. "No. But I figured out that sitting wasn't bringing him back. And it wasn't making me feel better. It was just sitting."

Walter looked at him. "So what did you do?"

"Started fishing again. Started talking to people. Started living, I guess, even though it felt like betrayal at first. Like I didn't deserve to keep going when he didn't."

"And does it feel like betrayal now?"

The man thought about it. "No. Now it feels like the only thing I can do that means anything. Keep going. Remember him. Try to be the kind of man he thought I was."

He stood up. "You don't have to fish. You don't have to talk. But at some point, you gotta decide if you're gonna stay a ghost or start being a person again."

He walked back to his dock.

Walter sat.

The sun moved across the sky.

The water lapped against the pilings.

That night, Walter opened his laptop for the first time since arriving at the cabin.

He searched for Catherine Mora.

Found an obituary. She had died sixteen months after his denial. The obituary mentioned her daughter, her grandchildren, her work as a teacher. It said she was loved. It said she would be missed.

It did not say she had died because someone in a cubicle decided her life was not cost-effective.

But Walter knew.

He searched for David Chen.

Found him alive. Found a news article about a fundraiser his community had held to pay for the cardiac procedure after insurance denied it. They'd raised enough. He'd survived. The article showed a photo of him surrounded by family, holding a sign that said Thank You.

Walter stared at the photo.

David Chen had lived because people had loved him enough to band together and override the system.

Catherine Mora had died because they hadn't.

Or maybe they had tried, and it hadn't been enough.

He would never know.

He started keeping a list.

Every name he could remember. Every claim he had denied.

He didn't know what he would do with the list. He just knew he needed to write it down. To see it. To make it real.

By the end of August, the list was forty-three names long.

He knew there were more. Hundreds more. But these were the ones he could remember. The borderline cases. The ones where the decision had required judgment, where he'd had to weigh medical necessity against policy language, where he'd chosen policy.

He printed the list.

He folded it.

He put it in his wallet.

September came.

The leaves began to turn.

The loons left.

Walter remained.

He sat on the dock in the mornings, the list in his wallet, Lydia's voice in his head.

I won't let you destroy everything you built.

But he had destroyed it anyway.

Not by withdrawing the money.

By saving it.

By building a future on a foundation of denials, of calculations, of systems that valued solvency over survival.

The cabin was his reward.

The retirement he had earned.

The proof that discipline worked.

And it was empty.

One cold morning in October, a year after Lydia's diagnosis, Walter walked to the end of the dock.

The water was dark. Still. The kind of cold that kills quickly.

He stood there a long time.

Then he walked back to the cabin.

He picked up his phone.

He called Joan.

"I'm sorry," he said when she answered.

There was a long silence.

"I know," she said.

"I should have fought harder."

"Yes."

"I should have quit. Should have liquidated everything. Should have—"

"Walter." Her voice was gentle. Tired. "You can't undo it."

"I know."

Another silence.

"What are you going to do?" she asked.

He looked out the window at the lake, at the empty dock, at the boat he'd never used.

"I don't know," he said. "But I can't just sit here anymore."

"Good," Joan said. "Because sitting isn't living."

"I don't know how to live with this."

"Neither do I," she said. "But we have to try."

Walter sold the cabin in November.

Took the money and donated it to a fund that helped families pay for denied medical treatments.

It wasn't enough.

It didn't bring Lydia back.

It didn't absolve him.

But it was something.

He moved back home. Started volunteering at a legal aid clinic that helped people appeal insurance denials. He wasn't a lawyer, but he knew the policies, knew the language, knew how to find the loopholes he'd once closed.

He helped twelve people in the first year.

Got seven approvals.

Five still died.

But seven lived who might not have.

It wasn't redemption.

It wasn't forgiveness.

It was just the work of trying to be something other than the man who had spent thirty years inside the machinery, saving for a cabin he would never enjoy, building a future on the bodies of people like his daughter.

On the anniversary of Lydia's death, Walter drove to the cemetery.

He sat by her grave.

"I'm sorry," he said. "I'm so sorry."

The wind moved through the trees.

No answer came.

He stayed until dark.

Then he drove home.

The next day, he went back to the clinic.

There was a new case. A woman with cancer. A denied claim.

Walter read the file.

He knew this policy.

He had written it.

And now he would unmake it.

One case at a time.

For as long as he had left.

It was the only accounting he knew how to give.

The only way to answer the question that haunted him in the night:

What will you do with what you built?

He would take it apart.

Brick by brick.

Denial by denial.

Until the machinery recognized that its calculations had always been incomplete.

That there were costs it had never measured.

Lives it had never counted.

Daughters it had buried.

And fathers left sitting on docks, staring at water, realizing—too late, always too late—that the system they had served had consumed them too.

That the barns they had built were full.

But their souls had been required.

And no one was coming to ask what would become of what they had stored.

*The Friend at Midnight*

*Luke 11:5–8*

The city stretched wide beneath the ink-black sky, its streets beating with the pulse of artificial life—neon signs flickering like synapses in some vast, indifferent brain, steam curling from subway grates as though the earth itself exhaled the accumulated breath of ten million souls, the rhythmic hum of traffic weaving like veins through an organism too vast to comprehend, too intricate to love, too necessary to abandon.

Nathaniel—Nate, though the abbreviated name always felt like an alias, like an attempt to outrun something deeper, something unspoken, the way a man might shed his given name after committing a crime he cannot confess—watched the distant skyline through his windshield, the coffee in his cup long since gone cold, its surface catching the reflected glow of passing headlights like a dark mirror refusing to reveal what lay beneath. There was a strange intimacy in the solitude of late-night rides, the silent confessions of passengers who would never see him again, the fragments of lives intersecting in brief exchanges of destination and departure, then vanishing into the rearview mirror like ghosts who had never fully materialized, leaving only the faint impression of their presence, the warmth of a recently vacated seat, the lingering scent of perfume or cigarette smoke or desperation poorly masked by cologne.

He had not planned on this life. No one plans on this life. Five years ago, he had been someone else entirely—a man with a voice that carried weight in crowded rooms, with convictions that stood firm as iron posts driven deep into frozen ground, with a future that stretched before him like a highway under open sky. But conviction, he had learned, was a luxury afforded only to those who had never been forced to choose between truth and survival. And when that choice had come—swift and merciless as a blade drawn in darkness—he had discovered that his iron posts were merely wood painted to look like metal, and the first strong wind had toppled them all.

A notification buzzed against the dashboard, the sound cutting through his reverie like a small, insistent knife.

One last ride.

He sighed, thumbed the acceptance with the resigned automaticity of a man who has long since stopped questioning the minor tyrannies of necessity. Another meaningless transaction. Another hour spent drifting through the city's arteries, though he wasn't sure anymore if it was his car moving or simply him, aimless, unmoored, a boat that had slipped its anchor and now moved only at the mercy of whatever current happened to catch it.

The coffee shop sat quietly in the amber glow of streetlamps, its windows fogged with breath and warmth, a sanctuary for those unwilling to go home just yet, for whom the emptiness of a rented room or the silence of an estranged marriage bed held terrors greater than the cost of one more overpriced latte, one more hour of borrowed company among strangers who asked nothing, knew nothing, expected nothing. The man stood outside, not waiting exactly, but positioned with purpose, as if the very moment had been appointed long ago, as if he had stood in this exact spot at this exact hour in some other version of reality and was now simply fulfilling an obligation written in a ledger Nate could not read.

He was older than most of Nate's passengers—sixty, perhaps, or that ageless quality some men possess where the spirit seems to have outgrown the body's attempts to mark time upon it. His coat was well-made but worn, the kind of garment that speaks not of poverty but of a man who has chosen substance over display, who values function over fashion, who has learned that true dignity requires neither announcement nor ornament. His face carried lines that suggested not hardship so much as attention—the deep grooves around the eyes of one who has spent a lifetime truly looking at things, truly seeing them, bearing witness to the world's unbearable beauty and its equally unbearable cruelty with the same steady, unflinching gaze.

He entered the car without urgency, settled into the backseat with a quiet deliberateness, fingers pressing lightly against the worn fabric as though reading something written there in Braille, some history of all the bodies that had occupied this space before him, all the stories that had been told and untold within these four doors and windows. He did not belong to the transience of rideshare culture, to the studied indifference and performative courtesy that characterized these exchanges. He belonged to something rooted, something ancient in its steadiness, as though he carried within him a continuity that stretched back through generations, back through centuries, back to a time when covenant was stronger than contract and promise was carved in stone rather than encrypted in the temporary algorithms of an app.

"Long night?" The voice was calm, leveled, not the casual observation of small talk designed to fill uncomfortable silence, but something deeper, something aware, a question that acknowledged the night's true length could not be measured in hours.

Nate nodded vaguely, pulling away from the curb, his eyes finding the familiar comfort of the road ahead, the white lines appearing and disappearing beneath his headlights in hypnotic rhythm. "Too long."

Silence stretched between them, fluid as the rain that had begun to fall, streaking across the windshield in diagonal paths that the wipers could not fully erase, leaving behind translucent trails that caught and fractured the city's lights into small, broken rainbows.

They drove for several minutes through the late-night city, past the bars where men his age drowned failures they could not name in whiskey they could not afford, past the all-night diners where waitresses with tired eyes served eggs and redemption to anyone willing to tip adequately, past the darkened storefronts where mannequins stood frozen in poses of impossible confidence, modeling lives that no one actually lived. The rain increased, drumming against the roof like fingers tapping out some ancient code, some message just beyond the threshold of comprehension.

Then, quietly, almost casually, as though it were merely another observation about the weather or the traffic:

"Nate… do you believe in second chances?"

The question arrived without preamble, without context, yet it landed with the weight of something prepared long in advance, a stone dropped into still water, the ripples moving outward in perfect, inexorable circles. A simple inquiry. An impossible answer.

Nate's grip tightened on the wheel, his knuckles whitening in the dashboard's glow. The words sat loaded between them, pressing against the air like a truth that demanded reckoning, like a debt that had come due after years of deferral. He had believed once—believed in the elasticity of grace, in the idea that mistakes were not immutable sentences but courses to be corrected, angles to be adjusted, trajectories to be altered before the final impact. He had believed in redemption the way children believe in fairy tales, with the uncomplicated certainty of one who has never tested whether the magic actually works when the wolf is at the door and the tower has no rope and the glass slipper fits no one's foot but the one who's already lost.

But reality had hardened that idealism the way winter hardens mud, transforming something soft and yielding into something rigid and unyielding, something that would break before it would bend. Second chances required someone willing to give them. And in his experience—in the long, bitter education of his thirty-seven years—the world was not so forgiving. The world kept accounts. The world remembered. The world had long memories and short mercies, and it inscribed your failures in permanent ink while writing your successes in disappearing pencil, easily erased, quickly forgotten.

Still, he answered, if only to push past the tension that had suddenly filled the car like a third presence, like something living and breathing in the space between them. "Yeah. I do."

The passenger nodded slowly, as though this response had been expected, as though it was merely the first movement in a longer composition whose full melody had yet to be revealed. "Then start again."

Nate let out a short laugh, not one of amusement but of disbelief, the bitter exhalation of a man who has heard too many easy answers to difficult questions, too many fortune-cookie philosophies dispensed by people who have never actually had to reconstruct a life from its scattered fragments. Start again. As if it were so simple. As if broken things could be willed back into wholeness by mere intention, as if scattered ashes could be commanded to reassemble themselves into the shape they held before the fire, as if Humpty Dumpty could be put back together by all the king's horses and all the king's men if only Humpty believed hard enough, wanted it badly enough, tried with sufficient sincerity.

"Easy to say," Nate muttered, his eyes fixed on the road ahead, on the wet pavement reflecting the traffic lights in smeared pools of red and green and amber. "Harder to do."

"Most things worth doing are."

The simplicity of the response irritated him, though he couldn't say exactly why. Perhaps because it was true. Perhaps because truth, when spoken plainly, has a way of stripping away the elaborate defenses we construct to protect ourselves from it, the complex justifications and sophisticated rationalizations that allow us to live with our failures by redefining them as inevitabilities, as things that happened to us rather than things we chose, however unconsciously, however reluctantly, however much we wish we had chosen otherwise.

The streets unwound before them, the rain murmuring against glass like whispered prayers in a language neither of them spoke, the tires humming against pavement in a low, steady note that might have been soothing if not for the tension coiled in Nate's chest like a spring wound too tight, ready to snap. Somewhere deep in the rhythm of the city—in the syncopated beat of windshield wipers and turn signals, in the bass-line thrum of the engine, in the percussion of rain on metal— Nate felt the past curling in around him, wrapping itself around his ribs like smoke, like fog, like something insubstantial that nevertheless made it difficult to breathe.

There was a time when he had stood for something. A time when his voice had meant more than the casual pleasantries exchanged between strangers in the confessional booth of a rideshare car, more than the automated responses and scripted courtesies that lubricated the machinery of service work. He had believed. Not just in second chances, but in justice, in truth, in the relentless pursuit of meaning, in the idea that words mattered, that testimony mattered, that standing up and speaking out when everyone else stayed seated and silent was not just a romantic notion but a moral necessity, the very thing that separated human beings from the animals and the machines, from creatures of pure instinct and devices of pure function.

He had been a journalist. Not one of the famous ones, not one of the names that appeared on television or commanded six-figure advances for tell-all memoirs. Just a reporter for a mid-sized paper in a mid-sized city, covering city council meetings and school board controversies and the occasional corruption scandal that would make waves for a week before being absorbed back into the general noise of civic dysfunction. But he had taken it seriously. He had believed that information was sacred, that truth was non-negotiable, that the public's right to know was not just a constitutional abstraction but a living obligation that demanded daily sacrifice, daily courage, daily refusal to look away from what was uncomfortable or inconvenient or dangerous to see.

And then he had seen something. Something that implicated people with power. Something that revealed rot at the foundation of institutions people trusted. Something that required him to choose between the truth he believed in and the security he depended on.

He had chosen security.

No—that wasn't quite accurate, and accuracy was what he owed himself even now, especially now. He had chosen survival. He had chosen his daughter's college fund and his mortgage payment and his wife's faith that the risks he took were calculated risks, managed risks, risks that would not leave her a widow or their child without a father. He had chosen to spike the story, to bury the evidence, to accept the whispered threat disguised as friendly advice, to look the other way while telling himself it was the reasonable thing to do, the prudent thing, the thing any responsible man with people depending on him would do.

Within six months, he had left journalism entirely. Within a year, his wife had left him, though she never said it was because of this, never even mentioned it. She didn't have to. The thing that had died in him—the thing she had loved, the fire she had been drawn to like a moth to flame—was gone, and what remained was merely the husk, the shell, the ash-outline of a man who had once been capable of burning.

"You're thinking about it," the passenger said quietly. Not a question. An observation.

"About what?"

"The moment you chose wrongly."

Nate's hands tightened on the wheel until his knuckles ached. "I don't know what you're talking about."

"Yes, you do."

They drove in silence for another five minutes, the city streaming past like footage from someone else's life, like scenes from a movie he had watched but not starred in. The rain continued its patient work, washing nothing clean but at least redistributing the dirt, at least moving it from one place to another, at least creating the illusion that something was being purified, something was being renewed.

Then, the second time.

"Nate." The voice was sharper now, not unkind but insistent, the way a surgeon's voice might sharpen when cutting near a vital organ, when precision becomes not just desirable but essential. "Do you believe in second chances?"

It was the same question. The exact same words. Yet somehow it landed differently, struck a different chord, resonated in a different register. Not a philosophical inquiry now but a personal challenge. Not abstract theology but concrete demand. Not "do people in general deserve redemption" but "do you, Nathaniel, believe that you—specifically you, particularly you, you with your particular history and your specific failures and your individual shame—do you believe that you can be remade?"

His jaw tightened, muscles bunching beneath skin, his teeth grinding together with enough force that he felt it in his temples. What was the point of this? Was the man looking for contradiction? For honesty? For confession? Was this some kind of therapy, some kind of intervention, some kind of spiritual ambush orchestrated by… whom? His ex-wife? His former editor? God himself?

The answer came slower this time, each word emerging reluctantly, dragged up from some deep place he had spent years trying to seal shut. "I do."

Even as he said it, he wondered if it was true. Belief was such a slippery thing, such an elusive quality. You could claim to believe something while living in perfect contradiction to it. You could profess faith while demonstrating through every action that you trusted nothing and no one, least of all the god or grace or mercy you claimed to believe in. Belief without embodiment was just noise, just vibration in the air, signifying nothing, changing nothing, mattering to no one.

The man's nod was nearly imperceptible, just the slightest inclination of his head, but Nate saw it in the rearview mirror, saw the way the man's eyes held his own reflected gaze, saw something in that look that was neither judgment nor approval but simply acknowledgment, simply witness, the look of someone who sees truly and does not turn away.

"Then make it matter."

Three words. A simple imperative. Yet they struck Nate with the force of physical impact, as though the man had reached forward and placed a hand on his shoulder, as though something tangible had passed between them, some transfer of weight or obligation or possibility.

Make it matter.

Nate swallowed hard, his throat suddenly dry despite the rain's liquid abundance everywhere around them, his eyes fixed on the road ahead with desperate intensity, as though the white lines might form themselves into an answer, into a map, into instructions for how exactly one went about making belief matter when belief had failed so catastrophically before.

How many times had he tried? How many times had he attempted to rebuild, only to find himself cut off before he even started? Three times he had applied for journalism jobs after leaving the profession, sending carefully crafted cover letters that acknowledged his departure without explaining it, that emphasized his skills without reference to why those skills had gone unused. Three times he had been called in for interviews. Three times he had sat across from editors who had looked at him with that peculiar expression—not quite pity, not quite contempt, but something worse: recognition. They knew. Perhaps not the specific details, perhaps not the exact nature of his failure, but they knew the general shape of it, knew he was one of the broken ones, one of the fallen ones, one of those who had looked into the abyss and blinked first.

Three times he had been thanked for his interest and shown the door.

After that, he had stopped trying. He had accepted that certain paths, once abandoned, cannot be walked again. He had taken the rideshare job because it required no explanation, no history, no accounting for the gap in his resume or the gap in his soul. The app cared only whether his car was clean and his driving record acceptable. The passengers cared only whether he knew the route and kept the conversation minimal. No one asked what he had been or why he had stopped being it.

There was no mercy in the world. Not really. Not the kind that actually restored, actually renewed, actually gave back what had been lost. There was only the mercy of forgetting, the mercy of moving on, the mercy of learning to live with a permanent diminishment, a chronic ache, a phantom limb where something essential used to be.

They approached the final destination, a quiet street corner bathed in the golden light of a single streetlamp standing sentinel over the intersection, an island of illumination amid the rushing darkness of the city at 2:47 AM. The address on his phone indicated they had arrived. Yet the man made no move to leave, sat perfectly still in the backseat, his presence somehow larger now, more substantial, as though the car had shrunk around him or he had expanded to fill all available space, his silence a pressure against Nate's chest, against his skull, against every defense he had carefully constructed over five years of exile and penance and hollow survival.

The man reached for the door handle. Then paused.

When he spoke, his voice was different—gentler somehow, yet more commanding, the way a father's voice might sound when asking the one question that matters most, the question upon which everything else hinges, the question that divides one kind of life from another kind of life entirely.

"One last time, Nate." The words fell into the space between them like stones into deep water, disappearing beneath the surface but sending ripples outward, outward, outward into regions neither of them could see. "Do you believe in second chances?"

Everything stilled.

The rain stopped its percussion against the roof. The engine's hum faded into background silence. The city's ten million souls seemed to hold their collective breath. Even time itself appeared to hesitate, to wait, to suspend its relentless forward march for just this moment, this question, this crossroads.

This wasn't about philosophy anymore. It wasn't about belief in theory, about abstracts debated in coffee shops over weary cigarettes and half-drunk whiskey, about the kind of intellectual exercise that allowed you to hold contradictory positions simultaneously without ever having to choose between them, without ever having to stake your life on one being true and the other false.

This was about action. About whether he would do something— anything—with what he claimed to believe. About whether his belief was a living thing that moved his hands and directed his steps or merely a dead thing he carried around like a talisman, like a lucky rabbit's foot that had brought no luck, like a prayer spoken in a language he didn't understand to a god he didn't trust.

Three times the question had come. Three times he had answered with words, with sounds shaped by tongue and teeth and expelled air, signifying everything or nothing depending on what he did next.

He thought of Peter. He didn't know why—he hadn't been to church since his daughter's baptism ten years ago, hadn't opened a Bible since college, when he'd taken a course on the New Testament as literature and been both moved and troubled by the strange, savage beauty of those ancient texts. But the story came to him now with perfect clarity: Peter in the courtyard, warming himself by the fire while his teacher stood trial inside. Three times asked if he knew the man. Three times denying it, each denial more vehement than the last, each disavowal more desperate, each betrayal compounding the one before until the rooster crowed and Peter met Jesus' eyes across the courtyard and saw in that gaze not accusation but something worse: sorrow. Grief for what Peter had become in that moment, for the distance between what he had promised and what he had delivered, between the man who had sworn he would die rather than deny and the man who couldn't even admit acquaintance when the cost grew too high.

But that wasn't the end of the story. There was a morning after, a beach, a charcoal fire, and the same question asked three times: "Do you love me?" Three chances to reverse three denials. Three opportunities to speak truth where he had spoken lies. Three moments of restoration offered to match three moments of betrayal committed.

"Feed my sheep," Jesus had said. Not as punishment but as calling. Not as penance but as purpose. Not "remember your failure" but "here is your work."

For the first time that night—for the first time in five years, if he was being honest—Nate truly considered the question. Not as an inquiry. Not as an intellectual exercise. Not as a theological proposition to be analyzed and categorized and filed away under "interesting ideas that have no bearing on actual life." But as a moment of decision. A fork in the road. A door standing open that would not remain open indefinitely, that would close and lock and never open again if he did not walk through it now, in this moment, in this rain-soaked car on this anonymous corner at this ungodly hour when only the lost and the seeking and the desperate were still awake.

Belief without action was nothing. Faith without works was dead. Hope without movement was merely wishful thinking, merely self-deception, merely the lie we tell ourselves to make comfortable peace with a status quo we lack the courage to disrupt.

Redemption required pursuit. Mercy required movement. Second chances had to be seized, not simply received—grasped with both hands, held tight, pulled close, embodied in flesh and deed and consequence.

He exhaled slowly, and it felt like the first true breath he had taken in years, like oxygen finally reaching tissues that had subsisted too long on stale air and broken promises. "Yeah." His voice was quieter this time, stripped of defensiveness, stripped of bravado, stripped of everything except the raw admission beneath. "And I need one."

The words hung in the air between them, confession and request, acknowledgment and plea. I need one. Not "I deserve one" or "I've earned one" or "I'm entitled to one." Just the simple, honest, devastating truth: I need one. I cannot continue as I am. I am drowning. I am dying. I am disappearing by degrees into a half-life that is not life at all but merely existence, merely time passing, merely waiting for death to make official what has already occurred internally.

The man smiled. Not smugly, not victoriously, not with the satisfied expression of someone who has won an argument or proven a point. But with the quiet, steady knowing of someone who had always understood the answer before it was spoken, who had known from the moment he entered the car—perhaps from before that, perhaps from some eternity preceding this temporal encounter—how this conversation would end, what truth would finally be voiced, what admission would finally break through the accumulated scar tissue of shame and pride and fear.

He placed something on the console between the front seats before opening the door and stepping out into the night. A business card, cream-colored, simple, elegant in its restraint. No corporate logo, no flashy design, just text in a clean, serif font.

Nate picked it up, turning it over in the dashboard's glow.

A name: Marcus Webb.

A title: Managing Editor, City Voice.

A phone number.

And beneath it, handwritten in blue ink, three words: We're still hiring.

Nate stared at the card, his vision blurring, though whether from tears or rain or the simple overwhelm of possibility he couldn't say. City Voice—he knew the publication, a scrappy independent news site that had launched two years ago, the kind of outfit that paid poorly but pursued stories the mainstream outlets wouldn't touch, that valued principle over profit, that still believed in journalism as a calling rather than merely a career.

He looked up, searched for the man in the rearview mirror, but the street corner was empty. The golden pool of streetlight illuminated nothing but wet pavement and falling rain. Marcus Webb—if that was even his real name—had vanished into the city as completely as if he had never existed, leaving behind only the card and the question and the choice.

Nate sat in the idling car, engine humming, wipers sweeping back and forth, back and forth, the rain showing no signs of stopping. He turned the card over and over in his fingers, feeling its weight, its texture, its simple material reality—proof that this had not been hallucination or dream or wish-fulfillment fantasy, that something had actually happened here, something that demanded response.

For five years, he had told himself the story was over. The choices had been made. The consequences had been paid. The path had been closed. All that remained was to serve out his sentence, to endure the years with whatever grace and dignity he could muster, to make peace with diminishment, to learn to be small where he had once tried to be large.

But perhaps—perhaps that story had been wrong. Perhaps it had been the lie he told himself to avoid the harder, more frightening truth: that the path was not closed but merely obscured, not ended but merely paused, not lost but merely waiting for him to find courage enough to walk it again.

Three times asked.

Three times answered.

And now, finally, truly: a choice.

He pulled up the phone app on his dashboard screen, the one connected to his rideshare account, the one that had directed him to this corner, to this passenger, to this moment. With a deliberate motion, he pressed the button to go offline. The screen confirmed: You are no longer accepting rides.

Then he opened his personal phone, the one he used for everything that wasn't work, the one that contained his daughter's photos and his ex-wife's old text messages and the remnants of the life he had lived before. His fingers hovered over the keypad.

It was nearly 3 AM. Calling now would be absurd. Would seem desperate. Would reveal the full extent of how much this chance meant to him, how badly he needed it, how little dignity he had left to lose.

But perhaps that was the point. Perhaps grace, when it finally came, demanded that you show up without pretense, without protection, without the armor of self-sufficiency that allowed you to pretend you didn't need saving.

He dialed.

The phone rang once. Twice. Three times.

Then: "Webb." The voice was alert despite the hour, as though its owner had been expecting this call, as though he kept vigil for exactly these moments when the lost and the broken finally found courage to reach out.

"Mr. Webb, this is Nathaniel Hayes. I… I just met someone who gave me your card. Said you were hiring. I don't know if you remember me, but I used to work for the Tribune, and I…" The words tumbled out, unpracticed, unrehearsed, truth spoken without preparation or polish.

"I remember you, Nathaniel." The voice on the other end was warm, impossibly warm for 3 AM, as warm as the coffee shop where the man had waited, as warm as the golden light of the streetlamp. "I've been waiting for your call. Can you come in Monday? Say, 9 AM? We'll talk about what you've learned in your time away. We'll talk about what you might write now that you couldn't write then. We'll talk about whether you're ready to try again."

"I'm ready," Nate said, and discovered as he said it that it was true, that readiness was not something you achieved but something you declared, not a state you arrived at but a door you walked through, not a feeling you waited for but a choice you made.

"Good," Webb said. "Monday then. And Nathaniel? Bring your best story. The one you couldn't tell before. The one that cost you everything. It's time to tell it."

The line went silent.

Nate sat in the car, the business card still in his hand, rain still falling, city still humming its endless song. But something had shifted. Some weight had lifted. Some door had opened.

He put the car in drive and pulled away from the curb, heading not toward another pickup, not toward another anonymous passenger and their anonymous destination, but toward home. Toward his small apartment with its single photograph of his daughter. Toward his laptop with its accumulation of dust. Toward the blank document he would open in a few hours, once the sun rose, once he had slept and showered and prepared himself for the work ahead.

The work of telling truth.

The work of restoration.

The work of becoming, once more, the man he had been before fear made him small.

In the rearview mirror, the city receded, its lights fragmenting in the rain-streaked glass into a thousand points of broken beauty. And Nate drove forward, into the darkness that was not darkness anymore but the space before dawn, the hour when night releases its grip and morning prepares to break, when anything might be possible, when even the dead might rise, when even the denied might be restored, when even the lost might find their way home.

Three times asked.

Three times answered.

And now, finally: three steps forward into the mercy that waits for those brave enough—or desperate enough—to receive it.

The rain continued to fall, washing the city clean.

## CHAPTER 18
### THE NIGHT THE RAIN STOPPED LYING

*The Mustard Seed*

*Matthew 13:31–32*

The rain had been falling for hours, the kind that didn't bother with theatrics. No thunder. No wind. Just a steady, unbroken descent that felt less like weather and more like a truth the sky had finally decided to tell.

The rest stop sat in the middle of it, a concrete island in the geography of in between, where people paused not because they wanted to but because their bodies or their cars or their lives required it. The facility offered nothing beyond function. Vending machines. Bathrooms around the back on the outside wall. A map behind scratched plexiglass that nobody consulted. The smell of wet pavement and exhaust and the particular loneliness of a place that was never designed for anyone to stay.

Inside the fluorescent glow, Daniel stood at a vending machine with a bag of something he didn't want in his hand. He had been staring at the rows of snacks long after he'd made his selection, as if the machine might suddenly offer him something else. Something that could reach into his chest and fix the thing living there. His car was parked outside with a duffel in the back seat and no destination programmed into the GPS. He had been driving since morning, telling himself he was clearing his head. He knew better. He was running. He just hadn't said it out loud yet.

The hum of the lights pressed against him. The smell of wet pavement seeped through the door every time someone passed through it. He didn't look at the travelers who came and went. He didn't look at anything.

Until he heard it.

A sound from somewhere beyond the concrete wall. Not a shout. Not a call for help. Just the sound a man makes when he has run out of everything except the ability to make that sound. A sound that didn't ask for anything. A sound that simply existed because it had nowhere else to go.

Daniel went very still.

The rain kept falling.

The sound came again.

He set the bag on the counter. He stood for a moment with the weight of what he was about to do settling over him like the rain itself. Eight months of driving away from things. Eight months of windows up and radio off and the interstate swallowing the miles without mercy.

He pushed through the door and stepped into the rain.

Around the back of the building, where the lights didn't reach and the travelers didn't wander, Raymond sat on the wet ground with his back against the wall. The rain had soaked through his jacket long ago. He didn't seem to notice. His knees were pulled up, his head bowed, his breath coming in the uneven rhythm of a man who has stopped trying to hold himself together.

He was forty-four years old and he had no idea how he had ended up here.

Not figuratively. Literally.

There were hours missing from the night before, torn from the sequence of events like pages ripped from a book. He remembered the motel room. He remembered the bottle. He remembered the familiar lie he told himself every time he poured the first drink. This one will be the last. Then the gap. Then the rain. Then the concrete and the cold that had worked its way into him so deeply it felt like it had always been there.

His car wasn't in the parking lot. He had checked. He didn't know where it was.

He didn't know where anything was anymore.

He realized he was crying without knowing when it had started. It felt like something that had been happening beneath the surface for years, pressing against whatever thin membrane had been holding it back, and had finally found the crack it was looking for.

He reached into his jacket pocket.

His fingers found the carving.

They always found the carving.

He closed his hand around it and bowed his head and the rain came down.

He had grown up on a farm in a rural county where the horizon was wide and the days were long and a man was measured by what his hands could do. His father had taught him the language of broken things. Engines that coughed. Fences that leaned into themselves with age. The wobbly leg of a kitchen chair. Fixing wasn't just a skill. It was a belief. A way of saying that nothing was beyond repair if you gave it your hands and your patience and your full attention.

He married Della young. Their life together lived in his memory as a series of small luminous moments he could no longer visit without the grief rising. Her garden. Her laugh. The way she touched his arm when she passed him in the kitchen as though confirming he was still there.

And then Thomas.

Thomas arrived with eyes that seemed older than his years. Quiet the way deep water is quiet. Not empty. Full of things you couldn't see but could feel if you stood close enough. He followed Raymond everywhere from the time he could walk and neither of them ever found words for how necessary they were to each other.

Raymond taught him to whittle on winter evenings at the kitchen table. Two pocketknives. A block of soft wood. Raymond's large hands guiding Thomas's small ones through the grain. The early attempts were crooked and lopsided and barely recognizable and Raymond kept every one of them in a coffee can on the workbench. He could not throw away anything Thomas's hands had touched.

Thomas got better. Quietly. Without announcement. The way he did everything.

By ten he could coax small animals from a piece of wood that looked like they might move if you stopped watching them.

Raymond remembered the morning Thomas first drove the tractor alone. The pride that rose in him felt like something with wings. The sense that something sacred was being passed from his hands into smaller ones that were ready to receive it.

He didn't remember the accident in sequence. He never had. It came in fragments the way trauma always comes. The sound. The silence after that was worse than the sound. The running across the field toward something he already knew he couldn't fix.

What he held onto was what survived.

In the boy's pocket. Untouched by the blades. A small carving of an animal. A rabbit he thought. Or maybe a dog. Thomas never got to tell him.

The door to Thomas's room had not been opened in ten years.

Not because they locked it. There was no lock. Just the understanding that passed between Raymond and Della in the weeks after the funeral, unspoken and absolute, the way some agreements are made in silence because saying them out loud would make them too real to survive.

The trophies still stood on the shelf above the desk. A relay ribbon. A spelling bee certificate. A soccer trophy with a figure frozen mid-kick that would kick nothing and no one forever. Objects that had meant everything to a ten year old boy and now meant something that had no name in any language Raymond knew.

The baseball glove on the desk still held the shape of Thomas's hand.

The boots beside the bed still carried the mud from the last morning.

Della had retreated to the couch sometime in the third year. Not dramatically. Not with an announcement. Just gradually, incrementally, the way a tide withdraws when the moon stops asking it to stay. Raymond understood without being told. They still ate together. They still spoke. They still loved each other in the way that love becomes more memory than motion when grief has taken up all the available space.

Raymond stood in the dark hallway many nights with his hand raised near the door. Not touching it. Just near it. Feeling the cold of the wood against his palm without making contact, as though the door itself was the border between the life he had lived and the life that had been taken, and to touch it was to admit that the border was real and permanent and would never open.

He never opened it.

He never stopped standing outside it.

Ten years of a marriage held together by the ghost of a boy until it wasn't held together anymore.

Raymond left because staying was drowning them both.

He had been living in a rented room three hours away for four months. He had a job interview in the morning. He had a bottle last night. He had been having too many bottles in the weeks before that, each one promising the same thing and delivering less of it every time. The silence of the rented room was a different silence than the silence of the farmhouse and he hadn't determined yet which one was heavier.

Daniel came around the corner of the building and stopped.

Raymond didn't look up. He sat against the wall with the carving held in both hands, rain running down his face in thin shining lines. A man reduced to his smallest dimensions by everything the night had taken from him.

Daniel didn't speak. He crouched down until they were at the same level.

Raymond lifted his eyes. They were red and worn and carried the particular exhaustion of a man who has been tired for a very long time. He looked at Daniel. He looked down at the carving.

"My boy made this," he said.

Just that.

Daniel didn't ask how old the boy was. He didn't ask where he was now. The way Raymond said it answered both questions.

Daniel sat down beside him. Not across from him. Beside him. Against the same wall. In the same rain.

They sat together in silence and the rain fell and the interstate hummed somewhere beyond the tree line and the vending machine inside kept its fluorescent vigil over an empty room.

Daniel was twenty-six years old. He had grown up in a mid-sized city with his father Marcus, who taught high school history. Marcus wasn't famous. He wasn't remarkable by any measurement the world typically used. He was a man who showed up every day believing that what he did mattered, and who somehow made the people around him believe it too.

Their life together had been easy in the way that the best relationships are easy. Not because nothing went wrong but because they understood each other without having to work at it. Saturday mornings. Baseball on the radio. Marcus teaching Daniel to cook because he said every man should know how to feed himself and the people he loved.

The argument came the way these arguments always come. Not from nowhere. From the slow accumulation of things left unsaid until they became too heavy to carry quietly. Daniel still at home at twenty-six.

Marcus worried in the way fathers worry when love has no other available outlet. It comes out sideways. As pressure. As criticism. As the wrong words landing at the wrong moment and neither person knowing how to stop what has already started.

Daniel said things he couldn't take back.

He no longer remembered the exact words. He remembered the heat beneath them. The way they came from somewhere deeper than the argument, from a place that had nothing to do with dishes or job searches or the future. They were the words of a young man in pain handing his pain to the nearest person and watching it land.

The last thing he said before Marcus picked up his keys was this.

Fine. Just go. That's what you always do. I hope I never have to see you again.

Marcus went to get milk and think.

He never came home.

The other driver ran a red light. The milk was still in the bag on the passenger seat.

Daniel had been living inside those last words for eight months. They were the first thing he heard when he woke and the last thing he heard before sleep, if the night's sleep came at all. They had become the whole story of who he was and what he had done and he could not find his way out of them no matter how many miles he put between himself and the place where they were said.

He had stepped into the rain because he recognized the sound of a man breaking.

He had been making that same sound for months. Alone in his car. Windows up. Radio off. The road taking everything he gave it and asking for more.

After a long time Daniel spoke.

"Where are you trying to get to?"

Raymond told him. The town. Three hours east. The rented room. The job interview he was going to miss. The car he couldn't find. The phone that had died sometime in the night. The complete inventory of a man who had arrived at zero.

Daniel stood.

He held out his hand.

Raymond looked at it for a long moment, the rain coming down between them, the carving still held in his other hand. Then he reached up and took it. Daniel pulled him to his feet.

They stood together in the rain. Two men upright. Which is not nothing.

"I'll drive you," Daniel said.

Not I'll call someone. Not I'll find you a ride.

I'll drive you. Three hours out of his way toward nowhere he had been heading. Three hours in a car with a stranger who was holding a dead boy's carving and had a job interview he might still make if the rain held and the road was kind.

Raymond looked at him for a long time.

"You don't even know me," he said.

Daniel shook his head slowly.

"Maybe that's why I can."

They walked together through the rain toward the parking lot. Raymond's hand was in his pocket, fingers around the carving. Daniel unlocked the car. They got in without ceremony. The engine turned over. The headlights opened a corridor through the dark.

They pulled out onto the interstate and the rest stop fell away behind them.

Two men in a car going east through the rain toward a town that was waiting without knowing it was waiting.

Raymond kept his hand in his pocket.

Daniel kept his eyes on the road.

The rain kept falling.

But it had stopped lying.

# CHAPTER 19
## THE WATCHERS OF THE DARKENED SKY

### *The Ten Virgins*

*Matthew 25:1–13*

There are people who wait for life to happen to them, and there are people who learn to read the sky.

I was the second kind. Not by choice, exactly. By geography. By the particular mercy of being planted young in the middle of tornado alley, where the earth itself teaches you that readiness is not a virtue — it is a survival skill. Where the difference between the prepared and the unprepared is not a matter of character but of consequence. Where five people can stand on the same stretch of road and only some of them will have thought to bring what they need for what is coming.

I moved with my new family to the Midwest, right smack into the land of storms, where you didn't just witness weather — you experienced it through every fiber of your being. And I learned, the way children learn things that will matter for the rest of their lives, to feel the electricity in the air before the first rumble of thunder. I learned to read the sky the way some children learn to read books. I learned to sense the shift in the wind, the subtle drop in pressure, the way the birds went silent before the world changed its mind.

This was my oil. This accumulated knowledge, this patient attention, this willingness to watch and wait and learn. I was filling my lamp one season at a time, one storm at a time, one silent bird and one darkening sky at a time. I did not know that was what I was doing. The wise virgins never do. They simply tend what they have been given and trust that the tending will matter when the moment arrives.

And the moments arrived.

To stand at the base of a dry line and marvel at the sheer height of a mesoscale, some 60,000 feet, is truly something to behold. It is like standing at the foot of a living mountain, except this mountain moves, breathes, grows, and sometimes decides to reach down and touch the earth. I would look out my bedroom window at night during a severe storm, as a child, and watch the streetlights turn off. Not flicker. Not dim. Turn off. The lightning would be so constant, so bright, that the sensors on the street lamps thought it was daytime. The world would flash white, then black, then white again, in a rhythm that felt almost alive. Almost like breath. Almost like something enormous was trying to get our attention.

One day, my father took me to get a haircut. It was noon when we arrived at the barber. The sky grew dark. In fact the sky turned black. All the streetlights came on at noon. The barbers paused mid-sentence. Men stepped outside, squinting upward, their faces lit by the unnatural glow of sodium lamps in the middle of the day. The air felt heavy, like the world was holding its breath. I remember the barber's hand trembling slightly as he held the scissors near my ear. I remember my father's calm voice saying we'll be fine, even though he kept glancing toward the window.

My father was a prepared man. He had oil. His calm in the face of what could not be controlled was its own kind of readiness — not the absence of fear but the presence of something steadier than fear. He had learned what I was still learning. That the storm will come whether you are ready or not. And that the only question worth asking is whether you have enough light to see by when it does.

One afternoon, during a tornado siren's wail, Dad placed me on the hood of the car and we watched twin tornadoes — sisters, they call them — both on the ground and black from their duration, from the dust and debris that had been swirling inside them for so long they had become the color of the earth they were unmaking. They moved slowly, deliberately, like ancient creatures deciding which part of the world to rearrange. I remember the sound — not the freight-train roar people talk about, but a deeper sound, a low resonant hum that vibrated in my chest like a second heartbeat. I remember the way the wind pulled at my shirt. I remember my father's hand resting firmly on my back, steadying me, as if he knew I would carry this moment for the rest of my life and wanted me to carry it upright.

I was not afraid. I was ready. The lamp was lit. The oil was sufficient.

This is what the prepared ones feel when the bridegroom finally arrives — not terror, but the fierce and wordless satisfaction of having watched long enough, faithfully enough, to be present for the moment the sky opens and the world reveals what it has been holding.

Later in life, when I started my career in broadcast television, I worked in master control. Right behind me was an old aircraft radar — a long tube of a thing with a scope on the end facing outward. The local meteorologist would use it during his weather forecast, and it displayed white blobs whenever rain or storms were in the area. The scope had concentric rings with a wand that swept in a circular motion, clockwise, steady, patient, always watching. The room smelled faintly of warm electronics and dust. The hum of the machines was constant, a low mechanical heartbeat that filled the space and felt, to me, like coming home.

I learned that the brighter the blob, the heavier the rain, the more severe the storm. I became friends with one of the maintenance engineers — a quiet man, steady, with the kind of calm that comes from knowing how things work. Machines. Roads. Storms. People. He told me that the distance between each concentric ring on the radar was ten miles. He told me that stacked bright white blobs meant something serious was happening in the atmosphere above, that the storm had organized itself into layers, that it had intention.

We became partners in watching. We tended that radar together the way the wise virgins tended their lamps — attentively, knowledgeably, with enough accumulated understanding to know what we were looking at when the moment came. We had learned to read the rings. We had learned to measure the distance between ourselves and what was coming. We had oil, both of us, and we knew how to use it.

One day I noticed stacked bright white blobs on the radar, only two rings away — roughly twenty miles. I asked the engineer if he knew where that was. He said he did, and that we could be there in half an hour.

So started our adventure in storm chasing.

The year was 1979. We had no laptops, no cellphones, no Doppler radar. We had an old aircraft scope for initial assessment and then we would simply follow the clouds. When you grow up in tornado alley, you learn the clouds the way a sailor learns the sea — what they mean, what they predict, what is coming. Mammatus clouds, those harbingers of transformation, pockets and puffs stuffed with ice that prevail before the onslaught of severe weather. The first time I saw them up close, the sky looked bruised and swollen, as if something enormous was pressing down from above, trying to get through.

My friend knew all the local roads. I knew the clouds. Together we were ready. Together we were enough. I drove. He navigated. We chased storms for two years, three windshields, and one terrifying core punch through a rain wall and into a hail shaft and the most intense cloud-to-ground lightning either of us had ever experienced. The hail left my car dented and cracked and beautiful. Battle-worn. Proof of presence. Proof of having been there when the bridegroom passed through.

But we rarely arrived at the perfect moment. We missed more than we caught. The storms would shift, evolve, dissipate, reorganize somewhere else. The technology of 1979 was honest about its limitations — it could tell you something was happening but not exactly where to stand. And so we stood in the wrong fields sometimes, watching the lightning from a distance, knowing the main event was somewhere we couldn't reach.

This is the part of the parable no one talks about. Even the prepared ones miss the moment sometimes. Even full lamps and steady hands and years of accumulated knowledge cannot guarantee arrival. The storm chooses its own path. The bridegroom comes at midnight, at the hour no one expects, and sometimes you are two fields over doing your best with what you have.

After two years, we called it quits as a team. Life pulled us in different directions, the way life does, the way it always does. The engineer had a family to consider. I had a career demanding more of my time. We extinguished the lamp together, quietly, and went our separate ways.

But the storms kept coming. They kept calling.

And this is where I must tell you about the night I left my oil at home.

I had been watching the radar at the end of my shift, as I always did, as I had trained myself to do. I noticed unusually bright, stacked blobs on the screen — three and four layers deep, twenty miles out. By the time my shift ended, the severe thunderstorm warnings were active. I could see the lightning already beginning to pulse on the horizon through the station windows.

I went alone. At ten o'clock at night. Without my partner. Without the roads he knew. Without the eyes that had always traveled beside mine.

I had knowledge without wisdom. I had the habit of watching without the infrastructure that made watching safe. I had the lamp but somewhere between the radar room and the car door, I had left the oil behind.

Never chase at night. This is the first rule of storm chasing, the rule every experienced chaser knows the way the wise virgins knew to tend their supply. At night the storm evolves faster than you can follow it. It reorganizes in the dark. It becomes something other than what it appeared to be when you first decided to pursue it. And by the time you arrive at the place where it was, it has already moved on, or worse, it has moved toward you, and you are standing in the dark on a road with no exits and no light except what the storm itself provides.

I followed the lightning. Then the lightning stopped. The storm appeared to vanish. I kept driving into a blackness so complete it felt thick, like a curtain pulled across the world. The road ahead was a narrow ribbon of gray in my headlights. The fields on either side were swallowed by darkness. The air felt wrong — too still, too heavy, too expectant. Like a room where someone has been holding their breath for a very long time.

This is what the unprepared ones feel when the bridegroom arrives. Not the fierce satisfaction of readiness. The cold dread of having nothing sufficient in hand. The door that will not open to them is not cruelty — it is consequence. You cannot light another person's lamp.

You cannot borrow someone else's years of patient watching. You cannot arrive at the moment of arrival without having tended what the moment requires.

Then the lightning returned.

A massive bolt to my left, illuminating the fields and fence lines and telephone poles in a single stark white flash. Before I could process it, another bolt slammed into the ground on my right. Then another left. Two more right. The storms were developing on both sides of me simultaneously, and I was in the middle, alone, with no partner to navigate and no roads to turn onto and no plan except the one I had failed to make.

And then I saw it in the rearview mirror.

In the continuous strobing of lightning, faint and ghostly and enormous, the shape of a funnel beginning its sweep groundward. The bridegroom arriving at midnight, and I was standing in the dark road with an empty lamp and nowhere to go.

I accelerated. The engine roared. The tires gripped the pavement with a desperation that had nothing wise about it. I watched the funnel in the mirror and understood, in a way I had never understood from the safe distance of preparation, what it means to have missed the moment of readiness. The funnel was getting bigger. When a tornado gets bigger in your rearview mirror it means only one thing. It is coming straight for you.

The telephone poles began to sway. Then they began to disappear. Vacuumed off the earth one by one as if the storm was erasing the landmarks I had always used to know where I was. The fence posts went with them. The familiar geometry of the world was being unmade at three hundred feet behind me, and I had no oil and no partner and no roads to turn onto and nothing between me and the door that was closing except speed and whatever mercy the night was willing to extend.

And then, as if the hand of something immeasurably patient had redirected what was coming, the funnel moved left. The telephone poles stopped disappearing. The fence posts remained in the ground. The door stayed open by a margin so thin I have never been able to measure it.

I drove home as fast as I could and I promised myself I would never chase a storm at night again.

It was the last chase I ever did.

The parable says the foolish virgins went to buy oil at midnight, while the door was already closing. They had the impulse toward readiness but they had it too late. What I had, standing in that dark road with the funnel filling my mirror, was something the parable does not name but every watcher of the sky understands — the terrible clarity that arrives only after the oil is gone. The knowledge of exactly what you failed to bring. The precise and irreversible understanding of what preparation means, purchased at the highest possible price, in the dark, alone, with the door swinging shut behind you.

I had spent years filling my lamp. I had tended the sky faithfully, learned its language, read its warnings, accumulated enough knowledge to stand on a car hood with my father's hand on my back and feel not terror but readiness. And then one night, in a hurry, in the ordinary momentum of a shift ending and a storm beckoning, I walked out without my oil.

The bridegroom does not wait.

The storm does not wait.

The moment of arrival does not announce itself in advance so that you can run out and make last-minute preparations. It arrives at the hour no one expects, in the dark, when the threshold between the ready and the unprepared becomes the difference between the door open and the door closed.

Watch, therefore.

Keep your lamp full.

Learn to read the sky while the sky is still readable.

Because the sisters are always out there somewhere, moving slowly, deliberately, like ancient creatures deciding which part of the world to unmake.

And midnight is always closer than it appears.

# CHAPTER 20
## THE BANQUET IN THE COLD

### The Great Banquet

*Luke 14:15–24*

Montana has a way of testing a soul before it ever tests a body. At high elevation, winter is not a season but a geography, an entire landscape carved from ice and silence. Forty-five below was not unusual. Snow fell sometimes ten months a year. The growing season lasted seventy-seven days on average when it lasted at all. Everything else was endurance.

And every morning at 4 AM, I stepped into that cold, turned the key of a school bus that belched black smoke like an aging dragon, and began the first movement of a daily liturgy: the pre-release run. Thirty-five miles each way. Downtown facility to the sawmill. Morning crew at 4 AM. Students to school. Students home. Evening crew to the sawmill. Day crew back. Two years of this rhythm. Two years of diesel and frostbite and headlights cutting through whiteouts. Two years of faces climbing aboard in the dark.

The first time I pulled up to the facility, the cold was so sharp it felt like it could carve bone. I expected stripes, orange jumpsuits, tattoos, scars. Instead, they came out in jeans and coats and hats, looking like anyone in town. Ordinary. Human. Cold. They climbed aboard quietly, stamping snow from their boots. I greeted each one the same way: "Good morning. I'm very happy to meet you and be of service by driving you." They looked at me strangely at first, no one expects warmth at 4 AM in a place built for punishment, but they softened.

They wanted to know their driver. I wanted to know them. Respect, I've always believed, is another form of love. And I had my own past years of addiction, crimes I should have done time for but didn't. I had no moral high ground to stand on. I never asked what they were in for. I wanted them to feel clean, absolved, given a fresh start. "There's not a human alive that hasn't made a mistake sometime in their lives," I told them once. They nodded. They understood.

Winter settled in like a long-term tenant. Whiteouts so thick I could barely see the road. Black ice that turned the bus into a question mark. The kind of cold that made metal groan and breath crystallize. At first, they worried. "You good up there?" "You sure we should be driving?" "Man, this looks bad." But after a few months, something shifted. "He's got this." "This dude's a good driver." "I bet he makes it up that hill." They weren't real bets, just playful confidence. But it warmed me more than the heater ever could. They trusted me. They saw me. And in the back of the bus, I overheard conversations, not about crimes or regrets, but about hope. Phone calls to loved ones. "I love you. I can't wait to see you." "I'm trying. I'm really trying." It surprised me at first. Then it humbled me. Then it changed me. A community was forming on that bus, one mile at a time.

Pre-releasers came and went, but one man carved himself into memory. Big Tom. He was a walking building, massive, formidable, with a scar down the left side of his face that made people keep their distance. He looked like what people expected a prisoner to look like. But he sat right up front, six feet behind me. "Hello," I said. "How are you doing?" "I'm doing great," he replied, cheerful as sunrise. And just like that, we were friends. He was articulate, intelligent, thoughtful, more so than most. He learned where I lived. I learned he lived in a small town tucked into the mountains. He learned my wife and I loved rock hounding. Six months in, he leaned forward and said, "I know a

place. Secret spot. Sapphires everywhere. I'll tell you how to find it."
Years later, my wife and I found that stream. We found sapphires,
many of them. But Tom was the jewel greater than anything we ever
pulled from the earth. I grew to love him. Truly. I still think of him
sometimes, wonder how he's doing, hope he's well.

One morning, early in those nine months, I had dropped the day crew
at the sawmill and was waiting for the overnight crew to come out.
They filtered onto the bus, one by one. I did a head count. One short.
"Who's missing?" I asked. Silence. Cold, heavy silence. Finally
someone muttered, "We should probably just get going." "Did they
flee?" I asked. "Are they officially MIA?" No answer. "You have to let
me know something," I said. "I can't leave without that person or a
reason. That means phone calls. That means police. I want nobody
getting in trouble. If we can fix this, I'll help. I won't say more than I
have to." More silence. Then someone finally said, "He's still inside.
He doesn't want to leave." They were terrified, of being late, of getting
him in trouble, of getting themselves in trouble. "Don't worry," I said.
"I'll take full responsibility. Go get him. Help him out." Ten minutes
later, they returned, him included. He looked like a man walking out of
a burning building, unsure if he'd made the right choice.

When we arrived back at the facility, the foreman was waiting,
checking his watch. He boarded the bus immediately, stern as a judge.
"Why are you late?" "Mechanical issues," I said. "Bus wouldn't start.
Took twenty minutes." Not a stretch, the bus was old, belched black
smoke like it was trying to quit smoking. He accepted it. The crew got
off.

In the days that followed, gratitude poured in. Especially from the man
who hadn't wanted to leave the sawmill. He thanked me again and
again. Later, I overheard someone say, "He's a cool dude. A good
driver." Eventually, I learned the truth. The one person waiting for

him, waiting to be reunited when he got out, was leaving him. Not because of anything he'd done. Or because of everything he'd done. I never got the full story. He was a shell of a man who realized he had nothing and no one waiting. He froze in panic. He couldn't move. An unwanted soul. I don't remember what happened to him after that. He drifted away like a face in the dark and cold. Usually only the people up front had any relationship with me. But I still wouldn't leave without him.

Nine months later, Big Tom completed the program. The day he told me, he stepped off the bus, and I jumped up and followed him. "Come here, you big lug," I said, pulling him into a hug. "I'm so proud of you." He nodded, eyes glistening. I think I saw tears, though he'd never admit it. "If I'm ever in your town," I said, "I'll look for you." He never told me his address. I respected that. I figured he'd be easy to spot, a walking building in a town dwarfed only by his big heart.

People think the Great Banquet is about the master. It isn't. It's about the servant sent to the roads and lanes, the one who refuses to come back without everyone. I didn't know it then, but that was me. Every morning at 4 AM in the Montana cold, diesel in my lungs, whiteouts on the windshield, black ice under the tires, I brought them all. Big Tom with his sapphires. The man frozen in the sawmill. The faces in the dark I can't recall. All of them invited. All of them counted. All of them brought to the table. The banquet wasn't the sawmill. The banquet was the bus. The place where an unwanted soul discovered he was wanted. Where a walking building discovered he was seen. Where pre-releasers looked like anyone in town because on that bus, they were. Grace is not about intimacy with everyone. Grace is about including everyone. And sometimes the Kingdom smells like diesel, sounds like betting on icy roads, and looks like a foreman accepting a lie. Because the servant sent to the margins knows: You don't leave anyone behind. Not the jewel up front. Not the face in the back. Not the one frozen in the sawmill. Everyone gets on the bus. Everyone comes to the banquet.

# CHAPTER 21
## THE FEAST OF ASH AND MERCY

### *The Prodigal Son*
*Luke 15:11–32*

In a town the world had long forgotten, hollowed out like a mine shaft, emptied of its ore, an aging widower named Martin kept vigil in the house where love once dwelt. The mines had closed a generation ago, their black mouths sealed with concrete and shame, leaving behind only dust and the skeletons of dreams. The young fled. The old remained, tethered to memory and mortgages they would never escape.

Martin had become what his shattered town needed most: a living hearthfire in a land of ash. His hands, gnarled by arthritis and decades of swinging a pickaxe in darkness, still opened his door to the desperate and the lost. His lungs, scarred by coal dust and time, still drew breath with a stubbornness that defied reason. He fed the hungry from his own meager pantry. He listened to confessions whispered over coffee at his kitchen table. He prayed for his neighbors in the small hours when sleep would not come, his words rising like smoke into a heaven that seemed, most days, too far away to hear.

What makes a man give when he has nothing left to give? The sages ask this, and the answer is simple, terrible, holy: Love. Love that does not count the cost. Love that pours itself out until the vessel cracks. Love that looks like foolishness to a world that worships survival.

Martin had two sons.

The oldest, Sam, bore his father's jawline and his mother's silence. He had stayed when staying meant sacrifice, when it meant watching his own life narrow to a single point: duty. Someone had to care for the old man when his knees gave out, when his cough turned bloody, when the bills piled high as gravestones. So Sam took a job at the town's last scrapyard, lifting rusted metal in the blistering heat, his body becoming a machine of labor and ache. He worked double shifts. He kept the lights on. He buried his dreams of opening a repair shop beneath the weight of necessity, and he never, never, complained aloud.

His silence was his pride. His sacrifice, his crown of thorns.

The youngest son, Ethan, had been born with his father's heart and a hunger for horizons wider than these dying hills. He fled westward the moment his feet could carry him, racing toward Los Angeles like a man chasing the sun itself. What drives a son to run from the hands that shaped him? Not cruelty, Martin's love had been gentle as rain. Not neglect, the old man's devotion was constant as dawn. No, Ethan ran because he could not bear the weight of his father's goodness, the unbearable knowledge that to stay was to inherit diminishment, to become another ghost walking these streets, another man whose dreams rotted in his chest.

So he chose the far country, where no one knew his name or the debts he carried in his blood.

At first, the far country smiled on him. A small role in an indie film. Bartending gigs in West Hollywood. Nights that tasted like freedom and mornings that promised more. But the world is a patient creditor, and it always collects. The pandemic came like a thief, stealing his work, his savings, his illusions. Rent skyrocketed. Auditions dried up. Ethan turned to schemes that skirted legality, to loans he had no intention of repaying, to lies that came easier than truth.

By 2025, Ethan was a hollowed man living in roadside motels, his phone full of unanswered calls from a father whose voice he could no longer bear to hear. He had squandered not just money, but time, the one currency no man can earn back. And when the last dollar was spent and the last friend turned away, Ethan stood at the edge of the continent, staring into the Pacific as though it might offer an answer.

It offered only silence.

So he bought a one way bus ticket east, back to the town he had sworn never to see again. Back to the father he had abandoned. Back to the brother whose silent judgment he could already feel like a blade between his ribs.

The bus pulled into town at sunset, the sky bruised purple and gold, a beauty so fierce it hurt to look at. Ethan walked the cracked streets with his head down, shame clinging to him like a second skin. The town had not changed. If anything, it had died a little more, another boarded storefront, another house with broken windows, another lot overgrown with weeds.

He stood at the door of his father's house, his hand raised to knock, and for a moment he considered running again. What right do I have to ask for anything? The question burned in his throat.

But before he could knock, the door swung open.

Martin stood there, his frame smaller than Ethan remembered, his face lined with years of worry. For a heartbeat, neither moved. Then Martin's eyes filled, not with anger, not with accusation, but with something Ethan had forgotten existed: joy.

The old man pulled him into an embrace so fierce it threatened to break them both, his arms shaking with the force of it, his voice cracking as he whispered, "You're home. Oh God, you're home."

Ethan had rehearsed a speech on the bus, words of contrition, of apology, of self, abasement. But his father's touch silenced him. In that moment, Ethan understood what mercy feels like when it first touches ground: unbearable, undeserved, undeniable.

When Sam came home from the scrapyard that evening, grime streaked across his face and exhaustion carved into his shoulders, he saw Ethan sitting at the kitchen table. His brother. The deserter. The prodigal. Laughing weakly as Martin ladled stew from an old pot, the smell of rosemary and thyme filling the small house like incense.

The sight stopped Sam cold.

It was as if Ethan had never left. As if those ten years of silence and betrayal had been erased, wiped clean by the old man's unthinking grace. Sam stood in the doorway, his hands clenched into fists, a thousand sacrifices rising in his chest like a flood.

Martin turned, his face bright with an emotion Sam hadn't seen in years. "Sam! Your brother's back! We need to celebrate, go tell the neighbors, we'll have people over, we'll—"

"No."

The word fell like a stone into still water.

Martin blinked. "Sam, I know you're tired, but this is—"

"I said no."

Sam's voice was quiet, but it carried the weight of a decade. He looked at Ethan, who could not meet his gaze, and then at his father, whose smile was faltering. And Sam felt something inside him crack, not break, not yet, but fissure, the first sign that a structure held too long under too much weight is about to collapse.

He turned and walked back out into the night.

The neighbors came anyway. They always did when Martin called. Old Mrs. Kowalski with her pierogi. The Hendersons with a bottle of cheap whiskey. The Ramirez family with their youngest child, who stared wide-eyed at Ethan as though he were a ghost made flesh. They filled the small house with noise and warmth, their laughter a fragile defiance against the cold dark pressing in from all sides.

Ethan sat among them, smiling when expected, nodding when spoken to, but inside he felt like a fraud. Do they know what I've done? Do they know I don't deserve this?

Martin moved through the crowd like a priest through a congregation, his joy infectious, his gratitude palpable. He kept one hand on Ethan's shoulder, as if afraid his son might vanish if he let go.

But Sam did not return.

He walked through the town's empty streets, past the shuttered church where his mother's funeral had been held, past the scrapyard where his youth had been ground to rust, past the sealed mine entrance where his grandfather had once descended into the earth's belly. He walked until he reached the edge of town, where the road disappeared into darkness and the stars hung low and cold.

Where is my feast? The question rose unbidden, bitter as gall. Where is the music for the one who stayed?

Sam had given everything. His time. His dreams. His body, which ached now in ways it shouldn't at thirty-five. He had been faithful when faithfulness cost him everything. And what had it earned him? Silence. Invisibility. The assumption that his presence was as inevitable as sunrise, requiring no acknowledgment, no gratitude, no celebration.

And now Ethan, Ethan, who had squandered a fortune and broken every promise, was feasted like a king.

The injustice of it burned in Sam's chest like coals. He wanted to scream. He wanted to weep. He wanted to strike something, to break the world the way it had broken him.

But he did neither. He stood at the edge of the dark and felt the weight of his own righteousness, heavy as iron, cold as stone. And for the first time in his life, Sam wondered if his faithfulness had been a gift or a cage.

When the neighbors finally left and the house fell quiet, Martin found Ethan still sitting at the table, staring into a mug of cold coffee. The old man lowered himself into the chair across from him, his joints protesting, and for a long moment neither spoke.

"He hates me," Ethan finally said, his voice barely above a whisper.

Martin shook his head. "He doesn't hate you. He hates what he's become."

"What do you mean?"

The old man sighed, a sound that seemed to carry the weight of years. "Your brother has spent his whole life doing the right thing. And somewhere along the way, he started believing that righteousness was a transaction, that if he gave enough, sacrificed enough, stayed faithful enough, the world owed him something in return." Martin's eyes were sad, ancient. "But mercy doesn't work that way, son. Grace isn't earned. It's given. And sometimes the hardest thing in the world is watching someone else receive what you think you deserve."

Ethan looked down at his hands, scarred and dirty. "I don't deserve this, Dad. Any of this."

"No," Martin said quietly. "You don't. None of us do. That's the whole point."

Sam returned near midnight, slipping into the house like a shadow. Ethan was still at the table, his head bowed. When he heard the door, he looked up, and their eyes met.

For a long moment, neither moved. The air between them was thick with everything unsaid, accusations and apologies, resentment and shame, the bitter fruit of years spent growing in opposite directions.

Then Sam did something he didn't expect.

He pulled out the chair across from Ethan and sat down.

The scrape of wood against linoleum was loud enough to wake Martin, who stirred in his recliner and opened his eyes. He saw his two sons sitting together in the dim light, neither speaking, neither moving. It wasn't reconciliation. It wasn't forgiveness. It was something quieter, more fragile, the beginning of what mercy looks like when it first touches ground: two men, broken and bound by blood, sitting in the wreckage, choosing not to leave.

Outside, the town slept its restless sleep, the darkness pressing close. But inside that small house, against all odds, three men breathed. And in the breathing, something ancient and holy stirred, not loud, not triumphant, but real.

A light that refused to go out, though the wind howled at every window.

Morning came softly, the sun breaking through clouds like a word spoken after long silence. The light fell across the kitchen table where Sam and Ethan still sat, exhaustion written into every line of their faces. Neither had slept. Neither had spoken much. But they had remained.

Martin rose stiffly from his chair and moved to the stove, his movements slow but deliberate. He filled the kettle, set it to boil, and began pulling out eggs and bread. The ritual of breakfast, simple and sacred.

"You staying?" Sam asked Ethan, his voice rough from disuse.

Ethan looked at him, searching for judgment in his brother's face and finding only weariness. "I don't know. I don't know what I'm doing here."

"That makes two of us."

The words hung in the air, not cruel, but honest. And in that honesty, something shifted, small as a seed, fragile as new growth.

Over the days that followed, a rhythm emerged. Ethan began to help around the house, fixing the front porch steps that had sagged for years, repainting the trim that had peeled away, clearing the gutters clogged with a decade of leaves. His hands, soft from years of avoiding real work, blistered and bled. But he kept at it.

Sam didn't thank him. But he didn't complain either.

One afternoon, Ethan showed up at the scrapyard unannounced, asking if Sam needed help loading the truck. Sam looked at him for a long moment, then nodded toward a pile of rusted metal. "Make yourself useful."

They worked side by side in the heat, sweat soaking through their shirts, their bodies moving in reluctant unison. When the truck was loaded, Sam tossed Ethan a bottle of water and said, "Same time tomorrow?"

Ethan nodded.

Word spread through the town the way wildfire spreads through dry grass: The Hartley boy is back. The one who left. He's trying to pull his weight.

Some scoffed. Some whispered about second chances being wasted on the unworthy. But others, those who had themselves been given mercy when they deserved judgment, watched with something like hope.

Martin, meanwhile, kept his door open. Sunday dinners became a fixture again, neighbors filing in with casseroles and stories, filling the small house with laughter and the clatter of mismatched plates. The old man would sit at the head of the table, his face lined with years but his eyes bright, and he would speak, not sermons, not lectures, but quiet truths about forgiveness, about the stubborn persistence of love, about how grace is the only force powerful enough to break the machinery of despair.

Some listened. Some didn't. But the words lingered, settling into hearts like seeds into soil, waiting for rain.

One evening, as autumn crept into the hills and the air turned sharp with the promise of winter, the three men sat around a fire pit in the backyard. The flames crackled and spat, sending sparks spiraling into the dark. Ethan stared into the fire, its light dancing across his face, and finally spoke the question that had been burning in him since he arrived.

"Dad… do you really think I deserve this? After everything?"

Martin was quiet for a long time, his gaze fixed on the flames. When he spoke, his voice was low, steady, carrying the weight of something older than himself.

"It's not about deserving, son. It never was. Mercy isn't a wage you earn or a prize you win. It's a gift given to the dying by the One who refuses to let death have the final word." He looked at Ethan, his eyes wet with firelight and something deeper. "You think you're the only one who's been broken? You think your brother hasn't fallen? You think I haven't?" He shook his head slowly. "We're all prodigals, Ethan. Every last one of us. The only difference is whether we're brave enough to come home."

Sam, sitting across the fire, said nothing. But for the first time since Ethan's return, his face softened, just a flicker, just a crack in the stone. It was enough.

The months turned. Winter came, bitter and unforgiving, and the town hunkered down against the cold. But something had shifted, imperceptible at first, like the first thaw beneath frozen ground.

The community center, long neglected, began to fill again. Neighbors helping neighbors. The Henderson boy organized a clothing drive. Mrs. Kowalski started a soup kitchen in the church basement. Sam, almost against his will, began hosting repair workshops in Martin's garage, teaching kids how to fix bikes and small engines, passing on the skills that had kept him alive.

And Ethan? He took a part time job at the scrapyard, his body growing lean and strong again, his hands calloused and sure. He didn't talk much, but his presence became a fixture, steady, reliable, proof that a man can be remade if he's willing to do the work.

One Saturday, as they were closing up the yard, Sam handed Ethan a wrench and said, "You're not half bad at this."

Ethan looked at him, surprised. "Thanks."

Sam shrugged. "Don't let it go to your head."

They both smiled, small, tentative, real.

Martin kept his door open. The smell of stew wafted through the air most evenings, drawing the lost and the lonely like moths to a flame. He knew the darkness would never fully recede, that the town would never return to what it once was, that his own body was failing him one breath at a time.

But he also knew this: Mercy gives life a fighting chance, even in the face of despair.

He saw it in his sons, in the quiet smiles exchanged over shared meals, in the work they did side by side without needing words. He saw it in the town, no longer waiting for salvation to arrive from elsewhere, but building it with their own scarred hands, one small act of kindness at a time.

Because grace doesn't erase pain. Mercy doesn't fix everything. But together, they do something more essential: they remind us that we are not alone in the dark.

And for Martin, for Sam, for Ethan, for their broken town and every soul who called it home, that was enough.

It was worth living.

In the Kingdom, the feast is not for the deserving. It is for the dead who have been raised, the lost who have been found, the broken who have been gathered up and held. And the music plays on, even when we cannot hear it, even when we stand outside in the cold, nursing our wounds and counting our sacrifices.

The door remains open.

The light still burns.

And the Father waits.

# CHAPTER 22
## *ENKRYPTONITE*

### *The Leaven*

*Matthew 13:33; Luke 13:20–21*

The waiting room breathed its own kind of silence. Not the peaceful kind. The held-breath kind. The kind that gathers in the corners of rooms where people come to say things they have never said out loud. A small office suite on the third floor of a building that could have been anywhere — Cleveland, Omaha, Sacramento, it didn't matter. The carpet was the color of oatmeal. The chairs were the color of resignation. A lamp on the side table cast a soft glow meant to feel comforting, though it never quite reached the corners. A white noise machine hummed outside the inner office door, its steady whispering meant to protect the privacy of the broken.

The door opened and a man stepped out. Forty years old. A face you could pass in a grocery store aisle and forget by the time you reached the dairy section. He nodded to the next patient, held the door, offered a small smile that didn't ask for anything and didn't give anything away. His name was Daniel. He was a psychologist. He treated the ones other therapists quietly referred out. The violent. The shattered. The ones whose histories were so heavy they bent the air around them. The ones who had been told, directly or indirectly, by the world and by their own accumulated evidence, that they were beyond repair. Daniel took them all. His colleagues admired him for it. Some found it unsettling. None of them understood where it came from. Daniel didn't either. Whatever drove him lived below language, below memory, in a place he had never visited and didn't know existed.

Thirty-nine years earlier, the world rearranged itself without warning.

Ruth was twenty-two. She worked the closing shift at a diner, took the bus home, and lived in a small apartment four blocks from the stop. She had moved to the city eight months earlier from a town where everyone knew her name, her mother's name, her grandmother's name, and the particular cadence of her laugh. She walked those four blocks every night. She knew the cracks in the sidewalk, the flickering streetlight on the corner, the stray cat that sometimes followed her halfway home. She did not know what waited for her between one streetlight and the next. We do not linger here. We do not give the darkness more attention than it deserves. We stay only long enough to understand the weight she would carry from that night forward. A man. A violence born of powerlessness. A moment that split her life into before and after.

What we stay with is Ruth afterward. Sitting in a hospital room under fluorescent lights that made everything look too sharp. Her mother Miriam driving three hours through the night to reach her. Miriam who had raised three children alone since Ruth was four. Miriam who had worked in a school cafeteria for twenty-two years. Miriam who had held her family together with the kind of strength that becomes invisible because it is constant. She held Ruth's hand and didn't say everything would be fine because she was too honest for that and Ruth was too broken for that and some moments require silence more than comfort. Six weeks later Ruth learned she was pregnant.

Those six weeks were their own particular country. Ruth moved through them the way a person moves through water — slowly, with more resistance than the air had any right to give. She went to work. She came home. She sat in her apartment in the evenings and listened to the city outside her window doing what cities do without apology, continuing, indifferent, full of lives that had not been rearranged on a sidewalk between two streetlights. She did not tell anyone what had happened. She carried it the way women carry things the world has not given them language for, inwardly, carefully, with the constant low-grade vigilance of someone transporting something fragile through a world that does not know it is fragile. When she finally called her mother it was not because she had decided to. It was because the silence had become heavier than she could hold alone.

Miriam was sixty-one years old and had lived her entire life in the trenches of necessity. She was not unkind. She was not unfeeling. She loved Ruth with a completeness that had no cracks in it. But when Ruth told her about the pregnancy Miriam decided with the speed of a woman who had spent decades triaging crisis. She found the clinic. She made the appointment. She drove Ruth there on a Tuesday morning in November with the heater on full blast and the radio off and her hand resting on Ruth's knee at every red light. She believed she was protecting her daughter. She believed she was preventing something from spreading. She did not know she was placing the leaven in the flour. Nobody ever knows when they do that.

The clinic was a low building set back from the street, the kind of place designed to be entered quietly and without spectacle. Inside, seven women sat in the waiting room. Different ages. Different stories. The same heavy silence pressing down on all of them equally. Carol worked the consultation desk. She was thirty-four and had been at the clinic for six years. She believed in the work. She still did. But something had been shifting inside her for months, a weight she couldn't locate precisely, a question she couldn't finish forming no matter how many times she reached for it. She watched the women come in and she did her job with competence and compassion and followed the protocol she had been trained to follow. Except for one thing. Lately, in the consultation room, she had been asking an extra question. One that wasn't in any script. One she had never discussed with her supervisor and couldn't fully explain even to herself. Is there anything else you want to talk about before we proceed? Most women said no and Carol proceeded. But sometimes, rarely, a woman said yes.

Ruth and Miriam sat across from Carol in the small consultation room. Carol went through the standard process. Options. Timelines. Information delivered with practiced warmth. Miriam answered most of the questions. Ruth sat with her hands folded in her lap and her eyes fixed on a point slightly above Carol's left shoulder. Carol reached the end of the script. She looked at Ruth. Not at Miriam. At Ruth. Is there anything else you want to talk about before we proceed? Miriam opened her mouth to say no but Ruth spoke first.

What came out of Ruth was not planned or polished or even fully formed. It arrived the way grief arrives when it has been held too long, in fragments, in contradictions, in the simultaneous presence of rage and sorrow and exhaustion and something else underneath all of those things. Something small and trembling and terrifying. What if it isn't what everyone says it is. Carol didn't answer immediately. She let the question sit in the air between them, heavy and alive, the way you let a frightened animal sit without reaching for it too quickly. Miriam went very still. The white noise machine hummed steadily outside the door.

Carol had been waiting months for a moment like this without knowing she was waiting. Her own unfinished question recognized Ruth's unfinished question the way one tuning fork recognizes another. She leaned forward slightly. She didn't reach for her intake forms. She didn't redirect toward procedure. She simply stayed in the room with both of them, in the full weight of what had been asked, and she said: tell me what you mean by that. And Ruth, who had been carrying something she had no words for since a night between two streetlights, began slowly and haltingly and with great difficulty to find the words at last.

What followed between these three women in that small room on a Tuesday morning in November was not a debate and not a lecture and not a conversion. It was three women sitting inside an impossible question together until the question changed its shape. Carol spoke from her own unfinished crisis rather than her training. She didn't tell Ruth what to do. She didn't promise anything would be easy or resolved or fine. She just left the door open a little wider than the script required. And Ruth walked through it.

The shift happened in Miriam. She had come to this clinic certain, the way she had always been certain when her family needed her to be. She was not a woman who reversed decisions carelessly or without cause. But watching her daughter speak a question she didn't know she had been carrying, watching Carol sit inside that question without flinching or redirecting or filling the silence with the efficiency of someone who had somewhere else to be, something moved in Miriam that had no name and required no announcement. She reached across the small space between their chairs and took Ruth's hand. Not to direct her. Not to decide for her. Just to say with the pressure of her fingers what words could not carry in that moment. Whatever you choose I am here and I will still be here and you are not holding this alone. That hand crossing that small space was the leaven hidden in the flour. Nobody would ever write about it. Nobody would ever know it happened. No record would carry it forward. Just a mother's hand finding her daughter's in a small consultation room while a white noise machine kept its steady vigil outside the door. And everything rose from it.

Ruth carried the pregnancy to term. The months were hard in the way that months are hard when a community has already rendered its verdict and is simply waiting for the evidence to arrive. The whispers came. The judgments delivered with the confidence of people who had never examined their own certainty. Devil baby. Damaged goods. You know what they say about children conceived in violence. Ruth heard all of it and absorbed it with a stillness that was not numbness and not acceptance but the particular endurance of a woman who had decided that what lived inside her was not defined by how it arrived. Miriam built a room. Literally converted the spare bedroom of her small house with the focused determination of a woman laying the foundation of something she understood mattered even when she couldn't yet say exactly why. A crib. A lamp. A window that caught the morning light. The baby arrived on a Wednesday in July. His name was Daniel. He was perfect. Not sentimentally. Clinically. All systems functioning. All indicators normal. Ruth held him and studied his face for a long time. He looked like nobody she could name. He looked like himself.

Daniel grew the way light moves across a room as the sun crosses the sky. Slowly. Inevitably. Illuminating everything in its path without announcing the movement. A quiet boy. Watchful. Drawn without explanation to the edges of rooms where the overlooked ones gathered. He listened more than he spoke. He sat with the kids nobody else sat with not because anyone taught him to but because something in him recognized something in them that he had no language for yet. His teachers noted it in the way teachers note things that don't fit the standard categories — a checkmark in a margin, a comment at the bottom of a report card. Daniel demonstrates unusual empathy for peers experiencing difficulty. What the comment didn't say, couldn't say, was that Daniel wasn't demonstrating anything. He was simply responding to something he could feel the way some people feel changes in barometric pressure before the weather arrives.

As a teenager he read voraciously and discovered psychology the way some people discover a language they already knew without knowing they knew it. At seventeen in his first introductory class something inside him clicked into place with the quiet authority of a thing finding its proper position after a long time of being slightly misaligned. In college he chose the hardest practicum cases. Violent offenders. Patients other students quietly avoided. His supervisor asked him once why he chose them specifically. Daniel thought about it for a long moment. I think I understand something about what people become when nobody believes they could become anything else, he said. His supervisor wrote something in her notes and didn't ask a follow-up question.

Years later he became the man in the third floor office. The unremarkable face. The white noise machine. The fifty minute hour. The patients other therapists referred out because the darkness was too concentrated or the history too heavy or the prognosis too discouraging. Daniel took them all. He sat across from the broken and the violent and the damaged and said with his complete unhurried presence what no textbook had taught him to say and no training had given him to give. I see you. I know what you contain. I know what you could rise into. Nobody in that office knew where this came from. Nobody knew about the consultation room or Carol's question or Miriam's hand crossing the space between two chairs. Nobody knew that Daniel had been almost not here. The leaven works in the dark. The bread rises without witnesses.

Somewhere in a small house three hours east an elderly woman named Miriam sat in a chair by a window that caught the morning light. She knew exactly what had risen from the thing she once believed she was protecting her daughter from. She had never told Daniel. She didn't need to. The bread already knew what it was. And on an ordinary

Tuesday in a third floor office in a city that could have been anywhere, Daniel opened the door for the next patient, offered a small smile that didn't ask for anything and didn't give anything away, and went back to his quiet invisible work of believing in what people could become.

The leaven was still working.

It always had been.

# CHAPTER 23
## *THE ONE THAT GOT AWAY*

### *The Net*

*Matthew 13:47–50*

The kingdom of heaven is like a net.

Not a beautiful net. Not the kind that gets painted into icons or pressed into stained glass with light coming through it in colors that have no business being that clean. A working net. Hemp and salt and the smell of everything the water has ever held. Heavy when wet. Indiscriminate by design. It does not know the difference between what the fisherman wants and what the fisherman does not want. It does not consult the fisherman before it closes. It simply opens in the water and takes what the water offers and brings it all to the shore, the beautiful and the broken, the keeper and the throwback, the one that will feed someone's family tonight and the one that will be discarded before it ever sees a basket.

The sorting happens at the shore.

Not in the water.

At the shore.

I have thought about this for a long time. I have thought about it in the particular way you think about things that you have lived from the inside, where the thinking is not academic but physical, where the parable is not a text you study but a place you have been. I have thought about it on cold Montana mornings with diesel in my lungs and a bus full of men behind me, every one of them caught in a net they did not design and could not escape, every one of them heading toward a shore that would decide what they were worth.

I was the driver. That was all. I was not the fisherman. I was not the net. I was certainly not the shore.

But I was there. Two years of 4 AM mornings, thirty-five miles each way through weather that had no interest in human plans, headlights cutting through whiteouts that turned the world into a single narrow corridor of visible road with nothing on either side but the dark and the cold and whatever was coming. I was there when they boarded and there when they arrived and there for everything in between, which is where most of the real things happen — not at the beginning and not at the end but in the miles between, in the particular suspended world of a vehicle moving through darkness toward a destination that has not yet decided what it will do with you when you arrive.

I drove the net. That is the closest I can come to it.

And in the net, I found Paul.

He boarded early in my third month of my second year, on a morning so cold the diesel had thickened overnight and the bus took four attempts before the engine turned over, belching its black complaint into the pre-dawn air like an old man woken before he was ready. The others came on in their usual way, heads down, boots stamping snow, the particular economy of movement that belongs to people who have learned not to take up more space than necessary. They filled the back rows first, the way people fill any room where the front carries risk.

Paul came on last.

He had an entourage the way certain men have entourages without trying — other men gravitating toward him, angling for proximity, wanting to be near whatever quality he carried. He didn't reciprocate much. He absorbed the attention without returning it, the way a stone absorbs heat without giving it back. He looked like a man who had learned, across a long and complicated life, that most of what people offered you had a price attached that you wouldn't discover until later.

He was not large. He was not small. He was the kind of man you could pass in a hardware store and forget, except for the eyes, which were doing something the rest of his face had decided not to do, which was pay full attention to everything.

He sat down four feet behind me, on the right side, closest to the aisle. Not because it was the best seat. Because it was closest to the driver. I understood this later. At the time I just said good morning and asked how he was doing.

He looked at me the way people look at you when they are deciding whether the question was real.

"You always ask everyone that?" he said.

"Every morning," I said.

He seemed to file this information somewhere useful. He settled into the seat. The bus pulled out into the dark.

The question he came back with, a few mornings later, was the one that opened everything between us.

"How long you been driving a bunch of criminals around?"

I laughed. I couldn't help it. Not at him but at the directness of it, the way it named the thing everyone else was pretending wasn't in the room. "I don't look at you guys that way," I said. "Lord knows I've made my share of mistakes. Only difference between us is you got caught and I didn't."

He was quiet for a moment. The bus moved through the dark. Snow ticked against the windshield.

"That's a hell of a thing to say," he said.

"It's the truth," I said.

He thought about that for the length of a mile or two. Then he said: "This isn't my first rodeo." He said it without shame and without pride, the way you state a fact about the weather. He had been through the pre-release program twice before. This was his third time. His last chance, he said. He had a wife. He had a daughter.

Her name was Sarah.

I know because of the phone calls. He made them without hiding anything, without cupping his hand over the phone or turning toward the window or lowering his voice to the conspiratorial murmur most men used when they called home. He just called. "Hello honey," he would say. "Please put Sarah on." And then his voice would do something it didn't do the rest of the time, which was soften all the way down to its foundation, down to whatever was left when everything else had been stripped away by years and choices and the particular education of a life that had taken him places he hadn't planned to go.

I never heard what Sarah said. I only heard his half of it, which was enough. Yes baby. I know. Soon. I promise. I love you too.

He would hang up and look out the window and say nothing, and I would say nothing, and the bus would move through the dark toward the sawmill where the day was waiting.

This was the rhythm of those months. The cold. The miles. The diesel. The calls to Sarah. The conversations that built themselves slowly, the way trust always builds, one small thing at a time, each one tested before the next is offered.

He told me about his background in pieces, the way you tell things you have carried a long time, carefully, checking each piece before you set it down. He had come from an abusive home. He said this the way he said everything — matter of fact, without drama, without asking for anything in response. He said he had tried not to let it define him.

I nodded. I drove. I thought about that word, define, and about what it costs a man to look at the thing that shaped him and say it does not own me, and about whether saying it was the same as it being true, and about all the things we tell ourselves in the dark that we genuinely believe and that are still, underneath the belief, doing their work on us whether we acknowledge them or not.

I did not say any of this.

I just drove.

There is a particular relationship that forms between a driver and the person four feet behind him that does not form anywhere else. You are not face to face. You are not side by side. You are moving together through the same darkness toward the same destination, one behind the other, the driver watching the road ahead and the passenger watching the back of the driver's head, and something about this geometry — the shared direction, the shared darkness, the inability to fully see each other — makes certain things easier to say than they would be across a table or in a room with nowhere to look except at each other.

Paul said things to the back of my head that I don't think he said to anyone else.

Not confessions. Not secrets. Just the ordinary things a man says when he is trying to locate himself in the world and has found someone safe enough to think out loud around. His daughter's laugh. The way his wife made coffee. The house he was going to have. The man he intended to become in the five years of probation that would follow the program, the slow patient work of rebuilding something from the ground up when the ground itself had never been entirely solid.

He had three months left when I first understood what was at stake. He said it quietly, between the usual things, the way you say the most important thing when you have first surrounded it with lesser things so it doesn't land too hard. Three months. Then home.

"You're going to make it," I said.

He looked out the window. "Yeah," he said. "I am."

The morning he didn't board, I felt it before I understood it.

The crew came on in their usual order, and there was a shape to their coming that I had learned the way you learn any daily ritual, not consciously but in the body, in the part of you that registers pattern without being asked to. When the shape was wrong I knew it before I counted heads. I asked if Paul was sick.

The silence that answered me was its own kind of answer.

I asked what happened. They told me. A 24-hour pass. A drug test on return. High levels of alcohol. He had come back drunk. They hadn't needed the test to know it — procedure required it anyway, and procedure had confirmed what his eyes had already announced. He was removed from the program and sent back to the facility. Placed under contract. Given one final chance.

I drove the rest of the route with the particular silence that settles over you when something you were watching carefully has broken anyway. Not surprise. Something worse than surprise. The recognition that the thing you feared was always going to happen and that the watching did not prevent it. That the watching was never going to prevent it. That the most you could do was witness it, and that witnessing it was not nothing, but it was not enough either, and you were going to have to find a way to carry that distinction for the rest of your life.

Two days later, Paul boarded the bus.

He sat in his seat, four feet behind me, right side, closest to the aisle. He didn't say anything. I didn't say anything. The bus moved through the dark.

After a while he asked me why I had never asked what he was in for. What the original offense had been. Why he had gone to prison in the first place.

I thought about it. "Are you still doing the things that got you there?" I said.

"No," he said.

"Then it doesn't matter," I said. "You paid your debt. What matters now is you. What you want. Who you're going back to."

He didn't talk the rest of the trip.

But he came back the next morning. And the morning after that. And for almost three more months he sat in that seat and made his calls and said hello honey please put Sarah on and watched the dark outside the window and moved through the days with the careful deliberate tread of a man who knows the ground is not entirely solid but is walking on it anyway because there is no other ground available.

One week left.

I know now what I did not know then, which is that one week is not safety. One week is still the water. The shore is not the shore until you are standing on it with dry feet.

Three days left.

Paul didn't board.

I did not ask what happened. I did not need to ask. There are moments in a life when the body knows what the mind has not yet been told, when the absence of a person has a shape you recognize because you have been paying attention long enough to know the precise weight of their presence and can therefore feel its removal the way you feel a change in barometric pressure, in the chest, before the storm announces itself.

I drove the route. I brought the crew to the sawmill. I drove back. I sat with it.

Two weeks later I heard what I had already known. A 24-hour pass. A car. Reckless driving. A field sobriety test. A DUI. The door of the program closed and behind it the door of something larger, the door of the life he had been building for six months, one cold morning at a time, with a daughter named Sarah on the other end of a phone and three days left between him and the shore.

I never heard of Paul again.

I want to tell you what I felt when he didn't board that last morning, because this is the part I have been the least willing to say out loud, the part that lived underneath the sadness for a long time before I found the words for it.

I felt anger.

Not at the system. Not at the circumstances. At Paul. At what felt, from where I was sitting, like weakness. Like a man who had been handed the shore on a platter and had thrown it back. Three days. A blink. And his daughter would grow up without him. Her first prom. Her first heartbreak. The goodbyes to college. The ordinary extraordinary architecture of a childhood that requires a father in it to be built the way it needs to be built — not because fathers are perfect but because their presence is a kind of grammar, a structure inside which certain sentences can be formed that cannot be formed without it. All of that. Gone. For three days he could not hold.

I sat with that anger and I let it burn and then I followed it back to where it actually came from.

It came from me.

It came from my own daughters, whom I was there to raise and who have not spoken to me in a decade, and from the particular grief of a father who did not leave and did not drink and was present in every physical sense of the word and still lost them anyway, in ways he cannot fully explain and has never stopped trying to understand. I needed Paul to make it because Paul making it would have meant something about the possibility of restoration. That daughters can have their fathers. That the shore can be reached. That the three days can be survived.

When Paul didn't make it, I lost that hope along with him.

And then the anger became sadness, and the sadness was the truer thing, and in the sadness I found what was actually there, which was not judgment but grief. Grief for Paul. Grief for Sarah. Grief for the man who had told me this wasn't his first rodeo and that this time was his last chance, and who had meant it, completely, in the way you mean the thing you are most afraid of failing at, and who had failed at it anyway because the net had caught him three times and the shore had been three days away and whatever was living in him that he had tried not to let define him had reached up in the final hours and done what it had been waiting all along to do.

I thought about the man I had known years before. The one in the treatment facility who had owned seven restaurants in Los Angeles and come to the program straight from the hospital with wet brain and sat in meetings with perfect posture and talked about return dates and reopening plans and the empire he was going back to. His wife had told me she wished her husband had what I had. She could already see what I couldn't see yet. He completed the program. He went out on a bender. He died from the complications.

The net catches everything. Not everything stays caught.

This is not a comfortable truth. It is not the truth we want when we are driving through the dark at 4 AM with a man four feet behind us who is making phone calls to his daughter and building something from the ground up and has three months left and then one week and then three days. We want the truth that says effort is sufficient. That presence is enough. That if a man wants it badly enough and has someone waiting for him and holds on for six months through the cold and the miles and the diesel and the bad coffee and the field sobriety tests on the way back from 24-hour passes — we want that truth to say he makes it. We want the shore to receive him.

But the net does not negotiate with our wants.

The net catches everything. The fishermen sort at the shore. And some mornings a seat that was filled is empty and you drive the route anyway and bring the others to the sawmill and bring them home and do it again the next morning and the morning after that, because the route does not stop for grief and the darkness does not wait for you to finish feeling what you feel about the fish that slipped back into the water three days from land.

Jesus does not explain the sorting. He does not tell us the criteria. He does not give us a rubric by which we can evaluate, from inside the net, which category we belong to. He says the angels will come and separate the evil from the righteous, and he says this with the confidence of someone who trusts the sorting to the sorter and does not feel the need to rehearse the methodology.

What he leaves us with is the net itself. The indiscriminate, patient, salt-soaked net that opens in the water and takes what the water offers and closes around all of it equally and brings it all to the shore. The beautiful and the broken. The ones who make it and the ones who don't. The ones who were three months away and the ones who were three days away and the ones who were three hours away and still didn't make it, and the ones who made it against every odds and every probability and every history that said they shouldn't have.

I was one of those. I know this. January 17th, 2000, is the date I know the way I know my own name, the day the net brought me to a shore I had been avoiding for years, and the shore received me, and I was one of the ones that made it. Not because I was stronger than Paul. Not because I wanted it more. Because the net brought me to the shore at the moment when the shore was ready to receive me, and the same net brought Paul to his shore at the moment when something in him was not yet finished with the water.

I do not know why.

I have stopped pretending I know why.

What I know is this. I drove the route. I said good morning and meant it. I told a man that the only difference between us was that he got caught and I didn't, and I meant that too. I listened to his calls to Sarah and I did not look away from the weight of what he was carrying and I let him talk to the back of my head about the house he was going to have and the man he was going to become, and I believed him, and believing him was not naïve. Believing him was the only thing I had to offer that was worth anything.

The net caught him three times. Three times it brought him close to the shore. Three times the shore did not receive him.

I do not know where Paul is now. I do not know if Sarah has a father. I do not know if the years the locusts ate were ever restored, if the abusive background he tried not to let define him ever found a healer patient enough to sit with it, if the man I drove through the dark for six months ever found a morning that held.

I hope so.

I hope it with the particular hope of a man who knows what it is to be in the net and to feel the shore approaching and to almost not make it and then to make it, and who understands, because of this, that the ones who don't make it are not less than the ones who do. They are the same fish, in the same water, caught in the same net, heading toward the same shore.

The sorting is not mine to do.

It never was.

I was the driver. That was all. I drove the net through the dark and the cold and the diesel and the miles, and I said good morning every morning and meant it, and I listened, and I believed, and some of them made it to the shore and some of them didn't, and the ones who didn't took something with them when they slipped back into the water that I am still, some mornings, reaching for.

Paul took something.

I am still reaching.

The route goes on.

The dark is still dark.

The morning is still coming.

And somewhere, in a world I can only hope for and cannot see, a daughter named Sarah is being told by someone who loves her that her father tried. That the net caught him and the shore was close and he tried with everything he had and it wasn't enough and that is not the whole story of who he was.

That the whole story of who he was included six months of cold mornings and phone calls made without hiding anything and a voice that went soft all the way down to its foundation when he said her name.

That he loved her.

That the net knows what it caught.

That the shore will have the final word.

Not me.

Never me.

I was only the driver.

# CHAPTER 24
## THE ONES THEY THREW OUTSIDE

### The Wicked Tenants

*Matthew 21:33–46*

She entered the order at twenty-two with a vocation so specific and so complete that the women who interviewed her for admission wrote in their records that they had rarely encountered anything quite like it. Not the vague spiritual restlessness that brought many to the order's door. Not the desire for structure or community or the particular safety of a life with clear purpose. Something more precise than any of those things. Something that looked, to the women who had spent their lives learning to recognize it, like the real thing.

Her name was Sister Catherine.

She taught for twelve years. Elementary school, the early grades, the ones where the children are still entirely themselves, before the world has taught them the performance of themselves, before they have learned to manage how they are perceived. She loved this work with the full weight of her vocation. She loved the specific children in front of her every morning — their names, their particular fears, the child who could not yet read but could draw horses with a fidelity that stunned her, the child who arrived every Monday with the weekend's evidence on her arms and who smiled with such determined brightness that it broke something in Sister Catherine every time she saw it. She prayed for these children. She stayed late to help them. She learned their families' names and called when the families needed calling and sometimes when they didn't, because she had learned that the families

289

who were hardest to reach were often the ones who most needed reaching.

She was, by every measure available to the institution that contained her, an exemplary servant of the vineyard.

She did not go looking for what she found.

It found her. The way these things always find the people who are paying the kind of attention she was paying. The child who said something in passing that was not in passing. The detail that did not fit the story it was embedded in. The specific quality of a child's stillness when a particular name was mentioned. Sister Catherine had spent twelve years learning to read children the way you learn to read any language you are immersed in — not through analysis but through accumulation, through the thousands of small observations that become, over time, a fluency. And the fluency told her, before she had language for what it was telling her, that something was wrong.

She went to the person she was supposed to go to. She said what she had observed. She said it carefully and specifically and with the particular humility of a person who understands that she might be wrong and wants to be wrong and is reporting what she has seen rather than a conclusion she has drawn. She was heard. She was thanked for her concern. She was told that the matter would be looked into.

She waited. She watched. She observed more. She went back.

She was heard again. She was thanked again. The language was patient and pastoral and entirely without urgency. The language of an institution that has learned, through long practice, to receive reports of this kind in a way that does not require action. The language that says we take this very seriously while doing the specific things that ensure it will not be taken seriously enough to require a response that costs the institution anything.

She did not go away.

She came back. She documented. She put the specific observations in writing in a letter addressed to the specific person whose institutional role required them to act on specific observations put in writing. She sent the letter through channels that were on record. She kept copies of everything.

The institution reassigned her.

Not with malice. With the particular pastoral care of an institution that has learned to frame every act of self-protection as an act of generosity toward the person being protected against. She was told it was an opportunity. A recognition of her gifts. A chance to bring her exceptional teaching to a community that needed her. She was moved far enough from the original location that her continued proximity to the situation could no longer be characterized as proximity. The people who delivered this news believed what they were saying. They genuinely experienced her reassignment as a kindness. This is the most important thing to understand about what happened to Sister Catherine and to the children she was trying to protect — it did not require cruel people to operate. It required only people who had learned, through long institutional habituation, to experience the institution's self-protection as identical with the institution's purpose.

She went to the new school. She taught the new children. She loved them the way she loved all children, specifically and completely, one at a time, by name. She called their families when the families needed calling.

She did not stop writing letters.

The children she had observed were not the first. They were not the last. They were part of a pattern that stretched back decades in every direction — backward through the institution's history, sideways through its geography, forward through the years still coming that nobody had yet lived. The pattern had its own institutional pathways, its own mechanisms for moving the problem from one location to another when it became too visible in the current one, its own language for explaining the movements in terms that sounded like opportunity and care and the institution's recognition of the gifts of the men being moved.

The men at the center of the pattern were not monsters in the way we imagine monsters. They were men who had served the institution faithfully in every dimension the institution could measure. They had built programs and raised funds and delivered homilies that made people feel the presence of something real. They had sat with the dying and counseled the grieving and baptized the children of families who loved them and trusted them with everything. The institution had measured them by these things and found them good and promoted them accordingly and moved them when necessary and explained the moving in the language of opportunity and need.

The children were not measured by these things.

The children were the vineyard's stated purpose — named clearly in every mission document and homily and strategic plan, the explicit reason the wall had been built and the winepress dug and the watchtower raised. But the children, when they became a threat to the institution's continuation, were not treated as its purpose. They were treated as its problem. And the solution to the problem was the same solution that had been applied to Sister Catherine. Movement. Distance. The manufacturing of explanations that made the movement look like something other than what it was.

They were thrown outside the vineyard.

Not in a single decision. Not by a single person. Through the accumulated weight of a thousand small decisions made by people who were, in their own minds and in many cases in reality, genuinely trying to protect something sacred. The decision not to call the police because the scandal would harm the faithful. The decision not to tell the new parish because the man deserved a fresh start. The decision to respond to the parents who came forward with the language of pastoral care rather than the language of institutional accountability. The decision, made again and again in rooms where the children were not present, that the institution's survival was worth the cost of their silence.

Each decision was a brick. Each brick was laid by a human hand. And the wall that was built from those bricks was not built to protect the vineyard.

It was built to protect the tenants' claim to it.

His name was David. He was fifty-three years old when he made the decision, and he had been carrying what was done to him since he was nine, and he had spent forty-four years deciding whether the telling was worth what it would cost. He had built a life on the outside of the vineyard — a real life, a good life, a life with a wife named Margaret and two daughters and work he was good at and a faith that had survived what the institution had done to it because he had understood, at great personal cost and over many years, that the faith and the institution were not the same thing. That the vineyard was real even when the tenants were not.

He came forward because his daughter was nine. The same age he had been.

He looked at her one morning across the breakfast table — her cereal, her backpack by the door, the particular absorption of a nine-year-old who is entirely present in the moment she is in — and something that had been waiting forty-four years finished its waiting. Not with drama. Not with the cinematic quality that stories about these moments are given when they are told afterward. Just a father looking at his nine-year-old daughter and understanding that the stone the builders had thrown outside the vineyard was still there, still carrying its weight, still waiting to become what the builders had rejected it from becoming.

He found a lawyer. He found others who had been thrown outside the same vineyard at the same age by the same hands. He found, in the particular way that the ones thrown outside always find each other when the moment arrives, that the outside of the vineyard was crowded with people whose existence the institution had been managing for decades. Men and women who had built their lives around the weight of what they carried. Who had raised children and held jobs and sat in rooms where they did not say what they knew, not because they were weak but because the institution had made the saying feel impossible, had surrounded the saying with enough legal weight and pastoral language and the specific shame that attaches to a child told that what happened to them did not happen, that the silence had become the shape of their lives.

The son was coming from a long way off.

The institution saw him. The institution had been seeing people like him for decades and had developed considerable expertise in the management of their approach. The lawyers were retained. The language was prepared. The pastoral response was calibrated with care — genuine compassion for the suffering of those who had come forward, deep commitment to healing and reconciliation, the institution's own grief at what had occurred, the importance of not letting the actions of individuals define the institution as a whole.

The lawyers worked. The language worked. And for a time it seemed that what had always worked would work again, that the machinery of institutional management, refined over decades of managing exactly this, would prove sufficient to contain exactly this.

And then it did not.

The walls came down.

Not all at once. Through the slow accumulation of testimony that could not be managed away. Through the particular quality of witness that arrives when the ones thrown outside have nothing left to lose and the truth they carry is the only thing they have left to give. Through the grand juries and the attorneys general and the journalists who had been filing the requests for years and the ordinary people in the pews who read the reports and decided that the language of pastoral response was no longer an adequate answer to what the reports were describing.

The institution was not destroyed. The vineyard was not destroyed. The faith of the people who sat in the pews and felt the presence of something real and refused to let what the tenants had done define what the vineyard was — that faith was not destroyed. The owner did not abandon the wall and the winepress and the watchtower. The sacred thing that the institution was built to tend was still there, beneath the corruption, older than the corruption, indestructible in the way that only the things that actually matter are indestructible.

What was destroyed was the fiction.

The fiction that the institution's survival was identical with the vineyard's purpose. The fiction that protecting the tenants was the same as protecting the harvest. The fiction that the children thrown outside the wall were less important than the institution that threw them.

This is the parable that Jesus told in the last week of his life.

He told it in Jerusalem, in the temple, to the religious leaders who were planning his death. He told it knowing they would recognize themselves in it. He told it knowing what recognition would produce — not repentance but acceleration, not reform but the finalizing of the plan. He told it anyway. Because the truth of the vineyard required its telling more than his safety required his silence.

A landowner planted a vineyard. He built a wall. He dug a winepress. He built a watchtower. He leased it to tenants and went away. When harvest time came he sent servants to collect his share. They beat the servants. They killed the servants. Finally he sent his son, believing that surely they will respect my son. The tenants saw the son coming from a long way off and said: this is the heir. Come, let us kill him and the inheritance will be ours. They threw him outside the vineyard. They killed him.

The religious leaders, when Jesus asked what the owner would do, answered their own condemnation. He will bring those wretches to a wretched end, they said, and give the vineyard to others who will produce its fruit. They spoke the verdict on themselves before they understood they had done so.

The stone the builders rejected has become the cornerstone.

This is not a comfortable parable. It is the angriest thing Jesus ever said, and he said it looking at the people who were going to kill him within the week, and he said it with the full force of everything he understood about what they were doing and why and what it would cost.

The church has spent two thousand years applying this parable to everyone except itself. To the Pharisees. To the first-century religious establishment. To other denominations. To the institutions of other traditions. The reading that requires the least from the reader is always the reading that locates the wicked tenants safely in the past, safely in someone else's tradition, safely removed from any institution the reader currently inhabits.

This chapter is not written from the outside of the church. It is written from the inside of the love for it. From the place where the vineyard is real and the faith is real and the kingdom that the institution was built to serve is genuinely, irreducibly real. It is written by someone who has felt the sacred descend in the architecture built to receive it, who has watched a priest lay hands on the dying and felt the presence of something that the building was designed to honor and sometimes does. The wall and the winepress and the watchtower were built for something genuine. The genuine thing does not disappear when the tenants corrupt their stewardship of it.

But the tenants corrupted their stewardship of it.

And the parable — the one Jesus told in the last week of his life to the people who recognized themselves in it and accelerated the plan — ends not with the institution reformed. Not with the tenants having learned their lesson. Not with the children restored to the vineyard from which they were thrown.

It ends with the vineyard given to others who will produce its fruit.

The others are the children who were thrown outside.

The others are David, looking across the breakfast table at his nine-year-old daughter.

The others are every person who came forward after David and before him and after them, who are still coming, in every diocese and every denomination and every institution that confused the protection of its own continuation with the protection of the sacred thing it was entrusted to tend.

The cornerstone the builders rejected is the child at nine, sitting in the room with the man the institution trusted and protected and moved when necessary and would not name.

That child is the cornerstone.

That child is the kingdom.

That child is what the wall and the winepress and the watchtower were always built to protect.

Sister Catherine was seventy-one when she read about the settlement in the newspaper. She was in her fourth reassignment, still teaching the early grades, still learning the specific children in front of her every morning, still calling the families when the families needed calling. She read the names. She recognized them. She thought about the letters she had written thirty years before and the children she had observed and what had been done with her observations.

She did not feel vindicated. Vindication is what you feel when you have been waiting for the other person to be proven wrong. She had not been waiting for that. She had been waiting for the children to be seen. For the ones thrown outside the vineyard to be acknowledged as the vineyard's purpose rather than its problem. For the institution to say, in whatever language remained available to it, that the children mattered more than its own continuation.

She did not know if that had fully happened. She suspected the institution's grief was genuine. She suspected its commitment to change was genuine. She suspected that the structural reckoning — the full acknowledgment of what the fiction had cost, the full weight of the accounting — was still, in the way that institutional reckonings always are, incomplete.

She closed the newspaper.

She went back to her classroom.

The children were arriving.

She loved them. Specifically and completely. One at a time. By name.

She kept the letters.

She always kept the letters.

The owner has not abandoned the vineyard.

The watchtower is still standing. The wall is still standing. The winepress is still there, waiting for the harvest that the vineyard was always planted to produce.

The tenants who confused their stewardship with ownership have been called to their accounting. The accounting is not finished. Accountings of this kind are never finished quickly or cleanly or in a way that fully satisfies the weight of what was owed. The children are still outside. Some of them have been welcomed back. Some of them will never come back. Some of them carried what was done to them until the carrying was no longer possible, and they are gone, and the weight of their going is part of the accounting that remains outstanding.

But the vineyard is still there.

The servants are sent out into the roads and the lanes and the highways.

Go out, the master says. Compel them to come in.

So that my house may be full.

The house that was built for the children the tenants threw outside.

The house that was always meant for them.

The house that will not be full until they are in it.

Into the Kingdom.

## CHAPTER 25
### THE LAST ORBIT

*The Wedding Banquet*

*Matthew 22:1–14*


Before I speak of thirteen, I must speak of one.

His name was Vladimir Mikhailovich Komarov, and in the spring of
1967, he climbed into a spacecraft called Soyuz 1 knowing, with the
particular clarity that belongs only to the very brave and the very
doomed, that he might not come back. The Soviet Union was in a
hurry. There are no more dangerous words in the history of human
ambition than those three: in a hurry. The spacecraft had over two
hundred known design flaws. Engineers had written letters. The letters
had been read and filed and forgotten, the way letters always are when
the machine that receives them is moving too fast to stop. Vladimir
knew all of this. He flew anyway, because the dream had chosen him,
and you do not refuse the dream when the dream chooses you. You
climb in. You strap down. You go.

A solar panel failed to deploy. Navigation systems flickered and died.
And then the Soyuz began to spin — not the clean correctable spin of a
craft making adjustments, but the slow maddening rotation of a
machine coming undone. Gimbal lock, the engineers called it from the
ground, speaking the words with the quiet horror of doctors delivering
a terminal diagnosis. The horizon disappeared. The stars wheeled past
without mercy. There was no up. There was no down. There was only
the spin, and the man inside the spin, and the cold indifferent universe
pressing in from every direction at once.

The ground crew did what ground crews do when the math has run out. They put his wife on the communications channel. Her name was Valentina. She said her goodbyes. She said her love. And Vladimir Komarov, still strapped into the machine that was killing him, received this love and answered it, and the whole of mission control stood in silence because there is nothing to say when the machine you built in your hurry is killing someone's husband and the whole world is a widow.

But Vladimir Komarov was not finished.

Orbit after orbit he fought it. Ninety minutes to circle the earth, and he used every second, firing his attitude thrusters, coaxing the wounded craft back toward something resembling control. The ground had written him off. The mathematics had written him off. History itself had already composed his epitaph. And still he fired the thrusters. Orbit after orbit. Fifteen. Sixteen. Seventeen.

On the eighteenth orbit, with three remaining before gravity's arithmetic became non-negotiable, the impossible happened.

The spin slowed. The stars steadied. The horizon reappeared in the porthole — that most faithful of promises, the line between the sky and everything below it — and Vladimir Komarov looked at it the way a man looks at the face of someone he feared he would never see again. He had earned it back. Against every calculation, against every probability, against the very machinery of his own destruction, he had earned it back.

"I am coming home," he radioed to the ground.

And he meant it with everything he had.

The reentry was legendary. A feat of piloting that no textbook had prepared him for, executed by a man running on will and love and the particular stubbornness of someone who refuses to let the universe have the final word. He had done the impossible thing. Now only the parachute remained. The soft deceleration. The fields of the Orenburg Oblast rising to receive him.

The parachute tangled.

It tangled because of the same spin that had plagued the mission from the beginning, the lines wrapped around each other in the dark with a patience that mocked every heroic thing he had done in the hours before. The reserve chute deployed and tangled too. And Soyuz 1, carrying the man who had done the impossible, fell.

In the fields near Orsk, a small group of elk lifted their heads at something approaching from the sky. They watched it fall. They lowered their heads. A barely audible thud. The soft extinguishing of a life that had, in its final hours, accomplished something the universe itself had ruled impossible.

The elk went back to rooting in the snow.

The sky said nothing.

I tell you this story first because it is the story of everything that follows. It is the story of the dream and the rush and the machine with two hundred flaws. It is the story of the parachute that was always tangled, waiting, patient as gravity, while the hero did his heroic thing. It is the story of the feast prepared and the banquet spread and the table set with every intention of welcome — and of who, in the end, was not there to receive it.

I tell you this story first so that when you meet the thirteen, you will already know, somewhere beneath your hope, how it ends.

You will know, and you will hope anyway. Because that is what we do. That is the most human thing we do.

On a Tuesday morning in October, in a city that had not yet decided to notice the cold, Carla Reyes stood in line at the Eastside Community Food Bank with a number and three children.

The number was forty-seven. She had been forty-seven before. She knew what forty-seven meant: an hour, maybe more, depending on whether the Tuesday volunteers showed up and whether the donation truck arrived on time and whether Marcus, her youngest, could hold himself together for sixty minutes without dissolving into the particular brand of four-year-old despair that arrived without warning and required everything she had to manage. She shifted the bag on her shoulder. She put her hand on Marcus's head. She did not look up at the sky.

She had learned, some time ago, that looking up at the sky was a thing that cost you something. You looked up and you saw the planes crossing the blue and you thought about where they were going and why, and before long you were doing the math of your own life against the math of those lives, and the math was never kind, and you couldn't afford unkindness on a Tuesday morning with three kids and a number and forty-six people ahead of you.

So she looked at the back of the head in front of her. She counted the cracks in the sidewalk. She waited.

Above her, without her knowing it, the world was preparing a feast.

They called the mission Horizon.

Thirteen astronauts. The International Space Station's final crew before its scheduled deorbit, and the first selected for what came after — a deep space proving mission, humanity's next sentence, the advance party of the species. The press called them the vanguard. The press releases called them the chosen. The invitations had gone out, as invitations always do, to the prepared and the credentialed and the celebrated, to the ones the king's messengers knew how to find.

They were magnificent. They were ready. And they were, in ways none of them fully understood yet, already inside the machine with its two hundred flaws.

Commander Elena Vasquez had wanted this since she was seven years old. She called her mother every Sunday, and her mother was unreservedly, embarrassingly proud. She had a gap between her front teeth she had always planned to fix and never did. She was, to her crew, a fixed point — the horizon within the mission named Horizon. On the morning of launch, standing in the gantry with the Florida sky going pink behind her, she pressed her palm flat against the cold metal of the structure and felt the vibration of the engines coming to life below, and she thought: we are going somewhere real.

She did not know, yet, what real would cost.

Mission Specialist Declan Byrne, from Galway, was the first one in the common area every morning, coffee already made. He had a laugh that arrived before the joke did. On the morning of launch, he said something to Elena that made her laugh so suddenly she had to grab the doorframe to steady herself, and the sound of it pulled the others out of their quarters one by one until thirteen people who were about to become history simply stood together in the corridor and laughed. It was Declan's last great gift to them before the ground fell away. He did not know it was a gift. He was just being Declan.

Dr. Yuki Tanaka had grown up in Hiroshima, granddaughter of a hibakusha, a woman who had been hanging laundry on the morning of August 6th, 1945, when the sky did the thing the sky was not supposed to be able to do. Yuki had become a doctor because of what her grandmother had transmitted to her in the evenings by the river: the knowledge of what invisible things released into the air can do to a human body. She was the mission's flight surgeon. She took her readings. She logged her data. She knew how to watch for the thing that announced itself only after it was already done.

Dr. Sarah Okafor had worked in refugee camps and disaster zones and the neighborhoods where the distance between crisis and help was measured not in minutes but in days. She had learned more from the people in those places than from any textbook. She noticed everything. Kenji's careful silences. Astrid going still at her data. Elena humming when she worried and going quiet when she was afraid. She wrote none of it in her official logs. She held it carefully, with both hands, without letting it become the thing that was carrying her.

Colonel Nikolai Volkov was the oldest of the thirteen, the one who had logged more hours in orbit than the rest combined. His grandfather had stood in mission control in 1967 and listened to Valentina Komarov say goodbye to her husband. On winter evenings in Moscow, over vodka, he had told Nikolai about the gimbal lock and the eighteen orbits and the voice saying I am coming home and the parachute and the field near Orsk and the elk. And then, in the last coherent conversation before the end, his grandfather had told him the thing he regretted most: that he had never learned the elk's names. That we are always so focused on the ones we send up, he had meant, that we forget to ask about the ones already there.

Nikolai pressed his palm against the observation window as the launch site fell away below. He held it there until his hand went cold.

The others had their own reasons for being here, their own invitations accepted, their own versions of the dream. Dr. Kenji Mori, planetary protection specialist, who apologized to furniture he bumped into and kept seventeen notebooks of concerns that the appropriate channels had not resolved. Yusuf Adeyemi, the alternate, who had been called four days before launch and who had watched Lagos disappear into the curve of the continent with complete and uncomplicated wonder, not knowing what else he was carrying aboard. Dr. Astrid Nilsson, physicist and Arctic daughter, who had stopped presenting her findings at certain conferences because the faces in the audience had begun to look like people who had already decided not to act, and who had come anyway because someone had to be up there with the instruments and the willingness to feel what the data meant. Marcus Chen, the robotics specialist, whose arms were the longest on the crew and whose Canadarm was the reach that made the assembly of everything else possible. Dr. François Beaumont, who pressed his palm against the observation window every day and stayed there, looking down at the planet they were leaving, keeping the record that he had long ago stopped hoping would change the decisions of people with the power to make decisions. Dr. Irina Volkova, geologist, who had spent three years studying a dying planet and who wrote things down with the precise conviction of a woman who understood that the record outlasts the recorder. Daniel Kowalski, who was the best listener any of his crewmates had ever encountered, and who had a nine-year-old daughter named Sophie who had asked him whether space was loud or quiet, and who had said: mostly quiet. But the quiet is full. And young Alexei Petrov, twenty-nine years old, who had told his mother he was coming back with the complete certainty of someone who has not yet encountered the thing that will teach him the difference between intention and outcome.

Thirteen. The feast was set. The table was full. The banquet had begun.

Below them, the line at the Eastside Food Bank moved the way lines move when the people in them have stopped expecting anything to be quick.

Carla's daughter Isabella, nine years old, was reading a paperback she had carried from home, holding it at the precise angle that blocked out her brother's fidgeting. Her other daughter Rosie, six, had found a crack in the sidewalk shaped like a river and was following it with one careful foot, arms out for balance, narrating quietly to herself. Marcus, four, had attached himself to Carla's leg with the tenacity of someone who understood on a cellular level that legs were the most reliable structure available.

The woman behind Carla had a number too. Sixty-one. They did not speak. They did not need to. There was a grammar to this line, a shared language of patience and dignity and the particular silence of people who are here because they are here, and who have made their peace with that, and who would prefer that peace not be interrupted by the expressions of people who had not yet had to make it.

A man near the front of the line had a phone pressed to his ear. "I love you," he was saying, quietly but not quietly enough. "I can't wait to see you." He listened. His face did something complicated. "I'm trying," he said. "I'm really trying."

Carla thought about her own phone. She thought about the calls she did not make because she did not know what to say that would not make things worse. She moved forward one step as the line advanced. She put her hand on Marcus's head. She waited.

On the fourteenth day of the mission, Dr. Yuki Tanaka noticed something in the routine blood panel.

It was small. Within the range of clinical variation. She took the reading again. And again. She looked at it the way her grandmother had looked at the laundry on the morning of August 6th — with the unhurried attention that ordinary things deserve, not knowing that the ordinary was about to become something else entirely.

She logged it carefully. She said nothing to anyone. Not yet.

On the fifteenth day, Marcus Chen noticed something in the arm's performance data. He ran the diagnostic three times. He went to dinner. He watched Yuki's eyes move to the medical bay door twice during the meal. He said nothing. He went back to his diagnostics after dinner and paid attention.

On the sixteenth day, Sarah Okafor went to find Yuki. She found her in the medical bay, at her instruments, with the expression of someone who has been looking at the same data long enough that the data has started to look back.

Sarah stood in the doorway. "How long have you known?" she said.

"Since the fourteenth day," Yuki said.

Sarah came in. She sat across from her. She looked at the data and did not look away and did not make the face. "Tell me everything," she said.

Yuki told her everything. When she finished, Sarah sat with it for a long time. Then she said: "You did the right thing."

Yuki said: "It won't be enough."

Sarah said: "No." She stood up and straightened her shoulders in the specific way of someone who has done this before, who has stood in the doorway of the thing that cannot be fixed and walked through it anyway because walking through it was the work. "Let's go find Elena," she said.

They went together down the corridor toward the commander's quarters, and they knocked on her door, and they went in. The before became the after.

Elena listened without interruption. She sat on the edge of her bunk with her hands folded and her face doing the thing a face does when it is absorbing something it cannot absorb and absorbing it anyway. When Yuki finished, Elena sat for a long moment in the full quiet. Then she said: "All right."

That was all. Two words. But her crew understood what lived inside them, because Elena was a fixed point, and fixed points do not shatter — they hold.

She called a meeting. All thirteen in the common module, floating in the specific weightless democracy of a space where there were no heads of tables, where the commander and the youngest crew member occupied the same relationship to up and down. She told them what Yuki had found. She told them what it meant. She told them what she did not know, which was everything else, and she told them this with the same steadiness with which she told them what she did know, because a commander who pretends to know more than she knows is more dangerous than the thing she is trying to manage.

Then she said: "We do the work. Every person, every system, every moment. We do not stop doing the work."

Kenji opened his seventeenth notebook.

Declan said: "Right then." He uncapped his coffee. He took a drink. He looked at Elena over the rim of the cup and there was something in the look that was not defeat and not bravado but the third thing, the thing his father had meant from the boat in the grey Atlantic swell, the thing about having the stomach for the crossing. "What's first?"

What was first was the work, and the work was what it had always been: the thousand small necessary things that held a mission together in the dark. Marcus at the arm. Daniel managing communications with the quiet efficiency of a man who had been doing the thing the moment required since before the moment required it. Astrid at the observation window, keeping the record, humming the joik her grandmother had given her, the melody without words that was not about anything specific and therefore about everything. Irina writing things down. François writing things down. Nikolai calm in the way that is not the absence of fear but the presence of something forged across nineteen years of orbit and one grandfather's kitchen and four words carried for thirty-seven years.

Yusuf floated to the observation window when his shift ended and looked down at the curve of Africa visible through the cloud. He had his grandmother's cloth in his hands, turning it over and over, the fabric moving between his fingers like a rosary. Sarah watched him from across the module. She did not go to him yet. She let him have the view.

She knew what he was thinking. She had always known. She had known it since before launch, the way she always knew things the instruments hadn't named yet. He was thinking about Lagos. About twenty million souls on streets that the mission budget had exceeded by a factor of four. About the distance between the feast up here and the hunger down there, and about the folded napkin in his pocket, and about whether the wonder was worth the price, and about who had set the price and who had paid it.

The questions were real. They deserved real answers. But the answers would not come tonight, and Yusuf knew it, and Sarah knew it, and so she let him stand at the window and hold his grandmother's cloth and look at the continent below until looking was enough.

Below them, the line moved.

Carla had reached the front. A volunteer, a college student with a lanyard and tired eyes, handed her a box. Canned goods. Pasta. A jar of peanut butter. A box of cereal with a cartoon toucan on it that Marcus immediately reached for with both hands. She let him hold it. She thanked the volunteer. She meant it.

She loaded the box into the cart. She gathered her children. Isabella, still reading. Rosie, still following her crack in the sidewalk, now extended beyond the food bank entrance and into the parking lot where, according to Rosie's ongoing narration, it had become a very important river indeed. Marcus with his cereal box, clutched to his chest like a trophy.

The air had turned. November coming through the back door of October, the way it did in this city, not with announcement but with the simple arrival of cold that had been scheduled all along and was only now making itself known.

Carla zipped Marcus's jacket. She did not look up at the sky.

She did not know, at that moment, that thirteen people were circling above her at seventeen thousand miles per hour in a station the size of a football field, that among them was a woman who had grown up in a neighborhood not entirely unlike hers, that another had packed his grandmother's cloth into a bag and thought about the twenty million people of Lagos every time the continent came into view, that a man named Daniel had a daughter named Sophie who was nine years old and who had asked her father whether space was quiet and that he had said yes, but the quiet is full.

She did not know any of this.

She pushed the cart toward her car. She buckled her children in. She drove home through the streets that the messengers had walked past on their way to find the invited guests.

On the nineteenth day, Alexei Petrov found the calculation.

He came to Elena's quarters at 0200, ship time, with the notebook and the numbers and the eyes of a man who had not slept in thirty-six hours and did not intend to until the universe gave him what he had asked for. "I found it," he said. "Look."

Elena looked. She looked for a long time. She was a better mathematician than she let people know, and the looking was not the looking of someone following along but the looking of someone checking, verifying, testing the joints of the thing for weakness. She handed the notebook back.

"Show Kenji," she said.

He showed Kenji. Kenji looked. Kenji was quiet for a long time in the way that Kenji was quiet, which was different from other people's quiet because in Kenji the silence was actively working, running the numbers against the seventeen notebooks, checking the solution against every concern he had ever written down.

"It assumes the secondary system holds," Kenji said.

"It will hold," Alexei said.

"You don't know that."

"I know the secondary system," Alexei said. "I built half of it. It will hold."

Kenji looked at him for a long time. "Okay," he said. "Okay. Let's show Elena."

They showed Elena. They showed Marcus and Daniel and Irina and François, and the module filled with voices, the first real voices — not managed voices, not work voices, but the voices of people who had been handed something to hold onto and were holding it.

Declan laughed. The real laugh, the one that arrived before the joke. "There it is," he said. "There it is boys."

Elena put her hand flat on the wall of the module in the specific way she had pressed her hand flat on the gantry on launch day, feeling for the vibration of the thing beneath. "All right," she said. "Let's build it."

They worked for sixteen hours.

Marcus at the arm, executing a repair sequence that had not been designed for these conditions, improvising with the tools available, the Canadarm moving with the patient mechanical precision of fifty-eight feet of purpose-built reach. Daniel at communications, keeping the channel open, talking Houston through every step in the calm unhurried voice of a man who had been taught by his mother that the necessary work is never finished but must be done anyway. Kenji at the systems console, every concern in his seventeen notebooks now organized into a single focused attention that was the opposite of worry, that was worry transformed by necessity into something useful and exact.

Yuki worked alongside them. She had stopped logging the blood panel data. She knew what it said. She had said what it said to the people who needed to know it. Now she did the next thing, because that was the training and the calling and the particular discipline of a woman who had grown up understanding that the membrane between life and death deserved the most serious attention available, and that serious attention meant doing the work in front of you until the work was done.

At hour fourteen, the secondary system held.

Alexei did not say I told you so. He looked at the readout, and something in his face went very still — not triumph, but the quiet of a man who has been running at full speed for thirty-six hours and has just been given permission to exhale. He floated to the observation window. Below them, the earth turned.

"Look at it," he said to no one in particular.

Nikolai floated up beside him. They stood together at the window and looked at the blue below, the terminator line moving across the surface with the clean unhurried authority of something that had never been in a hurry and had never needed to be.

"My grandfather," Nikolai said.

"I know," Alexei said.

Nikolai put his hand on the younger man's shoulder. They said nothing else. There was nothing else that needed saying.

On the twenty-first day, the data that Yuki had been watching since the fourteenth resolved into something that could not be managed by the solution they had built. It had been patient, the way such things are patient. It had waited for the secondary system to hold. It had allowed the moment of exhale. And then it had done what it was always going to do.

Yuki went to Elena.

Elena listened. She asked three questions. She received the answers. She sat for a moment and then she stood and she was the commander again, completely, without remainder.

"I need you to tell me we have time," she said.

"You have time to send everything you need to send," Yuki said.

"Then that's what we have," Elena said.

She called no meeting this time. She went from person to person, module to module, and she told each of them alone, because some things should be received in private before they are carried in company. And each of them, in their own way, received it.

Kenji opened his seventeenth notebook. He did not start a new page. He closed it.

François pressed his palm against the observation window and looked down at Paris, visible through a gap in the cloud, and thought about his daughter Élise, fourteen, who had asked him whether humanity deserved to go to Mars, and to whom he had given the answer that was not an answer, that was the truth, which is sometimes more useful. He thought about what he wanted her to know. He sat down. He started writing.

Irina wrote things down.

Daniel went to his quarters and finished his last message to Sophie at 0400, ship time, and sent it before the communications systems began to degrade. In Houston it arrived and was held in a server, patient and still, waiting for a nine-year-old girl who would read it ten thousand times and never find its bottom. In it he had written: the quiet is full, Sophie. That's what I want you to remember. The quiet is not empty. It is the fullest thing there is. It contains everything.

Declan made someone laugh. On the last full day, in the common area, with the earth turning below them and the data being what the data was, Declan Byrne from Galway made someone laugh. It was not the large, sudden laugh of the launch morning. It was smaller and quieter and harder-earned — the laugh that knows what it is up against and laughs anyway. The laugh that his father would have recognized from the boat in the grey Atlantic swell. The laugh that has the stomach for the crossing.

Yusuf sat with his grandmother's cloth and looked out the window and Sarah came and sat beside him and they did not speak for a long time, and then she took his hand and held it the way she held everything, carefully and without setting it down, and after a while he said: "It was still worth it. To see it. Even knowing."

"Yes," she said.

"Even knowing what we didn't fix. What we didn't change."

"Even knowing," she said.

He was quiet for a moment. "Carla," he said. He had never met her. He would never meet her. But he knew the way people who have spent their lives paying attention know, that there were Carlas everywhere, in every city the mission had orbited, in every country whose flag was on the station wall, in every language and every latitude, standing in lines the messengers had walked past on their way to find the invited guests.

He had carried this since before the launch. He would carry it until the end.

"Someone has to go back and do something about Carla," he said.

"Yes," Sarah said. "Someone does."

Alexei did not go gently. This was known and expected and accepted. He fought the way he had always fought, which was with everything, without reservation, past the point at which fighting made mathematical sense. He ran the calculations again and found new solutions and discarded them when they failed and found more solutions. He raged, in the end, with the particular rage of the species itself — refusing the unacceptable, refusing the door, demanding that the universe provide an exit it did not have. Four of them held him still while the thing ran through him and burned itself out. When it was over he was not diminished by it and neither were they. They understood what it was. They held him. He let them. He leaned his head back against the wall of the module and closed his eyes and said: "I told my mother I was coming home."

"I know," Nikolai said.

"I meant it."

"I know you meant it," Nikolai said. "I know."

Elena held the communications channel open herself. She did what commanders do when the math has run out and the work has reached its limit and the only remaining task is to be, completely and without reservation, what you have always been. She spoke to Houston with the clarity of a fixed point. She did not say I am coming home. She knew what happened to that sentence. She said what needed to be said in the time available to say it, and she said it with the precision of a woman who had wanted this since she was seven years old and would not dishonor it at the end by being anything other than what she had always been.

The channel was the last thing to go.

Then the silence.

Below them, in the city that had now committed to November, Carla Reyes sat at her kitchen table after the children were in bed and looked at the bills spread across the table and did the math she did at the end of every month, moving numbers around the way you move pieces on a board when the board has already been decided. The cereal box with the toucan sat on the counter. Marcus had refused to let it be opened, wanting to carry it like the trophy it was, and she had let him carry it to bed, and it was in his room right now beside his pillow.

She was not unhappy. This was important and she knew it was important. She had what she needed for the month. She had her children, which were the most important thing she had ever been given and which she guarded with the focused ferocity of someone who understands exactly what she is guarding. She had the line and the number and the volunteers and the crack in the sidewalk shaped like a river and the cereal box with the toucan. She had enough.

She did not have more than enough. She had never had more than enough. The feast, when she had heard about it the way people heard about feasts, had always seemed to be somewhere she could not quite reach, somewhere the messengers had not come, somewhere the invitation had not been issued, or had been issued and lost in the mail, or had arrived at the wrong address for reasons no one could fully explain and no one was quite willing to claim responsibility for.

She stacked the bills. She turned off the kitchen light. She went to bed.

Outside, the sky was clear. The terminator line moved across the surface of the earth with the patient authority of something that has never been in a hurry. The station orbited, silent now.

In the fields near Orsk, if you were there, standing in the snow in the place where the elk had been on a Tuesday in April in 1967, you would hear nothing. You would see nothing. The sky would be the sky: indifferent and immense and full of the light of stars that may no longer exist, full of the silence that is not empty, that is the fullest thing there is.

It contains everything we have sent into it.

It contains the palm prints on the cold glass of the observation window, the warmth of them already gone.

It contains Yusuf's grandmother's cloth and Astrid's joik and Daniel's message in the server in Houston and Sophie who will read it ten thousand times, and Declan's laugh that had the stomach for the crossing, and Alexei's rage that was the species at its most honest, and Elena's voice steady on the channel in the last minutes, and Nikolai thinking about the elk, thinking about the names of the ones already there.

It contains the parable without resolving it.

Many are invited, but few are chosen.

And then the silence.

The silence into which Élise, fourteen, in Paris, opened a notebook the morning after. She had asked her father whether humanity deserved to go to Mars, and he had given her the answer that was not an answer, and now she understood it, and she wrote at the top of the first page: I will keep the record. I will keep it for him. She began to write things down.

The silence into which Sophie, nine years old, in Scranton, read a message that said: the quiet is full. She read it again. She held it the way her father had taught her to hold things, carefully, with both hands, without setting it down.

The silence into which Carla's alarm went off at six in the morning and she got up and made lunches and got the children dressed and drove Isabella to school and Rosie to daycare and carried Marcus on her hip while she opened the cereal box that had been guarded all night and poured it into a bowl while Marcus narrated the process with the authority of someone supervising very important work.

She fed her children what she had to feed them.

She did not know the names of the ones who had orbited above her while she slept.

She would learn them later, the way people learn the names of the ones they were not invited to mourn, through a screen, through someone else's words, through the particular numbness that settles when something enormous happens and the world is required to absorb it while continuing to be the world. She would feel it — not distantly, not abstractly, but in the chest, the way you feel it when you learn that people were trying and it wasn't enough, which is the thing you know most clearly and most personally, which is the thing you have been living every month at the kitchen table with the bills spread out under the single light.

She would feel it.

And then she would pack the lunches and pick up the children and stand in whatever line was next, because the line was still there and the children were still hungry and the distance between the feast and the street had not been closed by the tragedy or the investigation or the names read in the halls of Congress or the flags at half-mast over the capitals of thirteen nations.

The distance remained.

It had always remained.

It was the oldest distance in the human story. The distance between the table and the street. Between the invited and the uninvited. Between the feast above and the hunger below. Between the ones the king's messengers knew how to find and the ones who stood in lines the messengers walked past.

The parable does not tell us how to close it.

Jesus tells the story and goes quiet. He does not resolve the feast or return the uninvited or rearrange the seating or repair the machine or untangle the parachute. He says: many are called. Few are chosen. And then he moves on to the next thing.

But the parable is not finished when Jesus finishes it. It never is.

It finishes in Élise opening her notebook.

In Sophie holding the message with both hands.

In Yusuf's voice saying: someone has to go back and do something about Carla.

In the answer Sarah gave him, which was yes. Not someday. Not when the mission is over and the investigations are complete and the committees have filed their reports. Now. Someone has to go back now and do something about Carla, because Carla is here now and the line is here now and the cereal box with the toucan is here now and the children are hungry now.

The banquet is set. It has always been set. The table is long enough. The food is sufficient. The feast does not end for lack of provision.

It ends, again and again, for lack of invitation.

The messengers keep going to the same addresses. The same streets. The same doors. And the ones at the other addresses — the ones on the roads and the lanes and the side streets and the food bank lines and the kitchen tables under the single light at the end of the month — keep waiting for a knock that does not come.

Go out, the master says. Into the roads. Into the lanes. Into the places you have not looked.

Compel them to come in. So that my house may be full.

Not so that the right people may come. Not so that the worthy may arrive. So that the house. May be full.

Carla is on the road. She has always been on the road. She is not waiting for rescue. She is not waiting for pity. She is waiting for the knock. The invitation. The voice that says: there is a place for you at this table. Not the table of charity. The table of the feast. The table where the food is abundant and the wine is real and the host is someone who will not require you to explain your number or how long you have been standing in line or what you did or did not do to find yourself here.

The table where the question is not whether you deserve it.

The question is whether the house will be full.

Above Billings, above Lagos, above Paris, above Scranton, above every city where the line is already forming and the numbers are already being handed out, the orbit continues.

Ninety minutes to circle the earth.

The earth turning below, patient and blue, wrapped in its thin miraculous breath, the terminator line moving across its surface in the clean authority of something that has never once, in all its revolutions, been in a hurry.

Go out, it says. Into the roads.

Compel them to come in.

So that my house may be full.

# ACKNOWLEDGMENTS

Most of what appears in these pages, I have lived.

The hospital corridors, the night shifts, the conversations in parked cars, the desperate phone calls, the quiet mercies extended by strangers who didn't know they were performing Kingdom work—these are not inventions. They are memory made sacred by attention.

I am a recovering addict with decades of sobriety. I know what it means to lose families, not to death, but to broken trust, to absence, to the wreckage addiction leaves behind. I know what it costs to be forgiven, and what it means to live in the tension between who I was and who I'm becoming.

That knowledge is in this book.

I cannot name all the people whose lives touched mine in ways that became these stories. Many would not recognize themselves. Some have passed on. Others would prefer to remain in the dignity of their anonymity. But they are here, in the welder's hands, in the mother's resolve, in the addict's last honest moment, in the stranger's unexpected kindness.

To those whose pain I witnessed and whose resilience I marveled at: thank you for letting me see what the Kingdom looks like when it breaks into the ordinary world.

And to Theresa, already named in the dedication but deserving every word again: you didn't just edit this book. You lived beside me through the long work of becoming. You are woven into every page.

# ABOUT THE AUTHOR

Bernd L Bergmann has lived many lives, each one preparing him for the work of listening deeply to the human soul.

He has been a welder shaping steel in the heat of California sun, a broadcast television technical director guiding stories through the glow of studio lights, a driver carrying strangers through the fragile crossings of their lives, and now, a newly certified Nursing Assistant tending to elders with hands that have learned the quiet language of dignity.

He is also a recovering addict with decades of sobriety—a man who knows what it means to lose everything, to be offered mercy he did not deserve, and to live in the tension between who he was and who he is becoming.

Across every chapter of his life, one thread has remained constant: a reverence for the sacred hidden inside ordinary people.

Bernd writes the way some people pray—not to explain, but to witness. Not to instruct, but to reveal.

His work draws from ancient Midrashic tradition, listening to Scripture the way one listens to a distant melody: with humility, imagination, and the belief that sacred stories are still alive.

He lives in Montana with his wife, Theresa—Episcopal priest, quilter, weaver, and the steady light by which he sees the world more clearly. She is his first reader, his fiercest editor, and the quiet grace that makes his writing possible.

His first book, Midrash Whispered By Stars, is a poetic retelling of Jesus's life from age five to thirty, drawing from gnostic gospels and Midrashic tradition to reveal the sacred mysteries hidden in His formative years.

Midrash: Into the Kingdom is his second major work, continuing his lifelong devotion to exploring the places where human suffering, divine mercy, and unexpected grace meet.

# ALSO BY BERND L BERGMANN

*Midrash Whispered By Stars*

A poetic retelling of Jesus's life from age five to thirty, drawing from gnostic gospels and Midrashic tradition to reveal the sacred mysteries hidden in His formative years.